GUY RITCHIE'S

GAME KEEPER ™

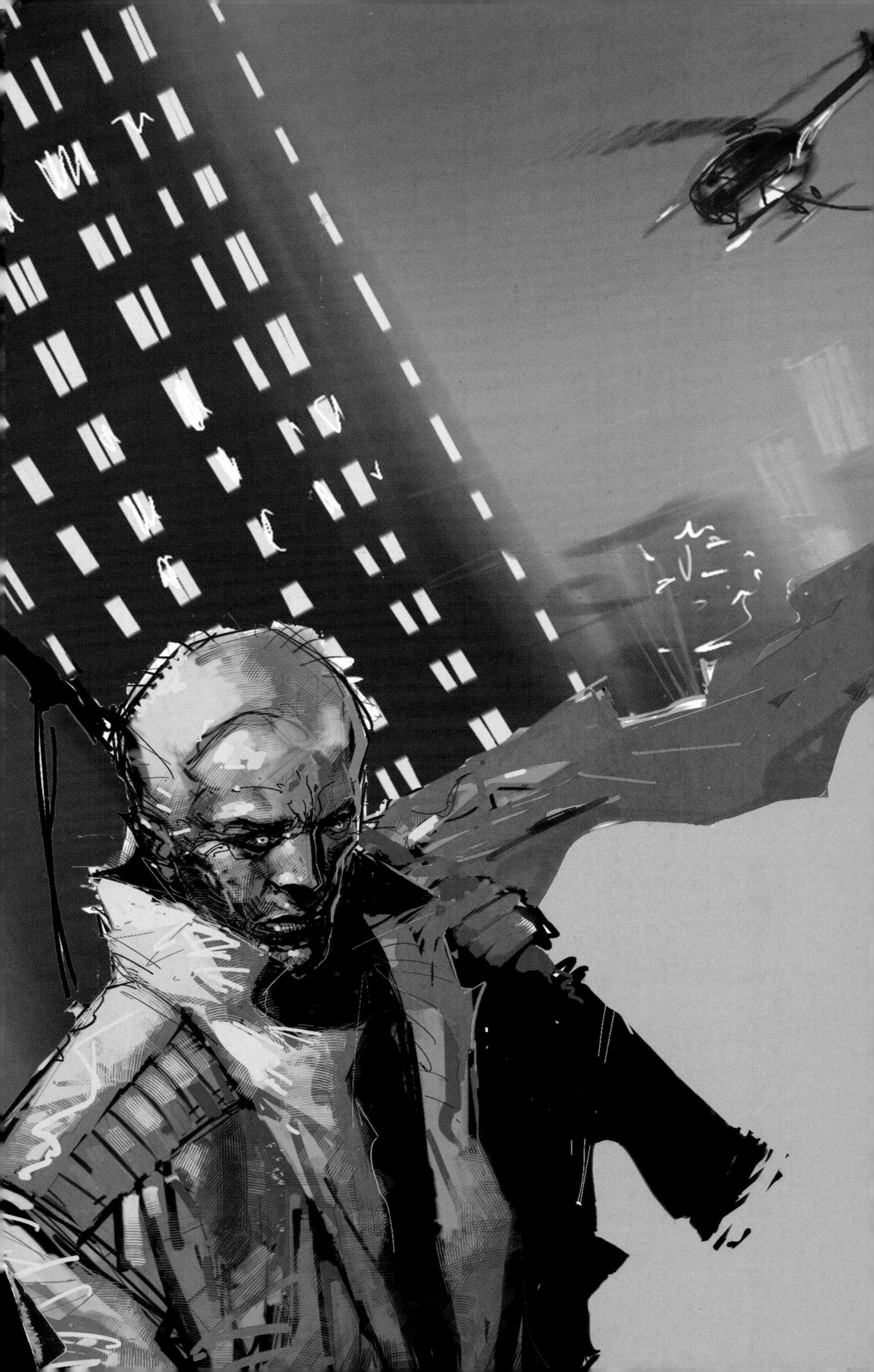

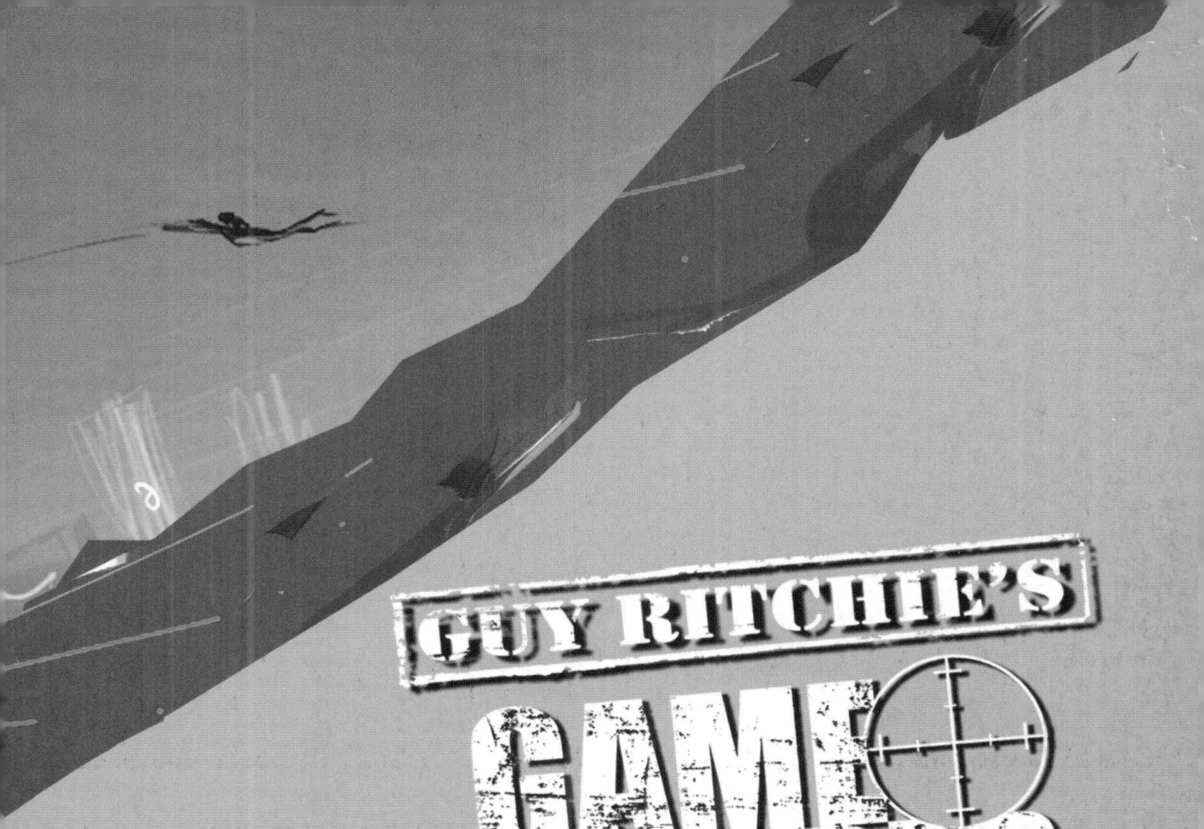

GUY RITCHIE'S GAME KEEPER™

Created by
GUY RITCHIE

Story by
GUY RITCHIE
ANDY DIGGLE

Art & Color
MUKESH SINGH

Cover Art
JOHN CASSADAY
with LAURA MARTIN

Additional Covers
MUKESH SINGH
GREG HORN
JONATHAN HICKMAN
NEELAKASH K.

Letters
RAVIKIRAN B. S.
NILESH S. MAHADIK
RAKESH B. MAHADIK
and SUDHIR B. PISAL

Project Manager
REUBEN THOMAS

Collected Editions Project Manager
SANDEEP NAIR

Assistant Editor
CHARLIE BECKERMAN

Collected Editions Editor
SANA AMANAT

Editor
MACKENZIE CADEN

Very Special Tha
LAUREN MEE

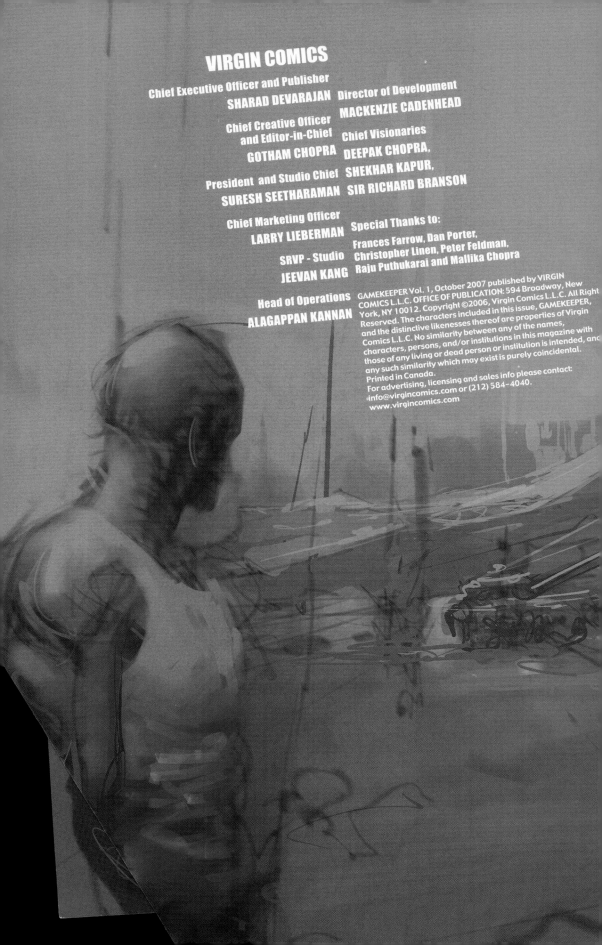

VIRGIN COMICS

Chief Executive Officer and Publisher
SHARAD DEVARAJAN

Chief Creative Officer and Editor-in-Chief
GOTHAM CHOPRA

President and Studio Chief
SURESH SEETHARAMAN

Chief Marketing Officer
LARRY LIEBERMAN

SRVP - Studio
JEEVAN KANG

Head of Operations
ALAGAPPAN KANNAN

Director of Development
MACKENZIE CADENHEAD

Chief Visionaries
DEEPAK CHOPRA, SHEKHAR KAPUR, SIR RICHARD BRANSON

Special Thanks to:
Frances Farrow, Dan Porter, Christopher Linen, Peter Feldman, Raju Puthukarai and Mallika Chopra

GAMEKEEPER Vol. 1, October 2007 published by VIRGIN COMICS L.L.C. OFFICE OF PUBLICATION: 594 Broadway, New York, NY 10012.
Printed in Canada.
For advertising, licensing and sales info please contact: info@virgincomics.com or (212) 584-4040.
www.virgincomics.com

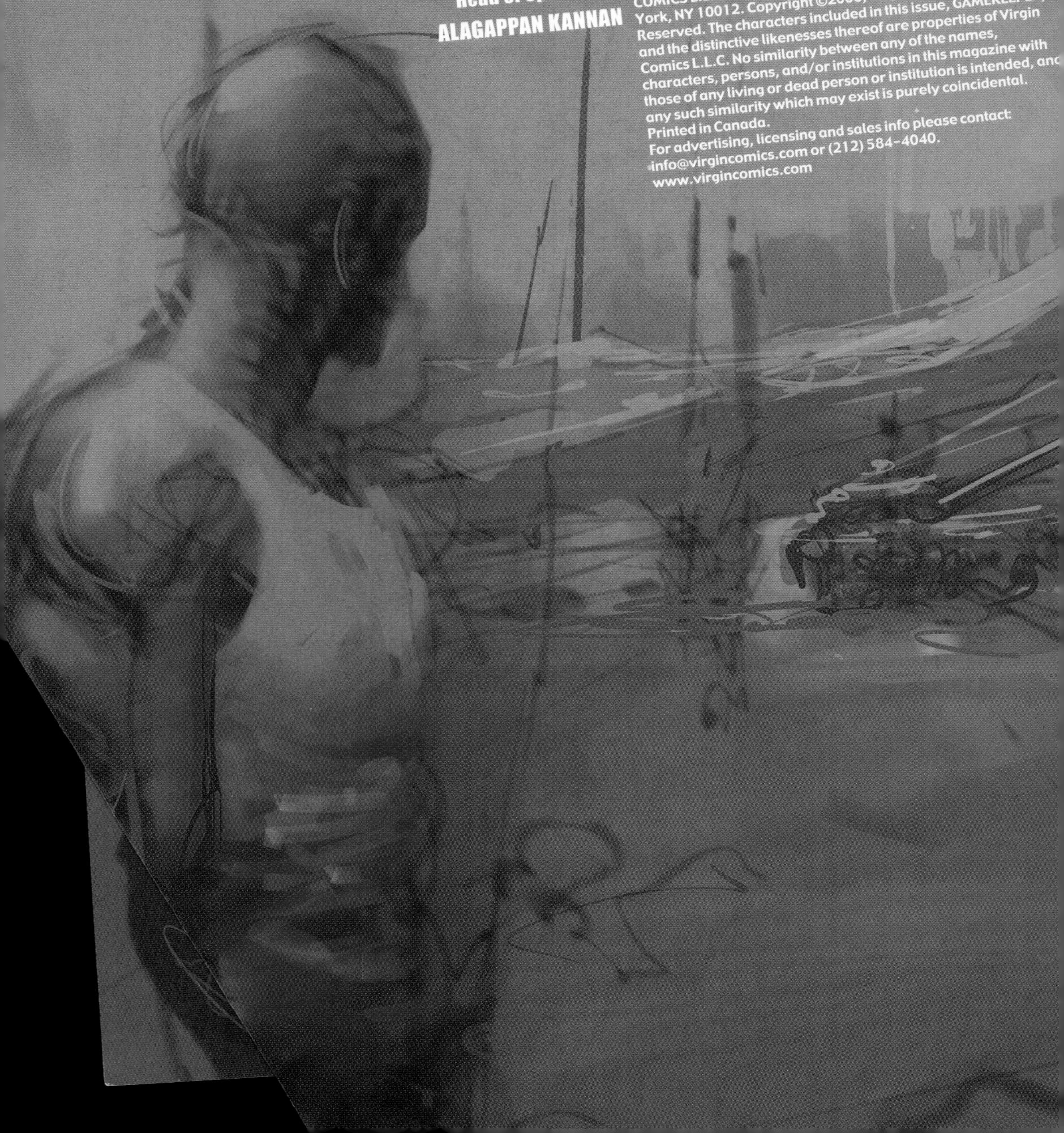

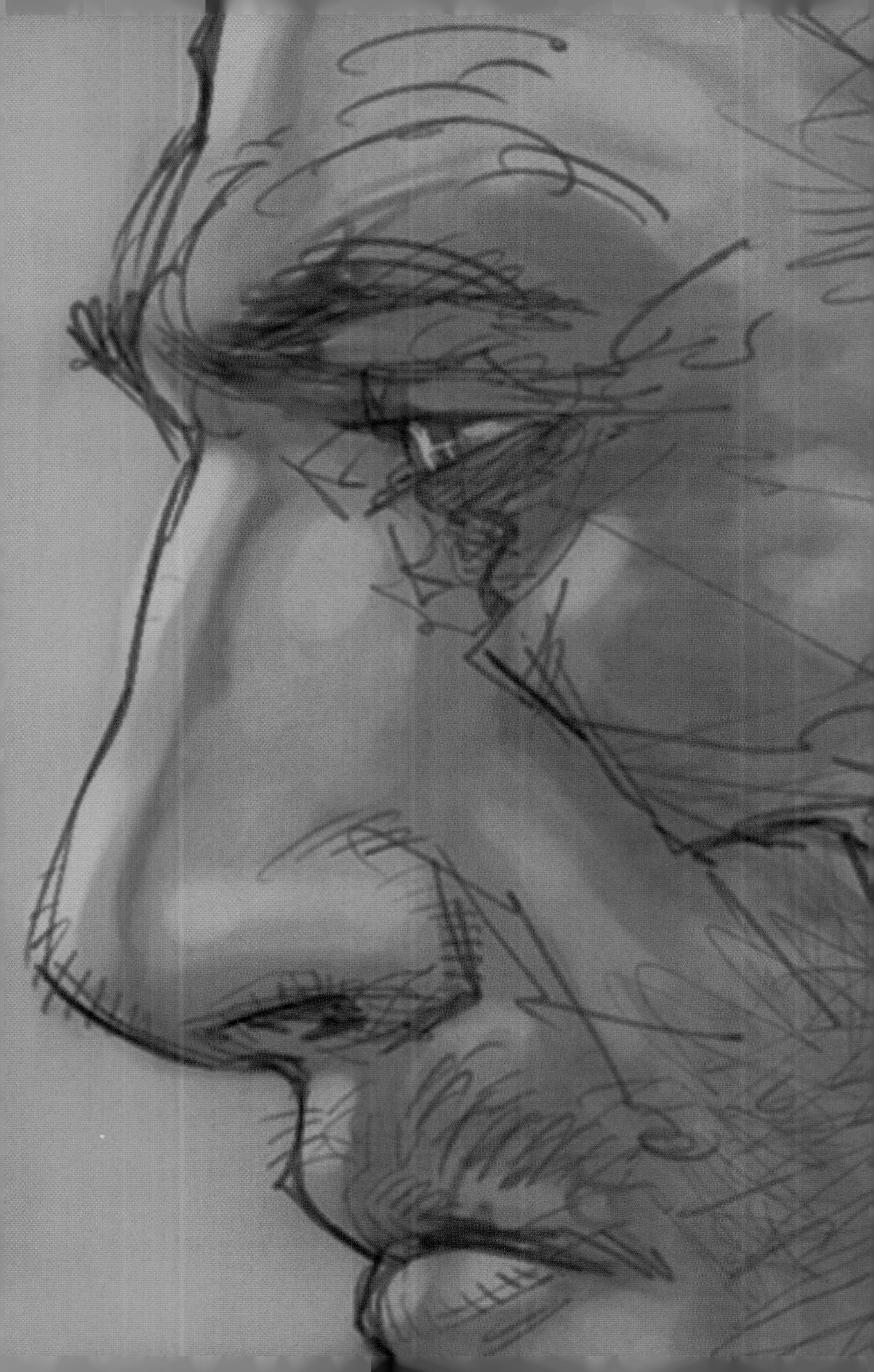

FROM GUY RITCHIE

In late April, Gotham Chopra, the fellow with whom I originally started brainstorming *Gamekeeper* over a year ago, showed up in London and together we sat down with a film executive from Warner Brothers who had expressed interest in our comic book.

It wasn't a typical pitch meeting, like many I have been in throughout my film career. There was no real pitching taking place, no act breakdowns or character profiles, nor elaborate discussions of things like conflict, theme, or even plot. Quite simply I opened up the comic to some of the first few pages from issue 1, pointed to the art of Mukesh Singh, some of the monochromatic scenes in the Scottish forests where Brock turns from prey to predator, and said: "See that bloody page? That's what I want to put on the screen."

That was it for me. There was likely some back and forth negotiation between agents and lawyers, executives from all sides and assorted producers, but I didn't get engaged in all that. For me, as a filmmaker, the moment I saw those pages, I had a cinematic vision for what I know will make a great film, so now I'm particularly happy to have Warner Brothers and Silver Pictures along with me for the ride.

Comics are fairly new to me—not as a reader, as I've always been a fan—but as a filmmaker who now understands how valuable they can be as an incubator of great storytelling and visual execution. I realize I am not the first. Forget *Spider-Man* and *Superman* and all of that usual comic fare. I do admire—or should I say am jealous of—the likes of *Frank Miller's Sin City* and Zach Snyder's cinematic vision of *300.* I like the way they've taken the published page to the screen.

In terms of the story of *Gamekeeper,* it's really about a man who understands the science of nature and who understands the ecosystem in which he exists better than most. But when that serenity is disrupted by some old urban enemies, Brock's rage is ignited and the action takes off from there. That's about all you need to know as you read these pages and until we bring Mukesh's visuals and Andy Diggle's story to the screen.

Until then...

Guy Ritchie
August 2007

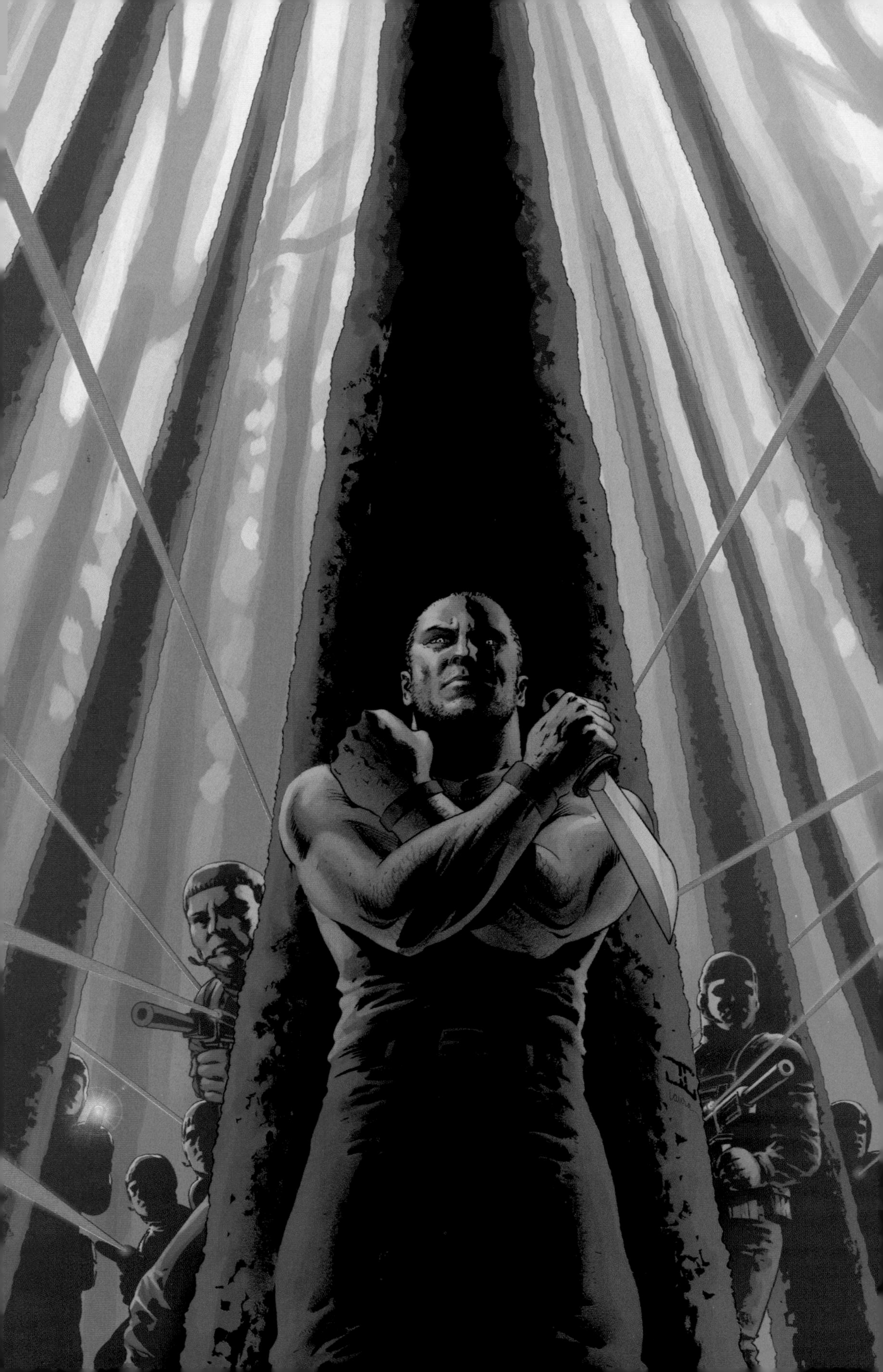

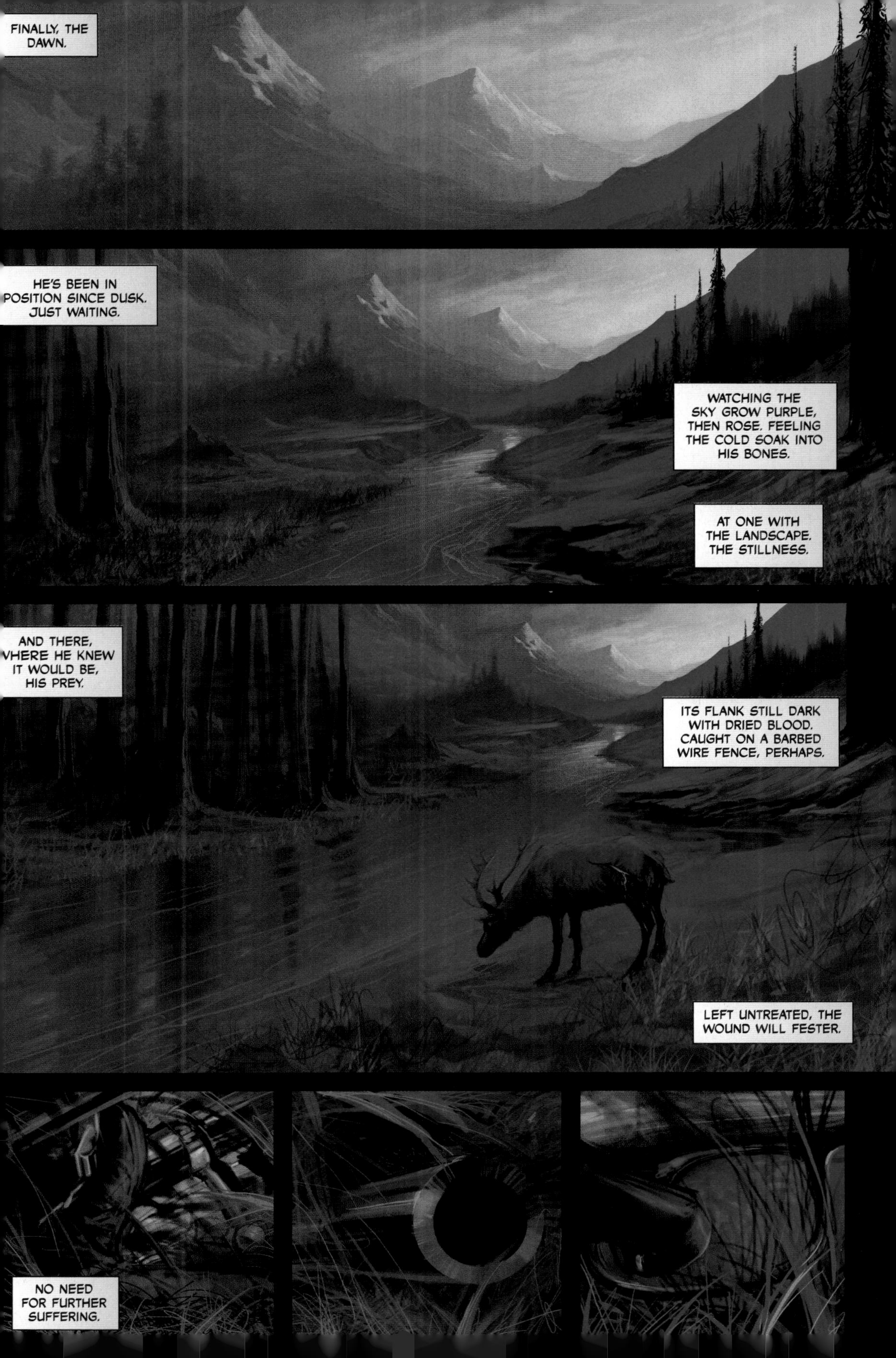
FINALLY, THE DAWN.
HE'S BEEN IN POSITION SINCE DUSK. JUST WAITING.
WATCHING THE SKY GROW PURPLE, THEN ROSE. FEELING THE COLD SOAK INTO HIS BONES.
AT ONE WITH THE LANDSCAPE. THE STILLNESS.
AND THERE, WHERE HE KNEW IT WOULD BE, HIS PREY.
ITS FLANK STILL DARK WITH DRIED BLOOD. CAUGHT ON A BARBED WIRE FENCE, PERHAPS.
LEFT UNTREATED, THE WOUND WILL FESTER.
NO NEED FOR FURTHER SUFFERING.

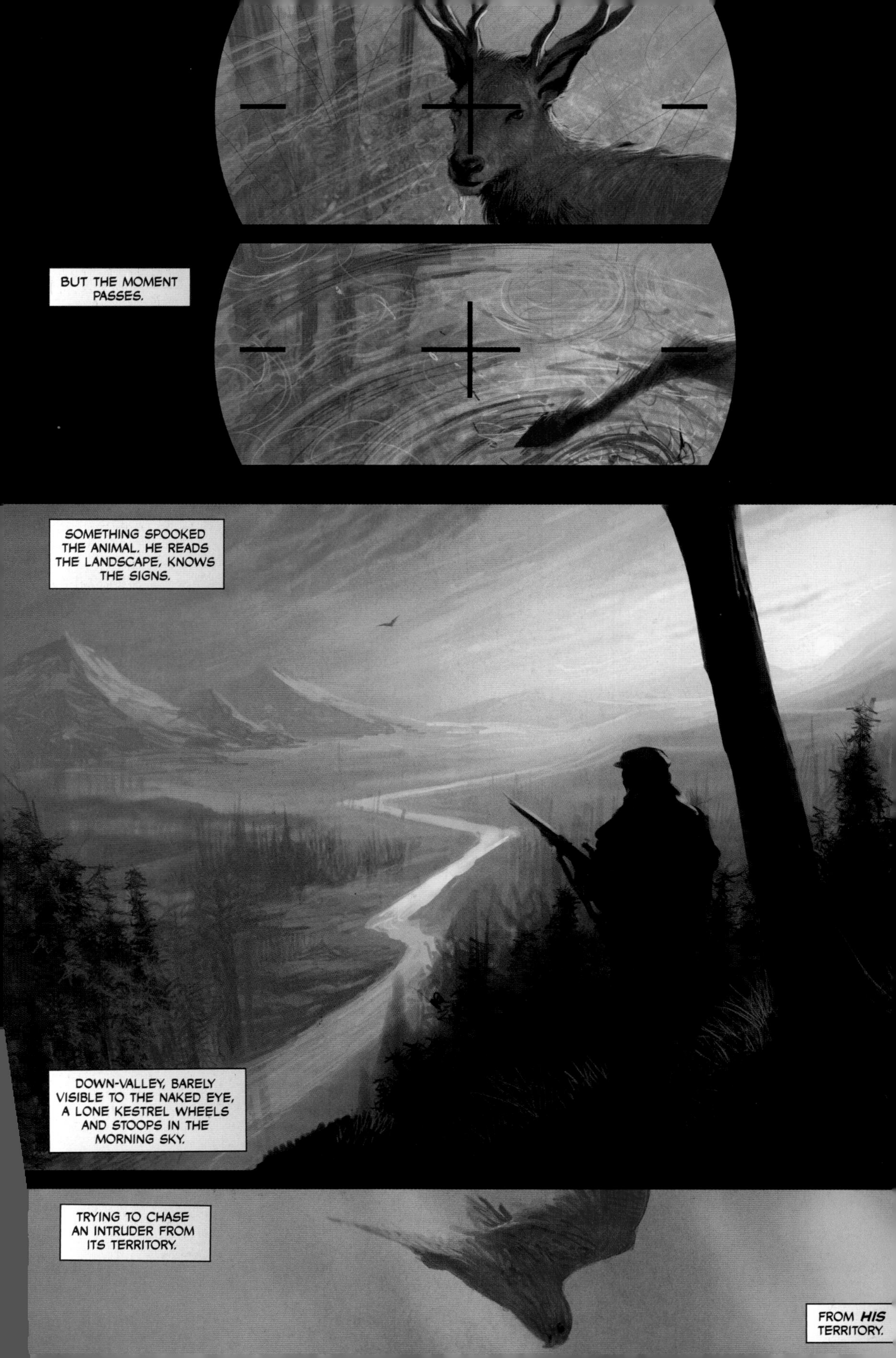
BUT THE MOMENT PASSES.
SOMETHING SPOOKED THE ANIMAL. HE READS THE LANDSCAPE, KNOWS THE SIGNS.
DOWN-VALLEY, BARELY VISIBLE TO THE NAKED EYE, A LONE KESTREL WHEELS AND STOOPS IN THE MORNING SKY.
TRYING TO CHASE AN INTRUDER FROM ITS TERRITORY.
FROM *HIS* TERRITORY.

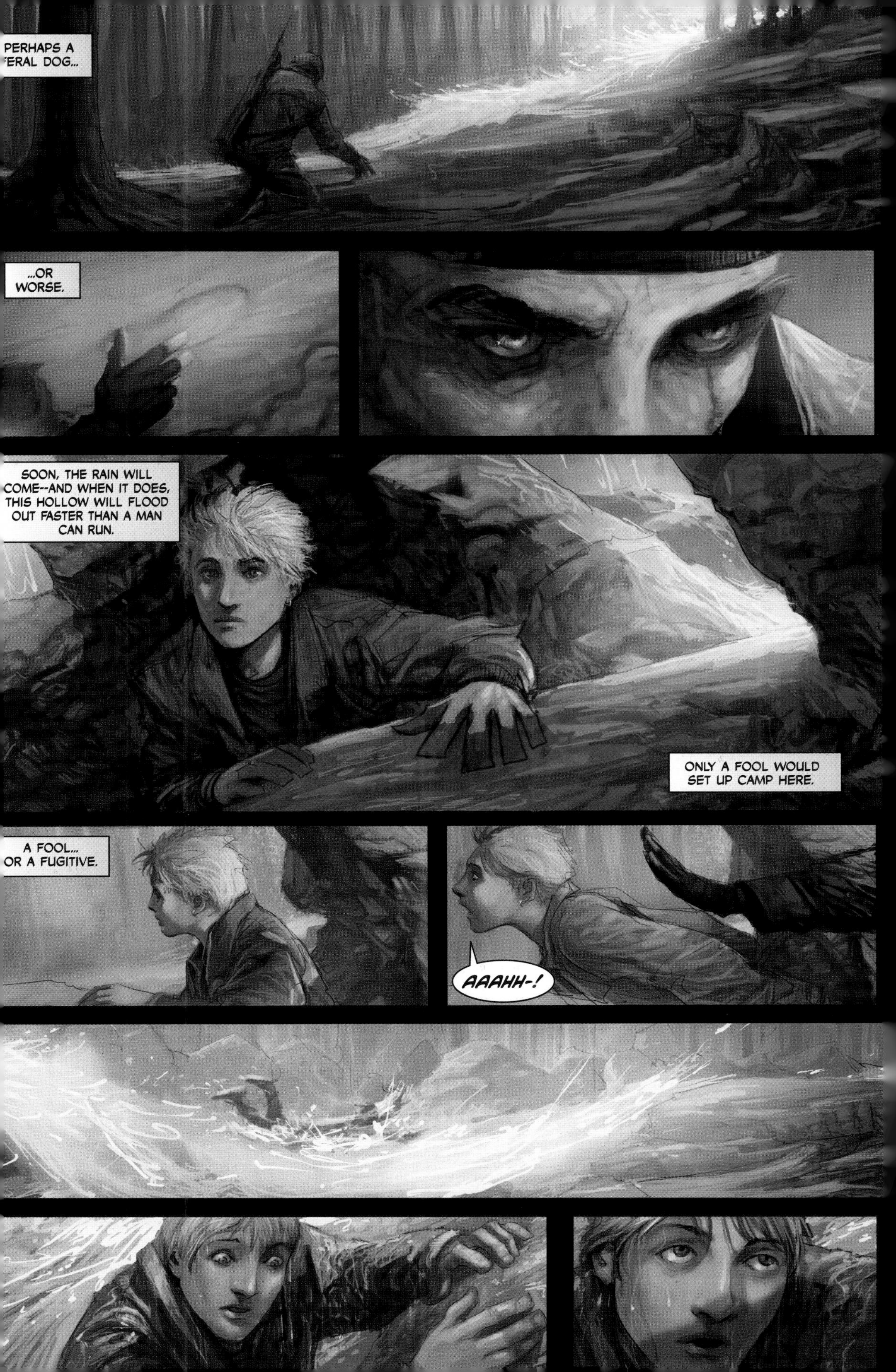
PERHAPS A FERAL DOG...
...OR WORSE.
SOON, THE RAIN WILL COME--AND WHEN IT DOES, THIS HOLLOW WILL FLOOD OUT FASTER THAN A MAN CAN RUN.
ONLY A FOOL WOULD SET UP CAMP HERE.
A FOOL... OR A FUGITIVE.
AAAHH-!

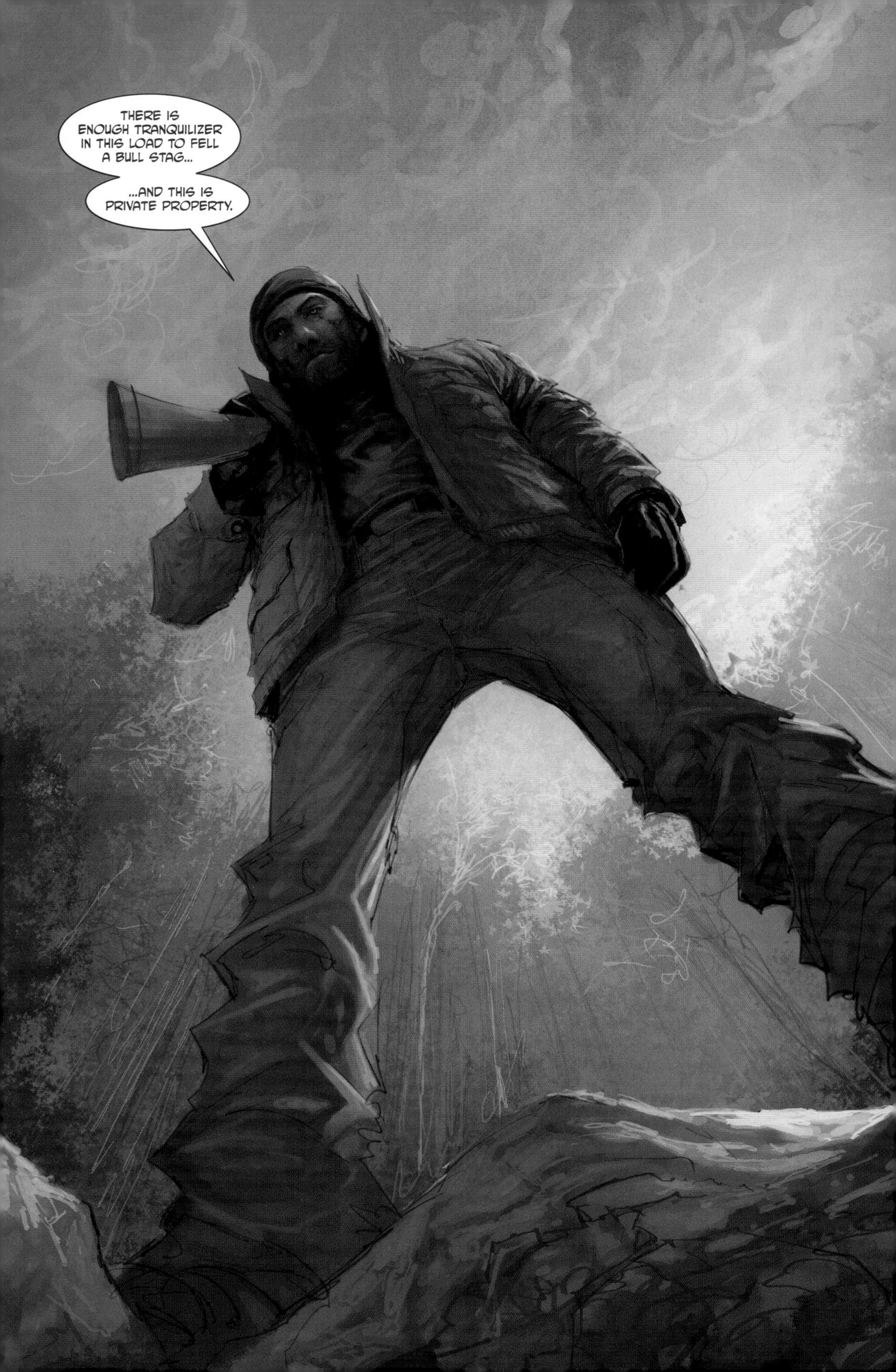
THERE IS ENOUGH TRANQUILIZER IN THIS LOAD TO FELL A BULL STAG...
...AND THIS IS PRIVATE PROPERTY.

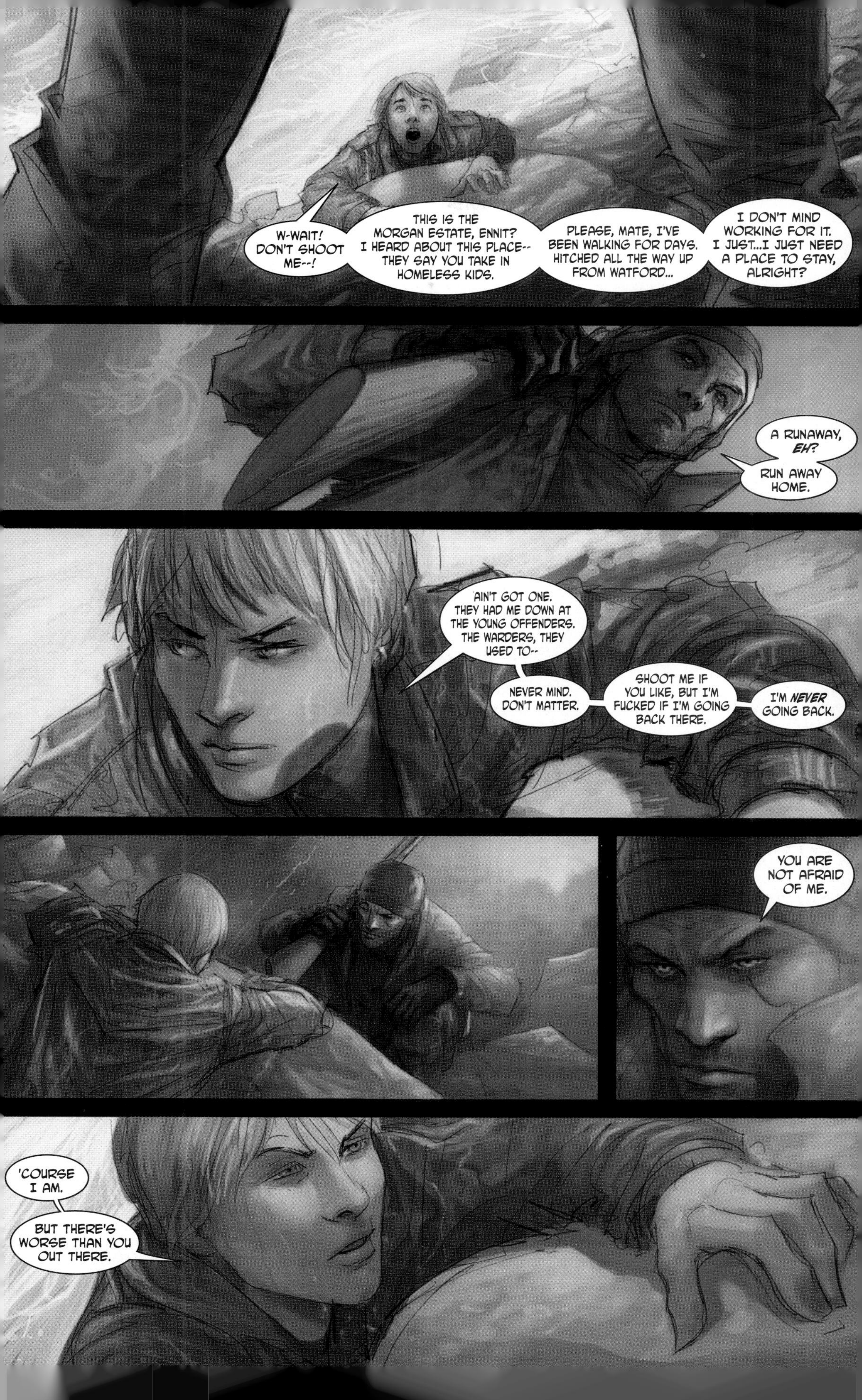
W-WAIT! DON'T SHOOT ME--!
THIS IS THE MORGAN ESTATE, ENNIT? I HEARD ABOUT THIS PLACE-- THEY SAY YOU TAKE IN HOMELESS KIDS.
PLEASE, MATE, I'VE BEEN WALKING FOR DAYS. HITCHED ALL THE WAY UP FROM WATFORD...
I DON'T MIND WORKING FOR IT. I JUST...I JUST NEED A PLACE TO STAY, ALRIGHT?
A RUNAWAY, EH?
RUN AWAY HOME.
AIN'T GOT ONE. THEY HAD ME DOWN AT THE YOUNG OFFENDERS. THE WARDERS, THEY USED TO--
NEVER MIND. DON'T MATTER.
SHOOT ME IF YOU LIKE, BUT I'M FUCKED IF I'M GOING BACK THERE.
I'M NEVER GOING BACK.
YOU ARE NOT AFRAID OF ME.
'COURSE I AM.
BUT THERE'S WORSE THAN YOU OUT THERE.

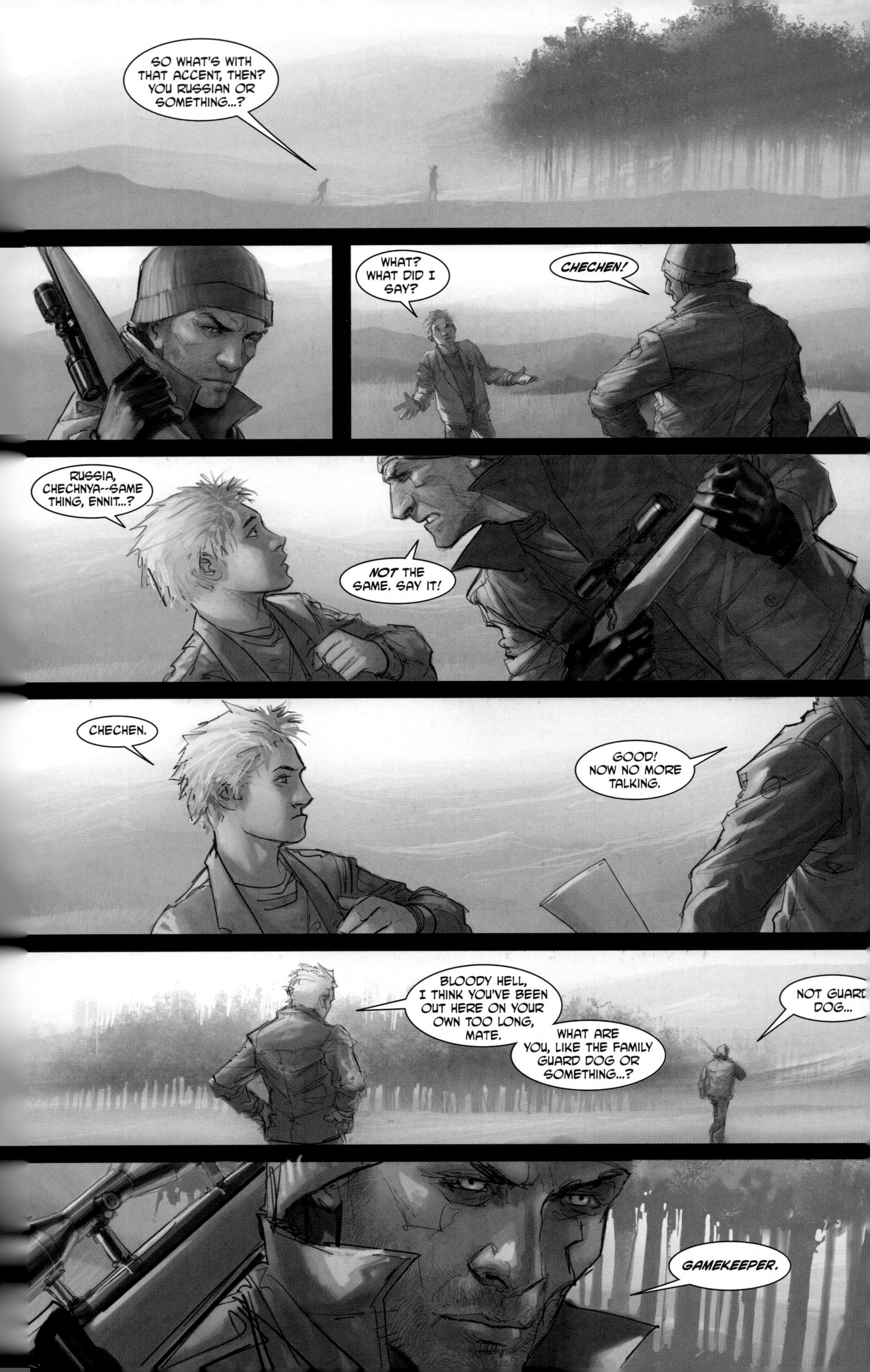
SO WHAT'S WITH THAT ACCENT, THEN? YOU RUSSIAN OR SOMETHING...?
WHAT? WHAT DID I SAY?
CHECHEN!
RUSSIA, CHECHNYA--SAME THING, ENNIT...?
NOT THE SAME. SAY IT!
CHECHEN.
GOOD! NOW NO MORE TALKING.
BLOODY HELL, I THINK YOU'VE BEEN OUT HERE ON YOUR OWN TOO LONG, MATE.
WHAT ARE YOU, LIKE THE FAMILY GUARD DOG OR SOMETHING...?
NOT GUARD DOG...
GAMEKEEPER.

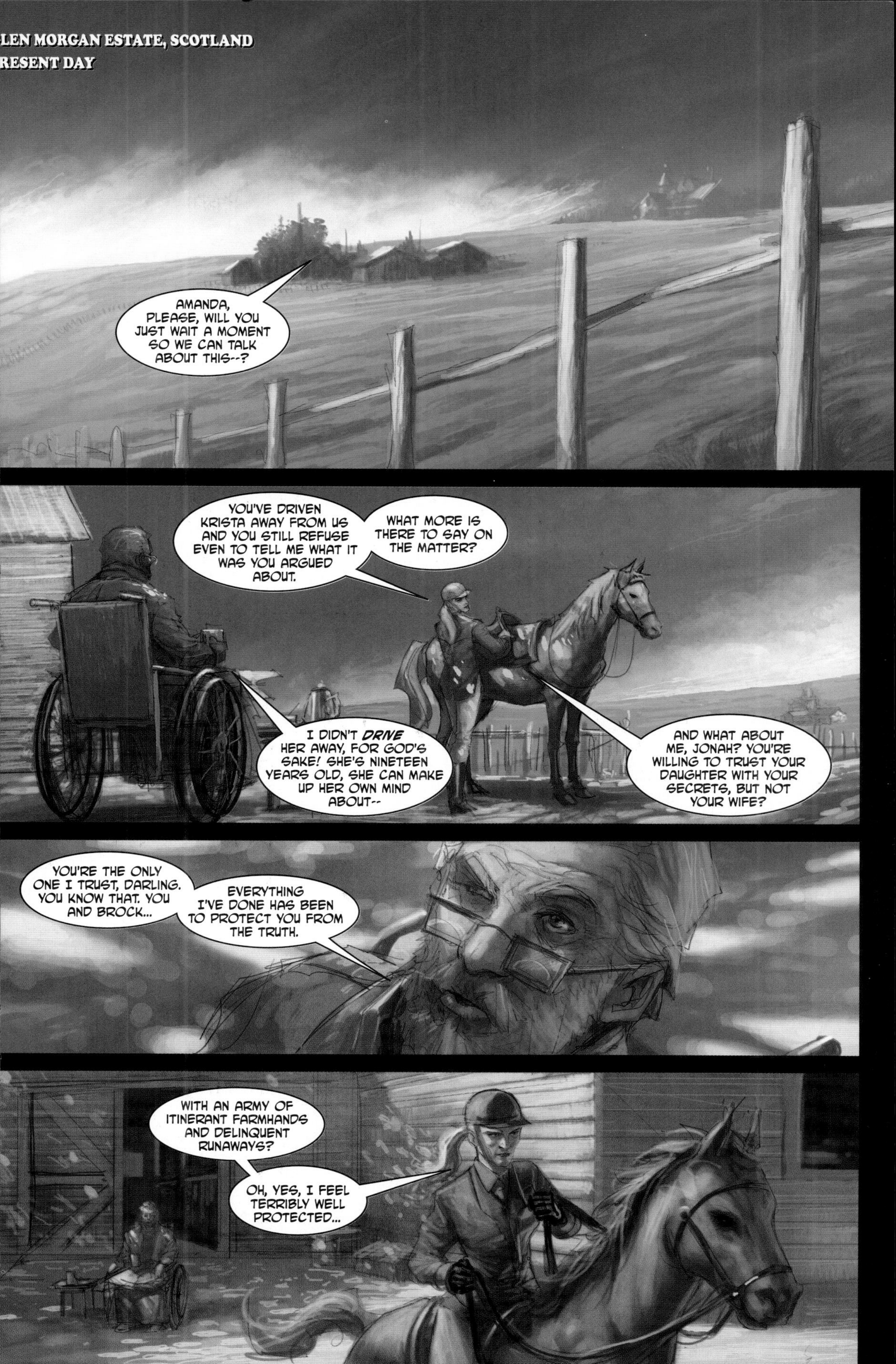
LEN MORGAN ESTATE, SCOTLAND
RESENT DAY
AMANDA, PLEASE, WILL YOU JUST WAIT A MOMENT SO WE CAN TALK ABOUT THIS--?
YOU'VE DRIVEN KRISTA AWAY FROM US AND YOU STILL REFUSE EVEN TO TELL ME WHAT IT WAS YOU ARGUED ABOUT.
WHAT MORE IS THERE TO SAY ON THE MATTER?
I DIDN'T DRIVE HER AWAY, FOR GOD'S SAKE! SHE'S NINETEEN YEARS OLD, SHE CAN MAKE UP HER OWN MIND ABOUT--
AND WHAT ABOUT ME, JONAH? YOU'RE WILLING TO TRUST YOUR DAUGHTER WITH YOUR SECRETS, BUT NOT YOUR WIFE?
YOU'RE THE ONLY ONE I TRUST, DARLING. YOU KNOW THAT. YOU AND BROCK...
EVERYTHING I'VE DONE HAS BEEN TO PROTECT YOU FROM THE TRUTH.
WITH AN ARMY OF ITINERANT FARMHANDS AND DELINQUENT RUNAWAYS?
OH, YES, I FEEL TERRIBLY WELL PROTECTED...

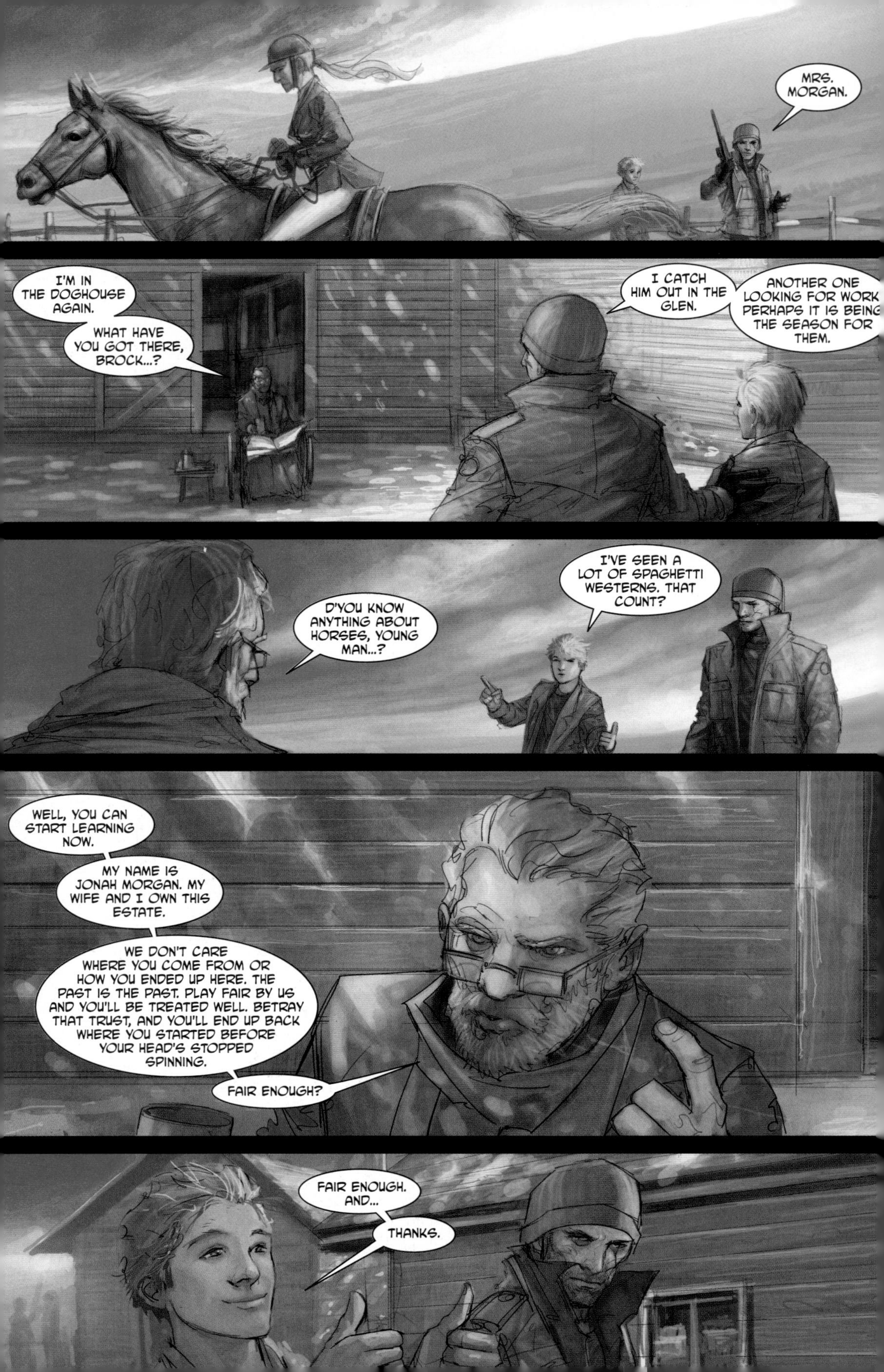
MRS. MORGAN.
I'M IN THE DOGHOUSE AGAIN.
WHAT HAVE YOU GOT THERE, BROCK...?
I CATCH HIM OUT IN THE GLEN.
ANOTHER ONE LOOKING FOR WORK PERHAPS IT IS BEING THE SEASON FOR THEM.
D'YOU KNOW ANYTHING ABOUT HORSES, YOUNG MAN...?
I'VE SEEN A LOT OF SPAGHETTI WESTERNS. THAT COUNT?
WELL, YOU CAN START LEARNING NOW.
MY NAME IS JONAH MORGAN. MY WIFE AND I OWN THIS ESTATE.
WE DON'T CARE WHERE YOU COME FROM OR HOW YOU ENDED UP HERE. THE PAST IS THE PAST. PLAY FAIR BY US AND YOU'LL BE TREATED WELL. BETRAY THAT TRUST, AND YOU'LL END UP BACK WHERE YOU STARTED BEFORE YOUR HEAD'S STOPPED SPINNING.
FAIR ENOUGH?
FAIR ENOUGH. AND...
THANKS.

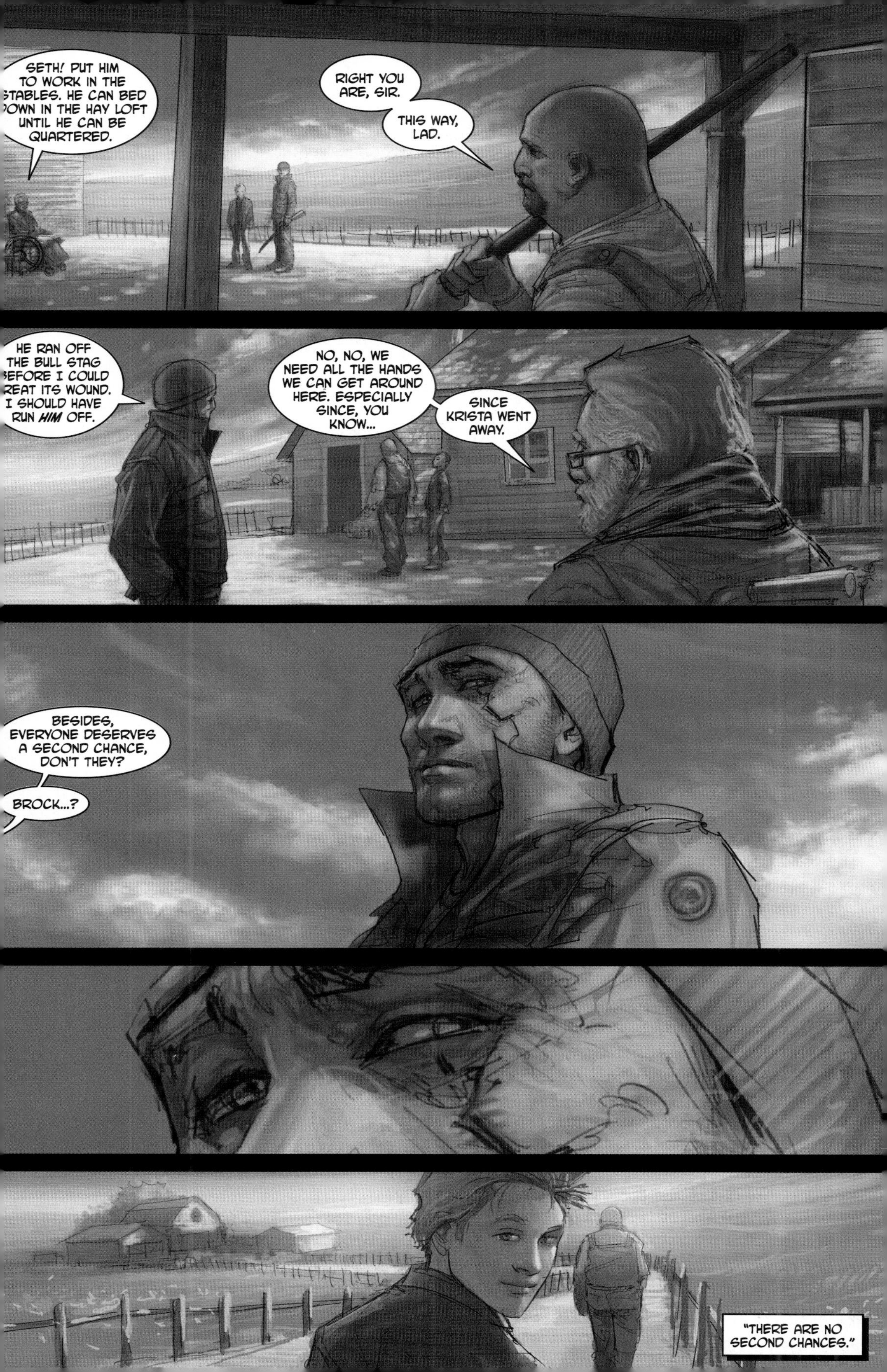
SETH! PUT HIM TO WORK IN THE STABLES. HE CAN BED DOWN IN THE HAY LOFT UNTIL HE CAN BE QUARTERED.
RIGHT YOU ARE, SIR.
THIS WAY, LAD.
HE RAN OFF THE BULL STAG BEFORE I COULD TREAT ITS WOUND. I SHOULD HAVE RUN HIM OFF.
NO, NO, WE NEED ALL THE HANDS WE CAN GET AROUND HERE. ESPECIALLY SINCE, YOU KNOW...
SINCE KRISTA WENT AWAY.
BESIDES, EVERYONE DESERVES A SECOND CHANCE, DON'T THEY?
BROCK...?
"THERE ARE NO SECOND CHANCES."

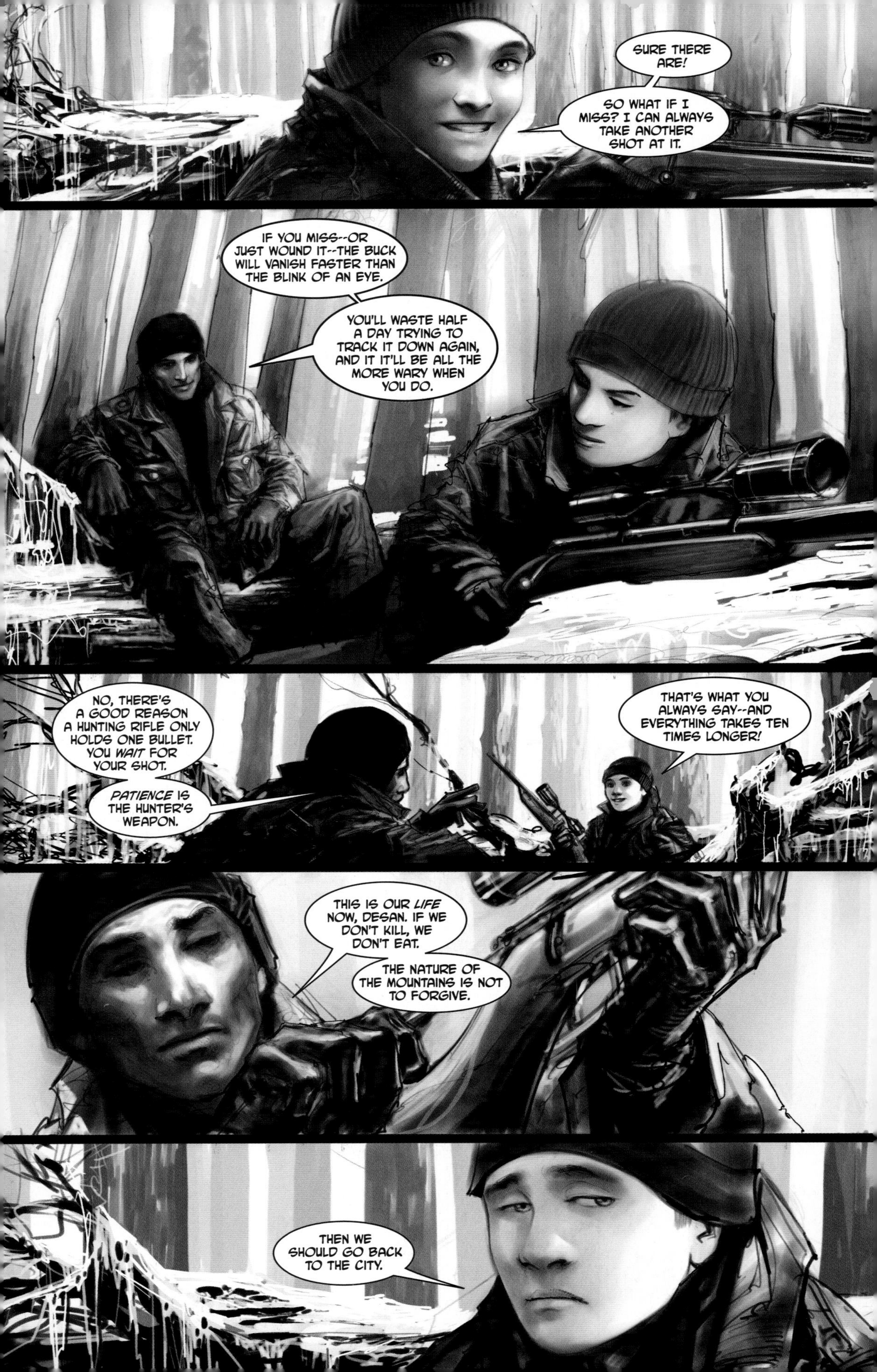
SURE THERE ARE!
SO WHAT IF I MISS? I CAN ALWAYS TAKE ANOTHER SHOT AT IT.
IF YOU MISS--OR JUST WOUND IT--THE BUCK WILL VANISH FASTER THAN THE BLINK OF AN EYE.
YOU'LL WASTE HALF A DAY TRYING TO TRACK IT DOWN AGAIN, AND IT IT'LL BE ALL THE MORE WARY WHEN YOU DO.
NO, THERE'S A GOOD REASON A HUNTING RIFLE ONLY HOLDS ONE BULLET. YOU *WAIT* FOR YOUR SHOT.
PATIENCE IS THE HUNTER'S WEAPON.
THAT'S WHAT YOU ALWAYS SAY--AND EVERYTHING TAKES TEN TIMES LONGER!
THIS IS OUR *LIFE* NOW, DESAN. IF WE DON'T KILL, WE DON'T EAT.
THE NATURE OF THE MOUNTAINS IS NOT TO FORGIVE.
THEN WE SHOULD GO BACK TO THE CITY.

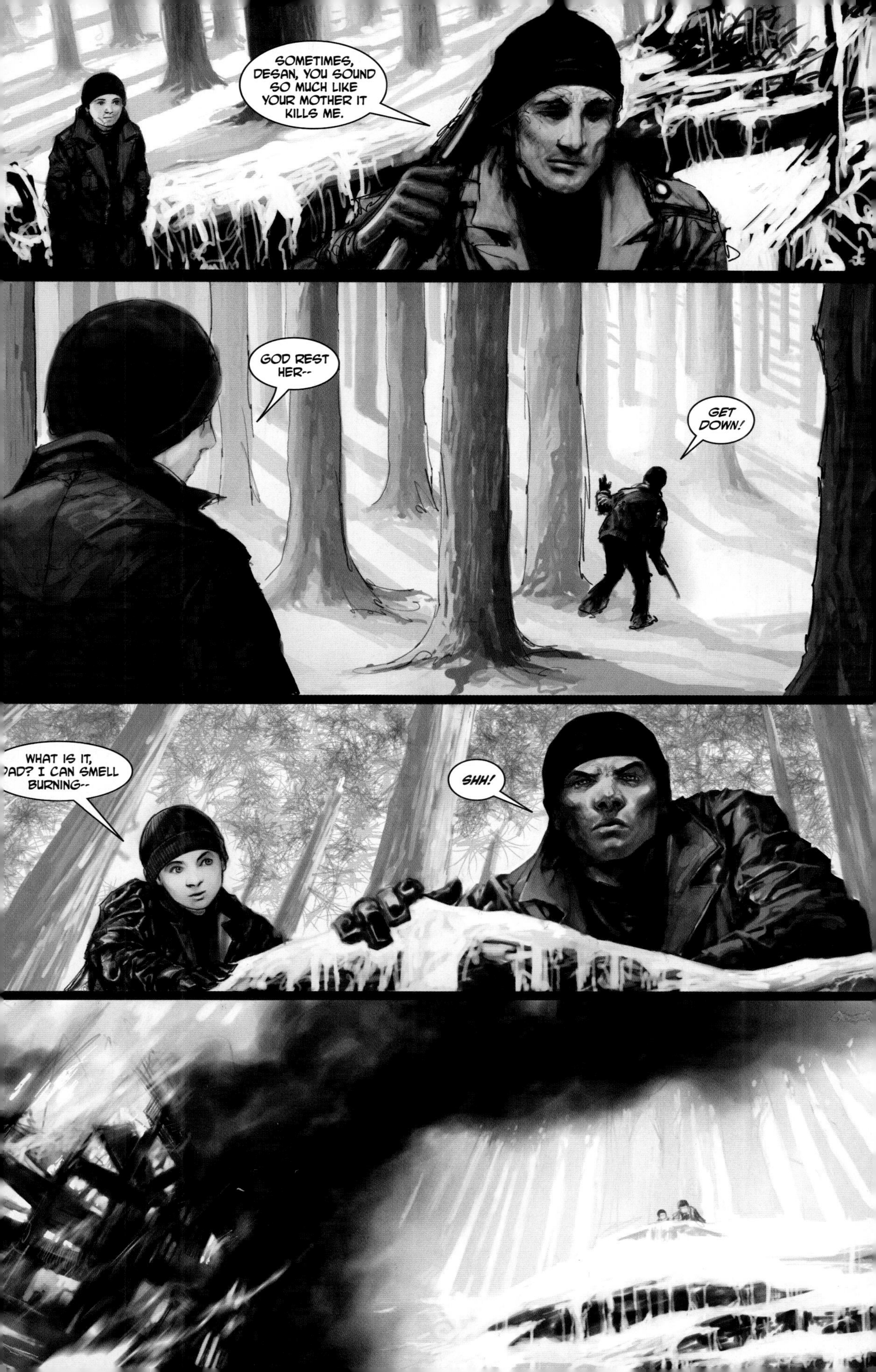
SOMETIMES, DESAN, YOU SOUND SO MUCH LIKE YOUR MOTHER IT KILLS ME.
GOD REST HER--
GET DOWN!
WHAT IS IT, DAD? I CAN SMELL BURNING--
SHH!

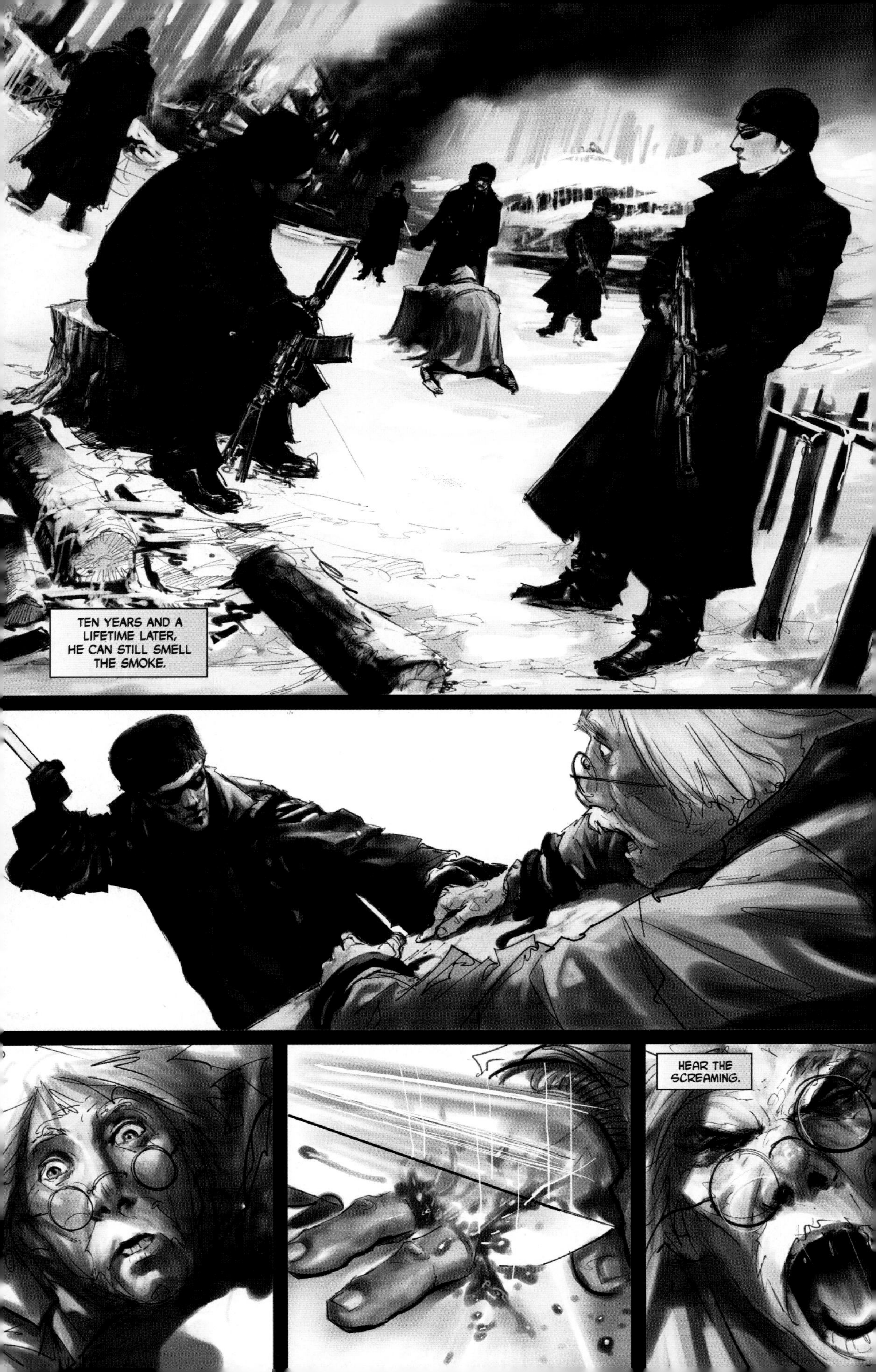
TEN YEARS AND A LIFETIME LATER, HE CAN STILL SMELL THE SMOKE.
HEAR THE SCREAMING.

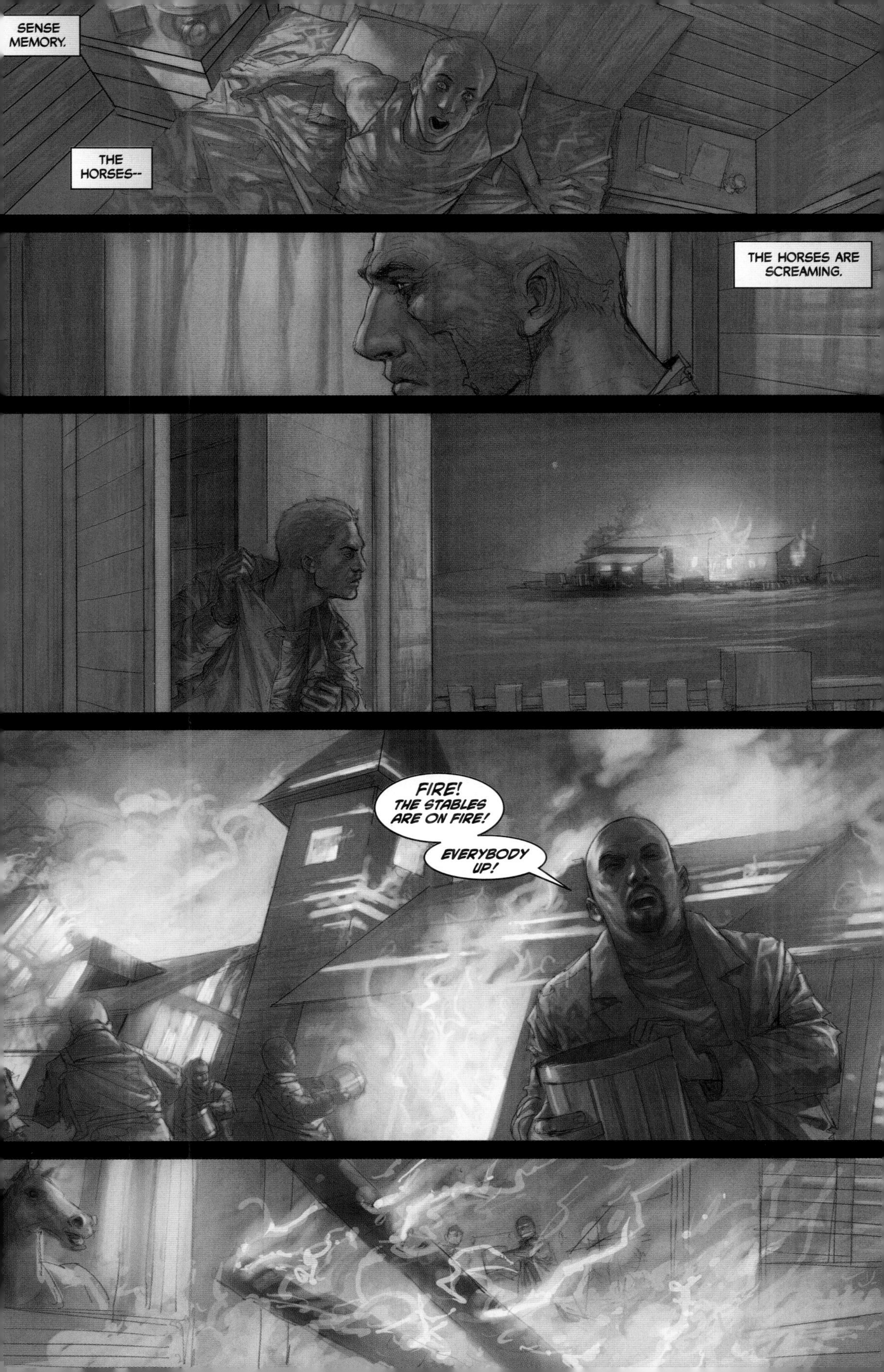
SENSE MEMORY.
THE HORSES--
THE HORSES ARE SCREAMING.
FIRE! THE STABLES ARE ON FIRE!
EVERYBODY UP!

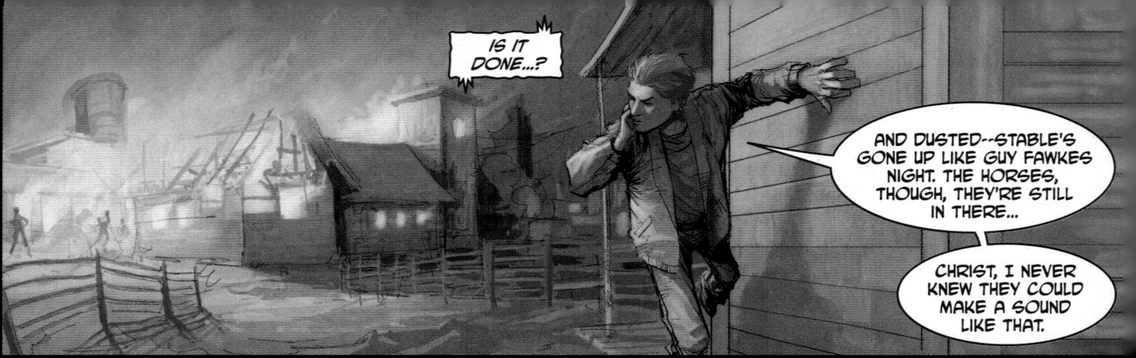
IS IT DONE...?
AND DUSTED--STABLE'S GONE UP LIKE GUY FAWKES NIGHT. THE HORSES, THOUGH, THEY'RE STILL IN THERE...
CHRIST, I NEVER KNEW THEY COULD MAKE A SOUND LIKE THAT.

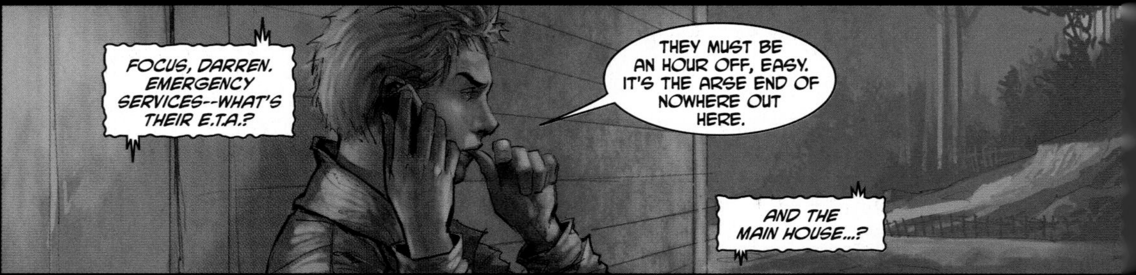
FOCUS, DARREN. EMERGENCY SERVICES--WHAT'S THEIR E.T.A.?
THEY MUST BE AN HOUR OFF, EASY. IT'S THE ARSE END OF NOWHERE OUT HERE.
AND THE MAIN HOUSE...?

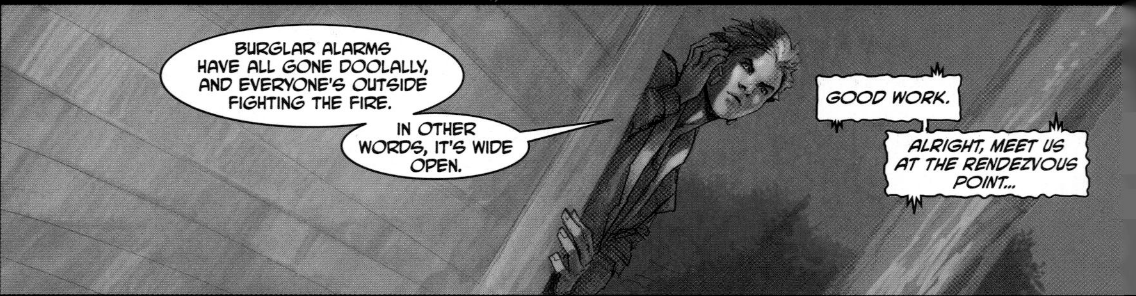
BURGLAR ALARMS HAVE ALL GONE DOOLALLY, AND EVERYONE'S OUTSIDE FIGHTING THE FIRE.
IN OTHER WORDS, IT'S WIDE OPEN.
GOOD WORK.
ALRIGHT, MEET US AT THE RENDEZVOUS POINT...

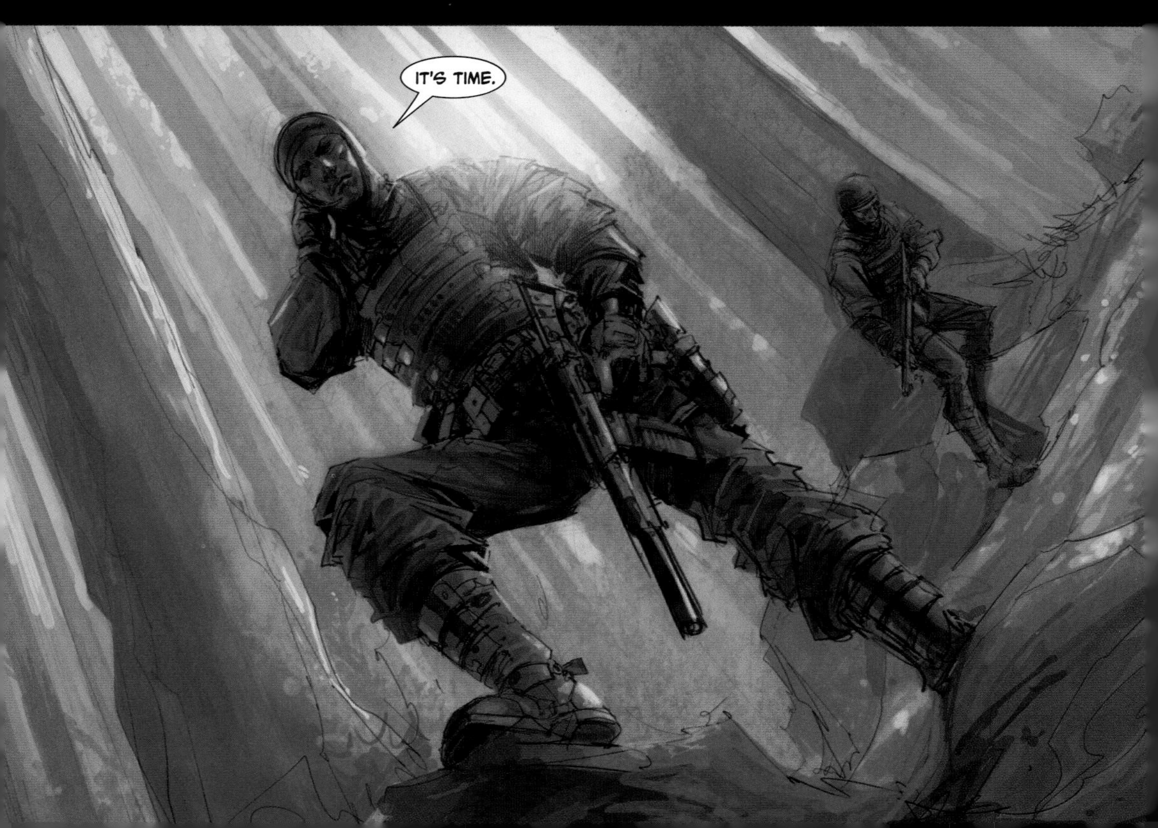
IT'S TIME.

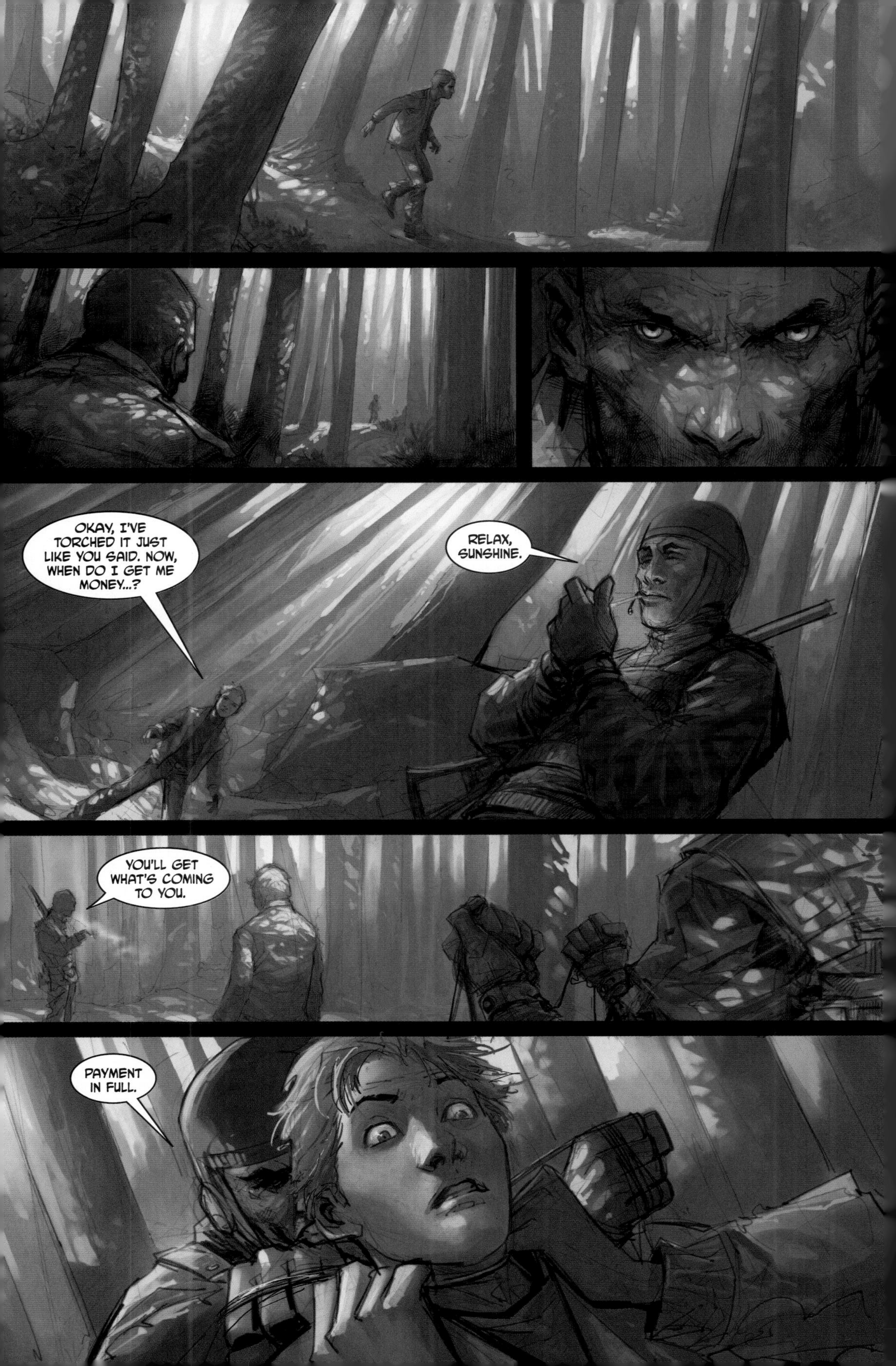
OKAY, I'VE TORCHED IT JUST LIKE YOU SAID. NOW, WHEN DO I GET ME MONEY...?
RELAX, SUNSHINE.
YOU'LL GET WHAT'S COMING TO YOU.
PAYMENT IN FULL.

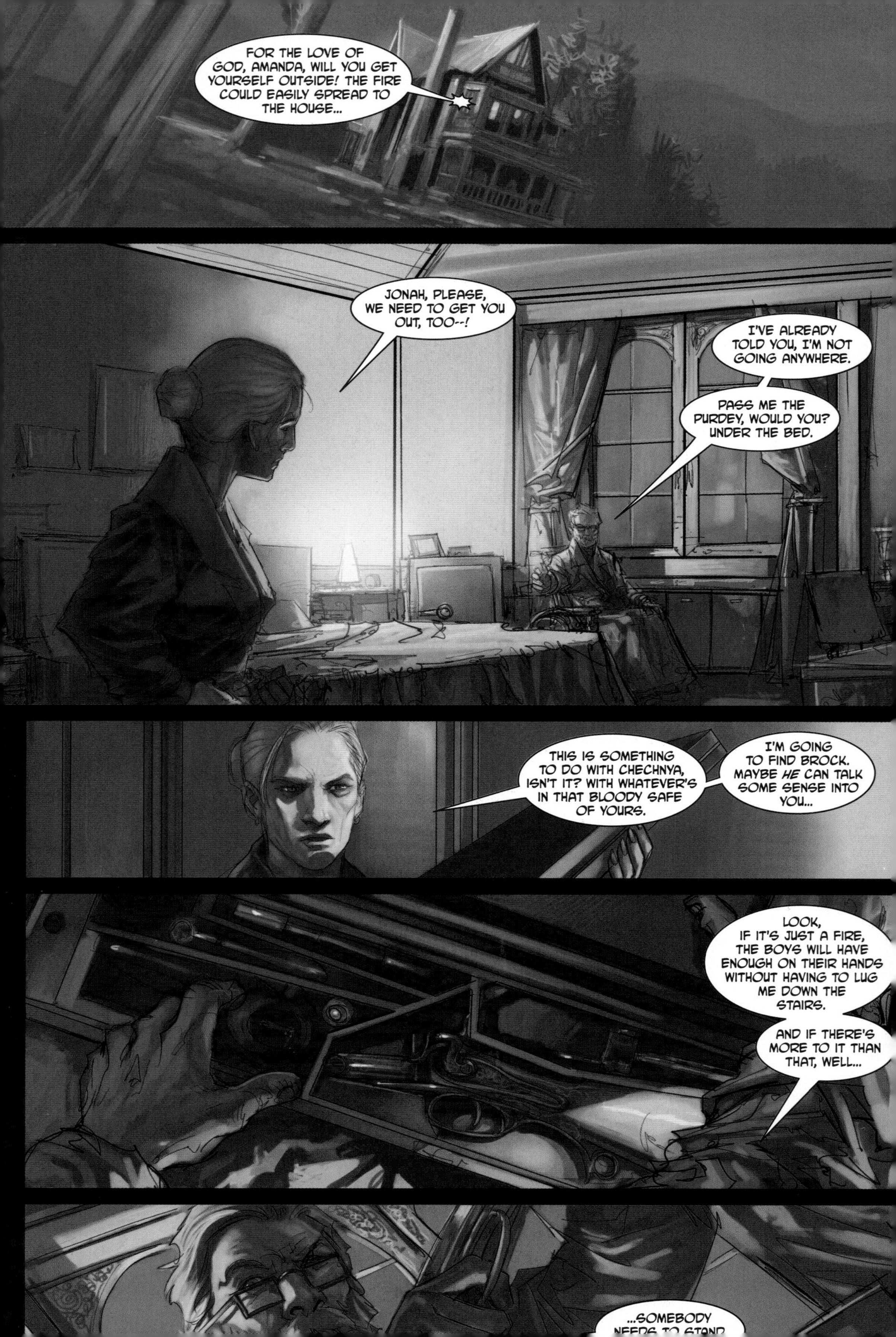
FOR THE LOVE OF GOD, AMANDA, WILL YOU GET YOURSELF OUTSIDE! THE FIRE COULD EASILY SPREAD TO THE HOUSE...
JONAH, PLEASE, WE NEED TO GET YOU OUT, TOO--!
I'VE ALREADY TOLD YOU, I'M NOT GOING ANYWHERE.
PASS ME THE PURDEY, WOULD YOU? UNDER THE BED.
THIS IS SOMETHING TO DO WITH CHECHNYA, ISN'T IT? WITH WHATEVER'S IN THAT BLOODY SAFE OF YOURS.
I'M GOING TO FIND BROCK. MAYBE *HE* CAN TALK SOME SENSE INTO YOU...
LOOK, IF IT'S JUST A FIRE, THE BOYS WILL HAVE ENOUGH ON THEIR HANDS WITHOUT HAVING TO LUG ME DOWN THE STAIRS.
AND IF THERE'S MORE TO IT THAN THAT, WELL...
...SOMEBODY

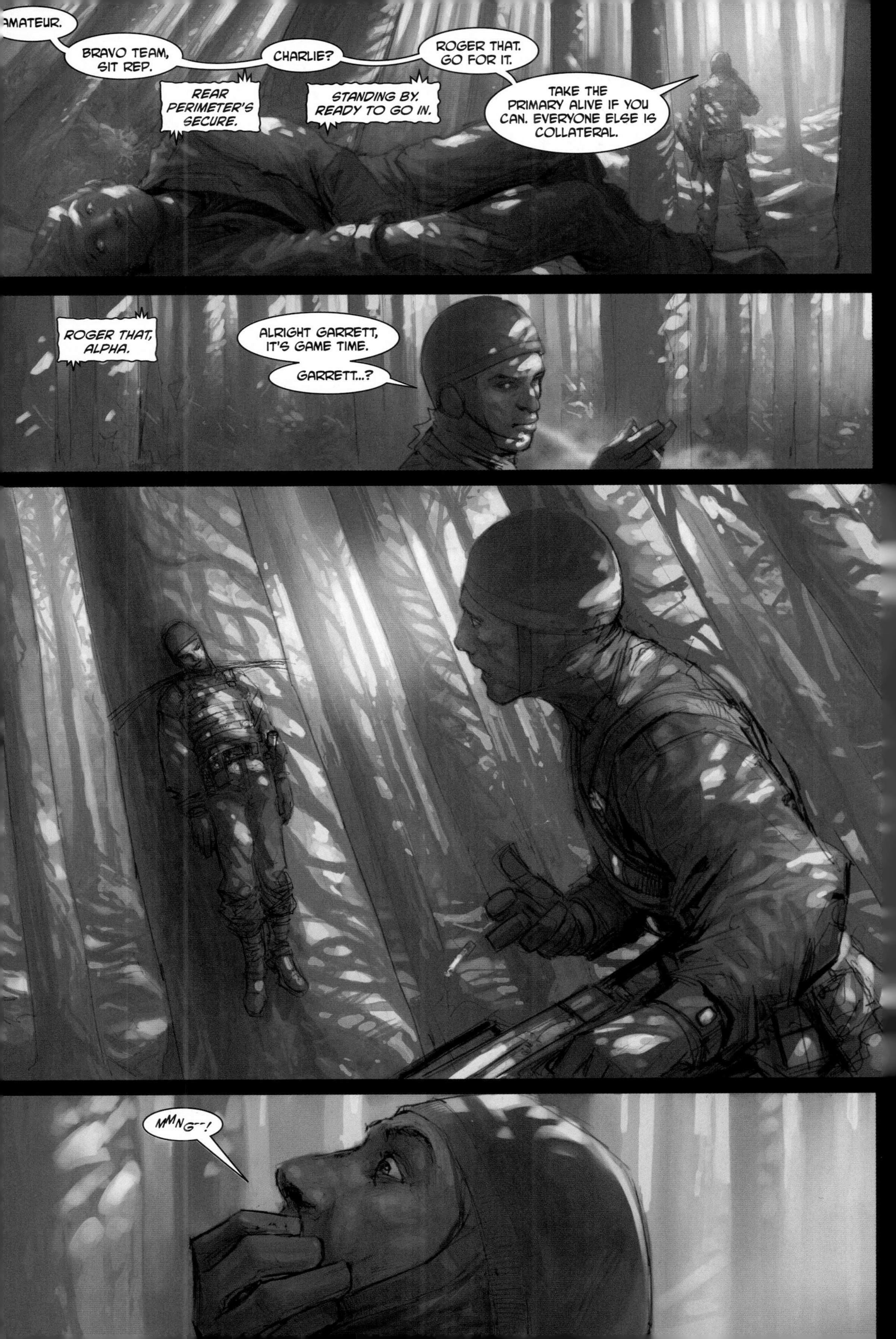
AMATEUR.
BRAVO TEAM, SIT REP.
REAR PERIMETER'S SECURE.
CHARLIE?
STANDING BY. READY TO GO IN.
ROGER THAT. GO FOR IT.
TAKE THE PRIMARY ALIVE IF YOU CAN. EVERYONE ELSE IS COLLATERAL.
ROGER THAT, ALPHA.
ALRIGHT GARRETT, IT'S GAME TIME.
GARRETT...?
MMNG--!

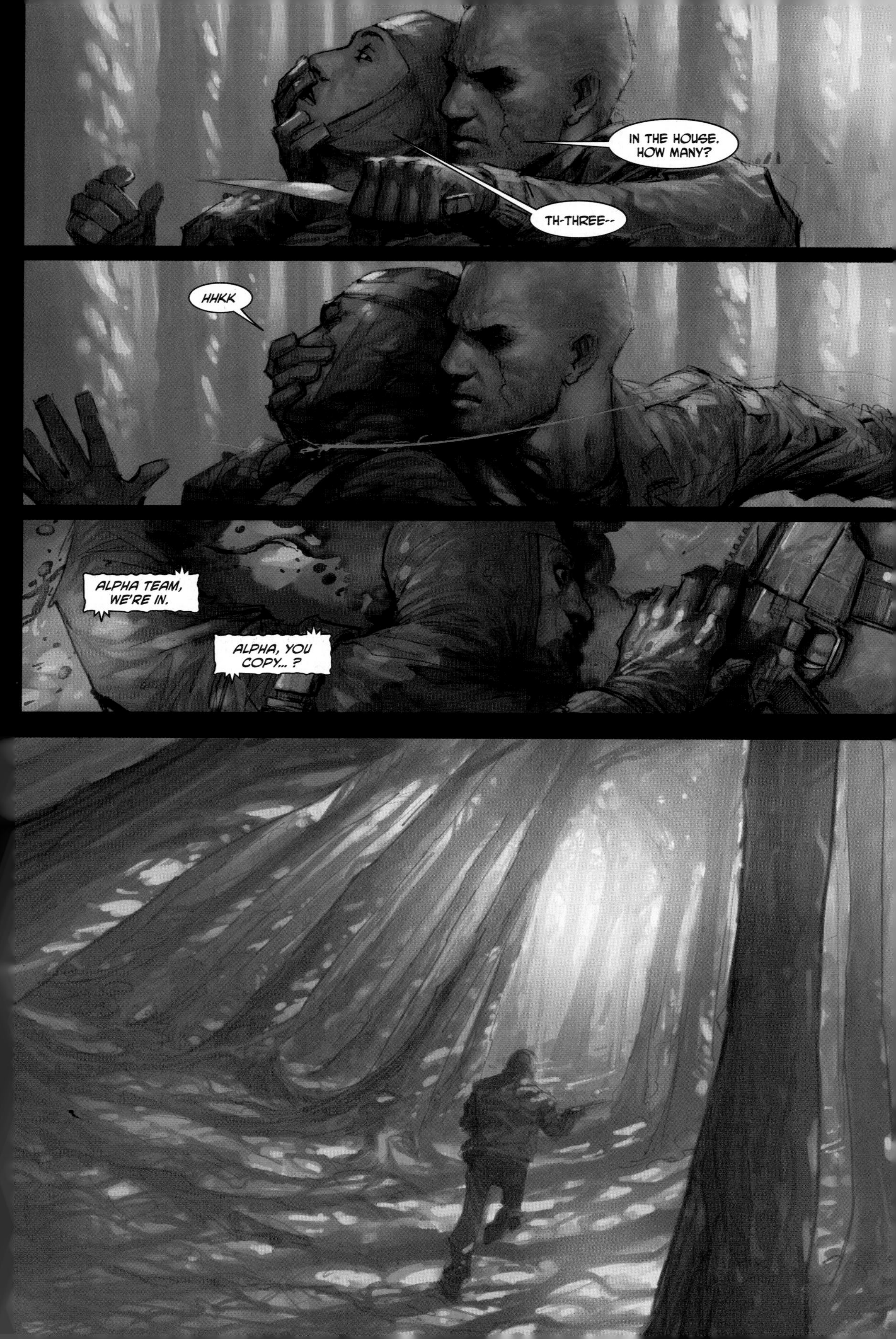
IN THE HOUSE. HOW MANY?
TH-THREE--
HHKK
ALPHA TEAM, WE'RE IN.
ALPHA, YOU COPY... ?

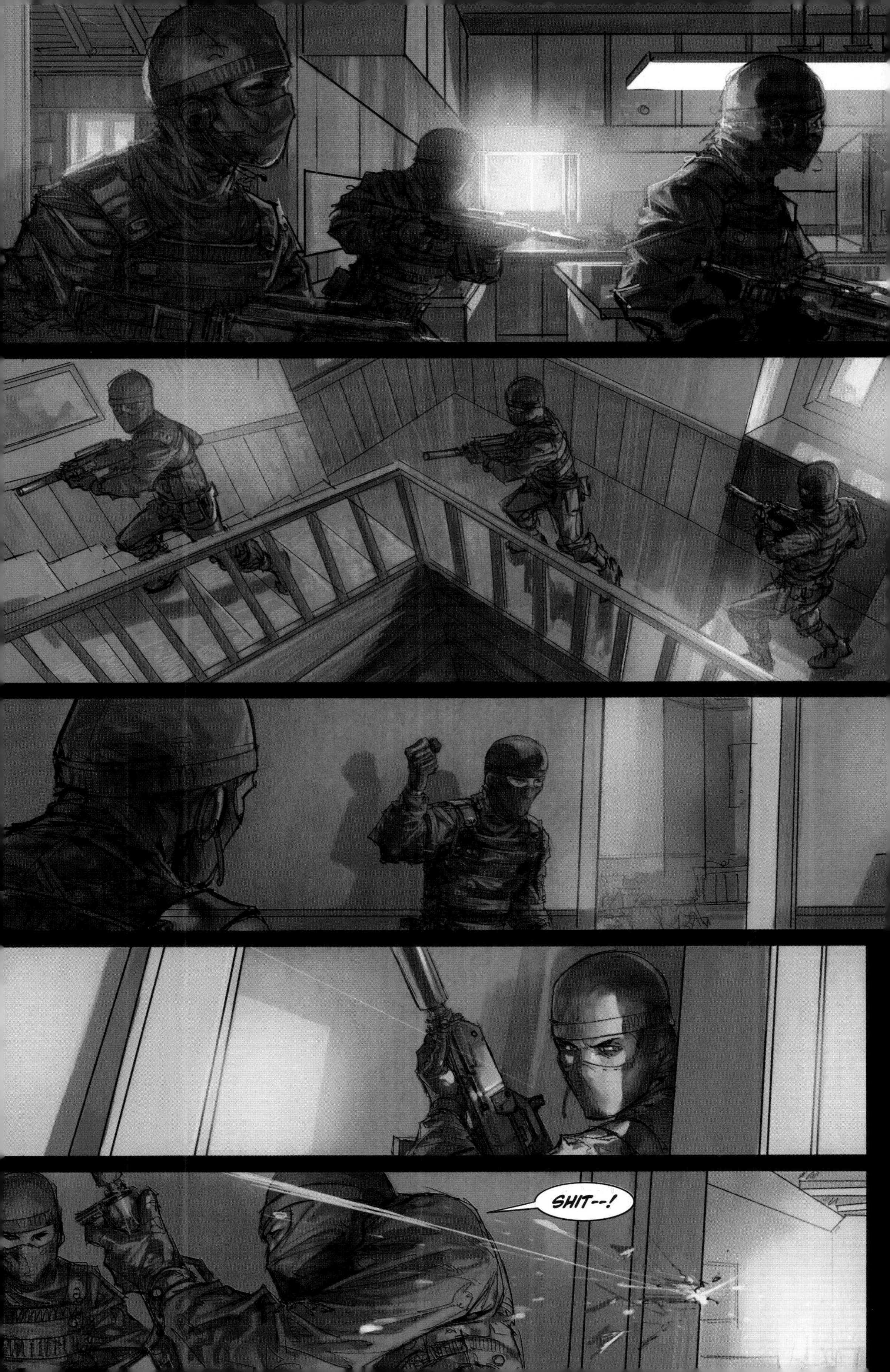
SHIT--!

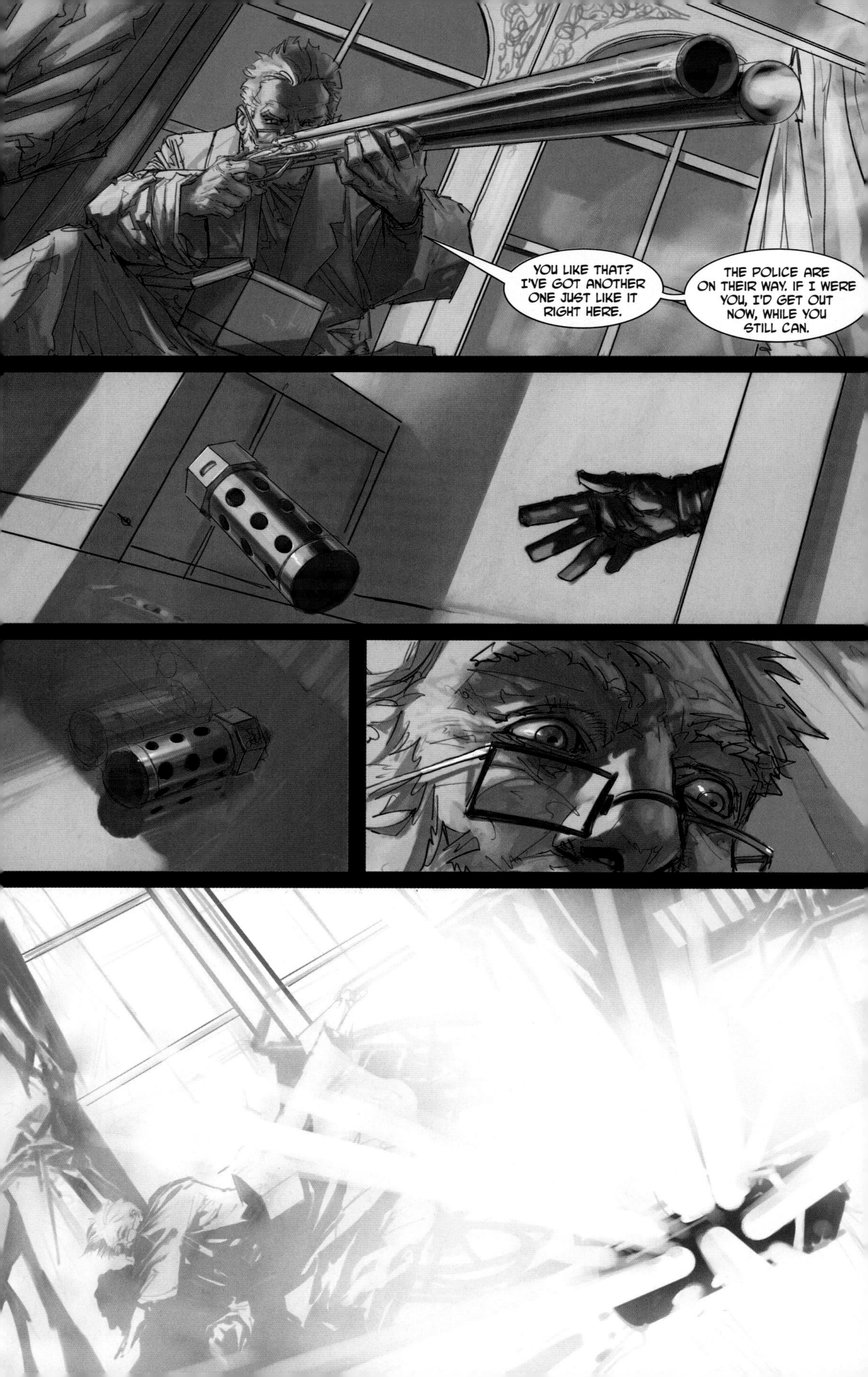
YOU LIKE THAT? I'VE GOT ANOTHER ONE JUST LIKE IT RIGHT HERE.
THE POLICE ARE ON THEIR WAY. IF I WERE YOU, I'D GET OUT NOW, WHILE YOU STILL CAN.

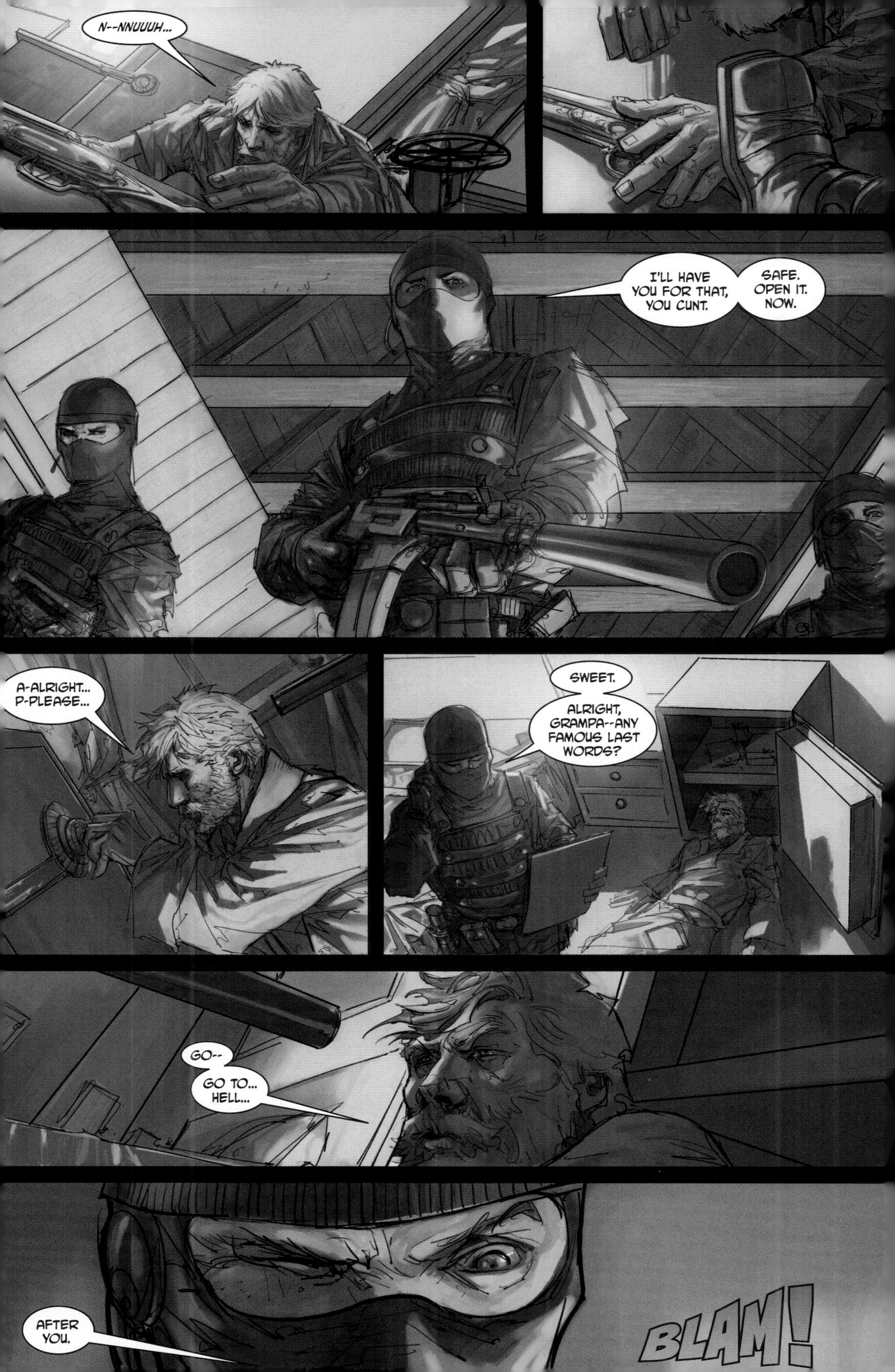
N--NNUUUH...
I'LL HAVE YOU FOR THAT, YOU CUNT.
SAFE. OPEN IT. NOW.
A-ALRIGHT... P-PLEASE...
SWEET.
ALRIGHT, GRAMPA--ANY FAMOUS LAST WORDS?
GO--
GO TO... HELL...
AFTER YOU.
BLAM!

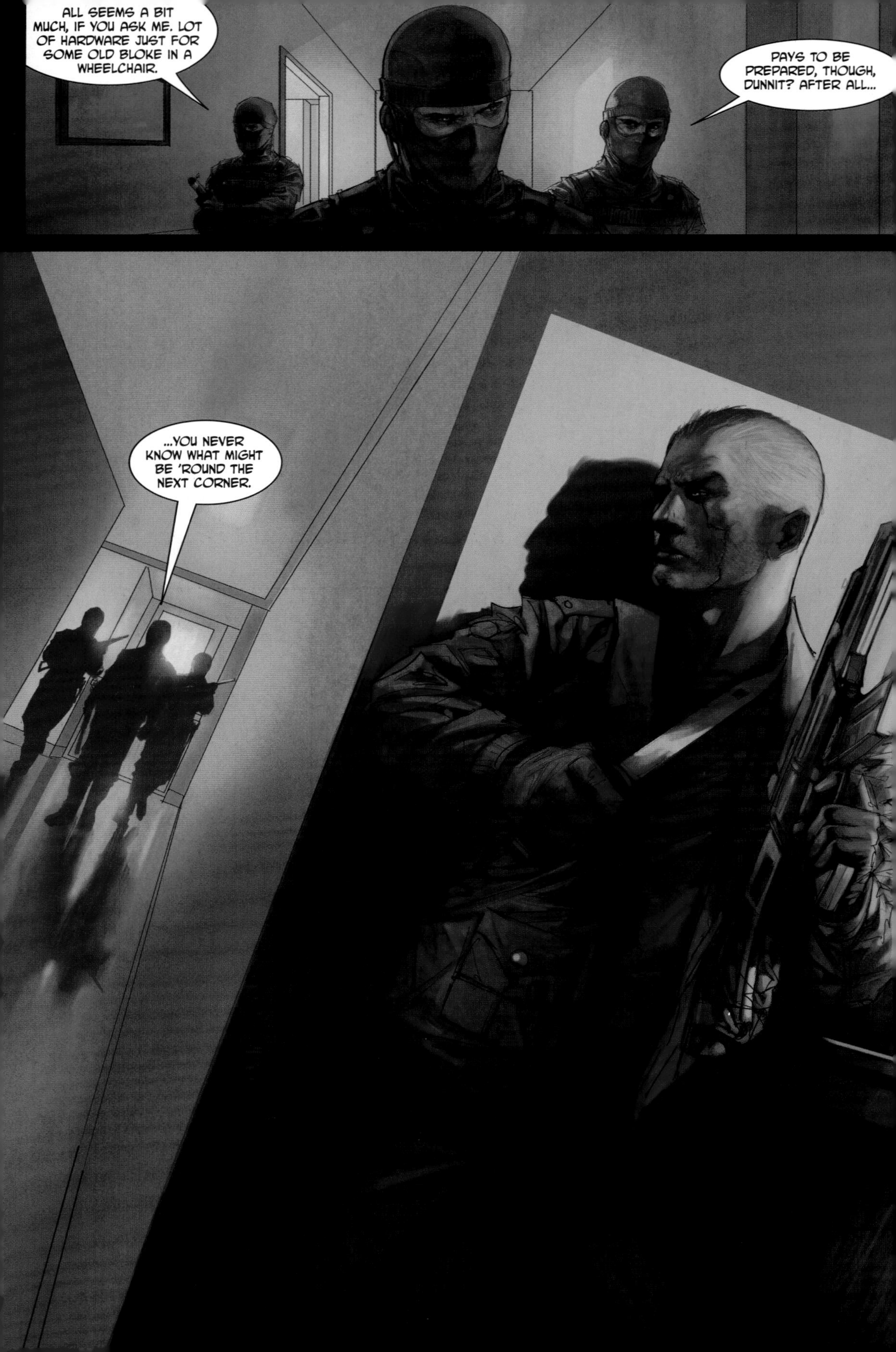
ALL SEEMS A BIT MUCH, IF YOU ASK ME. LOT OF HARDWARE JUST FOR SOME OLD BLOKE IN A WHEELCHAIR.
PAYS TO BE PREPARED, THOUGH, DUNNIT? AFTER ALL...
...YOU NEVER KNOW WHAT MIGHT BE 'ROUND THE NEXT CORNER.

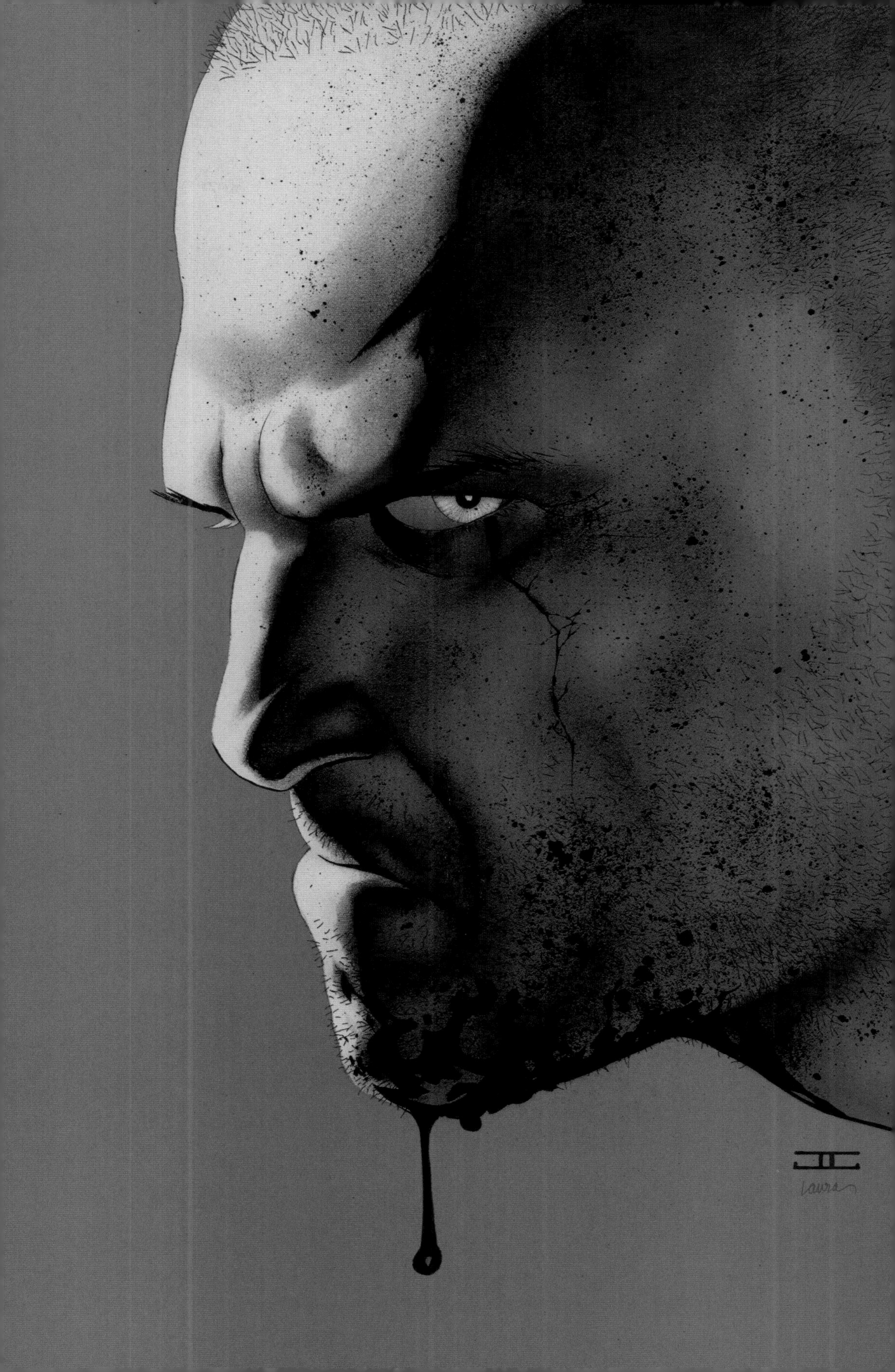
Laura

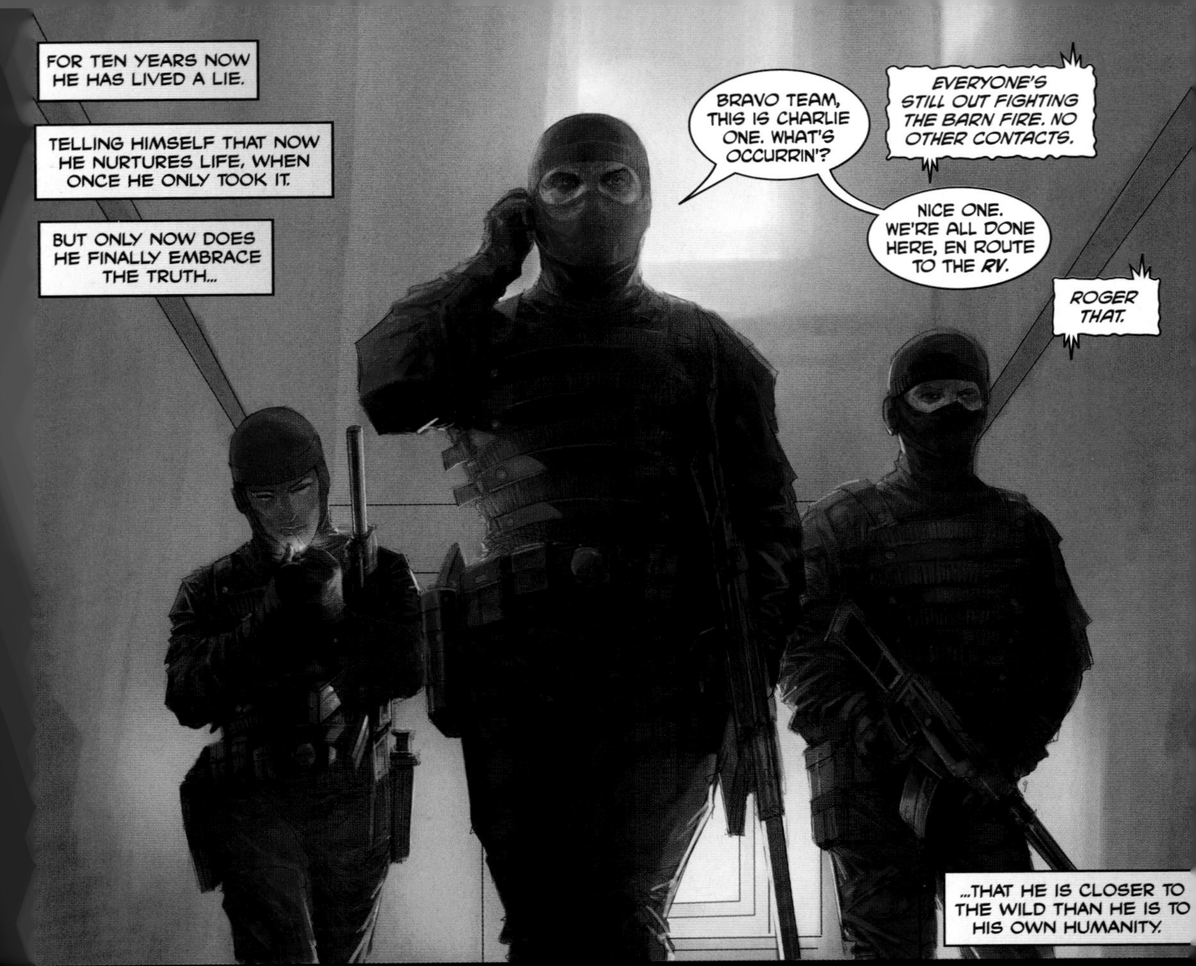
FOR TEN YEARS NOW HE HAS LIVED A LIE.
TELLING HIMSELF THAT NOW HE NURTURES LIFE, WHEN ONCE HE ONLY TOOK IT.
BUT ONLY NOW DOES HE FINALLY EMBRACE THE TRUTH...
BRAVO TEAM, THIS IS CHARLIE ONE. WHAT'S OCCURRIN'?
EVERYONE'S STILL OUT FIGHTING THE BARN FIRE. NO OTHER CONTACTS.
NICE ONE. WE'RE ALL DONE HERE, EN ROUTE TO THE RV.
ROGER THAT.
...THAT HE IS CLOSER TO THE WILD THAN HE IS TO HIS OWN HUMANITY.
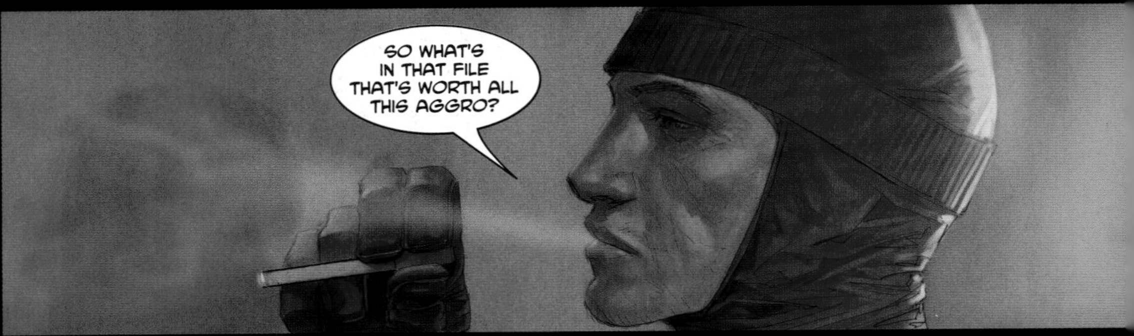
SO WHAT'S IN THAT FILE THAT'S WORTH ALL THIS AGGRO?
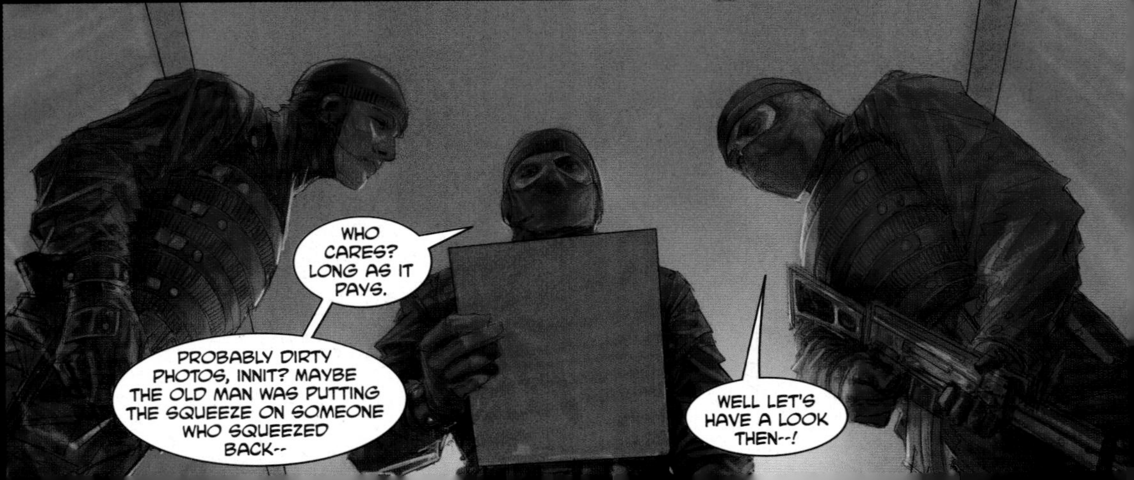
WHO CARES? LONG AS IT PAYS.
PROBABLY DIRTY PHOTOS, INNIT? MAYBE THE OLD MAN WAS PUTTING THE SQUEEZE ON SOMEONE WHO SQUEEZED BACK--
WELL LET'S HAVE A LOOK THEN--!

$$0n + {}^{235}_{92}U \rightarrow {}^{236}_{92}U +$$
$$\rightarrow {}^{141}_{56}Ba + {}^{92}_{36}Kr + 3({}^{1}_{0}n)$$
$$P + {}^{11}B \rightarrow 3\ {}^{4}He + 8.7\ Mev$$

IT'S NOT DIRTY PICTURES, IT'S...I DUNNO, *GREEK* OR SOMETHING.

THAT'S NOT GREEK, YOU MUPPET! IT'S *AN EQUATION*.

WHAT, A MATHS EQUATION? IS THAT REALLY WORTH A BODYCOUNT...?

IN THE WILD THERE IS NO CONSCIENCE.

NO MORALITY.

ONLY NECESSITY.

ONLY *SURVIVAL*.

AT ANY COST.

YES.

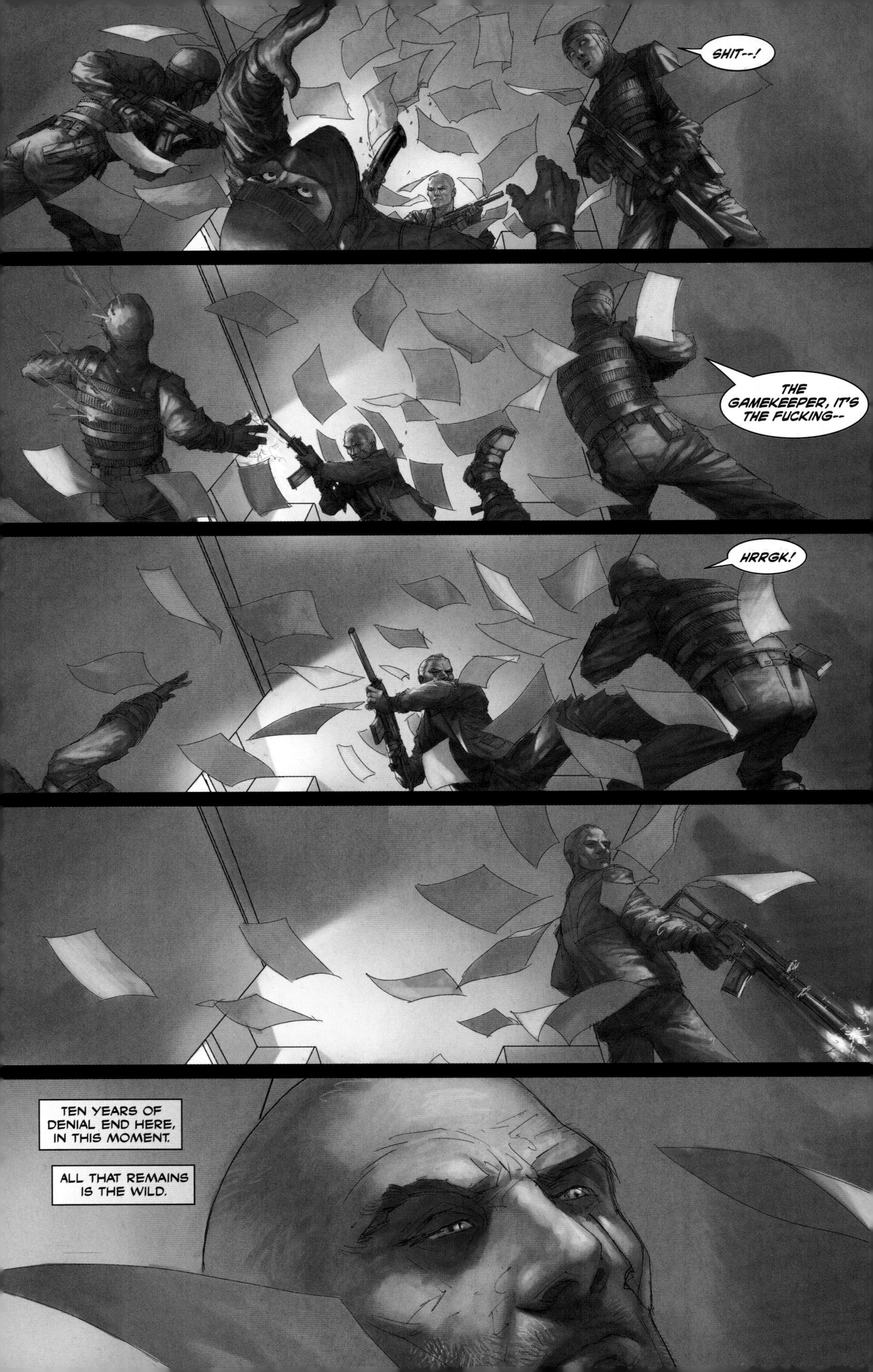
SHIT--!
THE GAMEKEEPER, IT'S THE FUCKING--
HRRGK!
TEN YEARS OF DENIAL END HERE, IN THIS MOMENT.
ALL THAT REMAINS IS THE WILD.

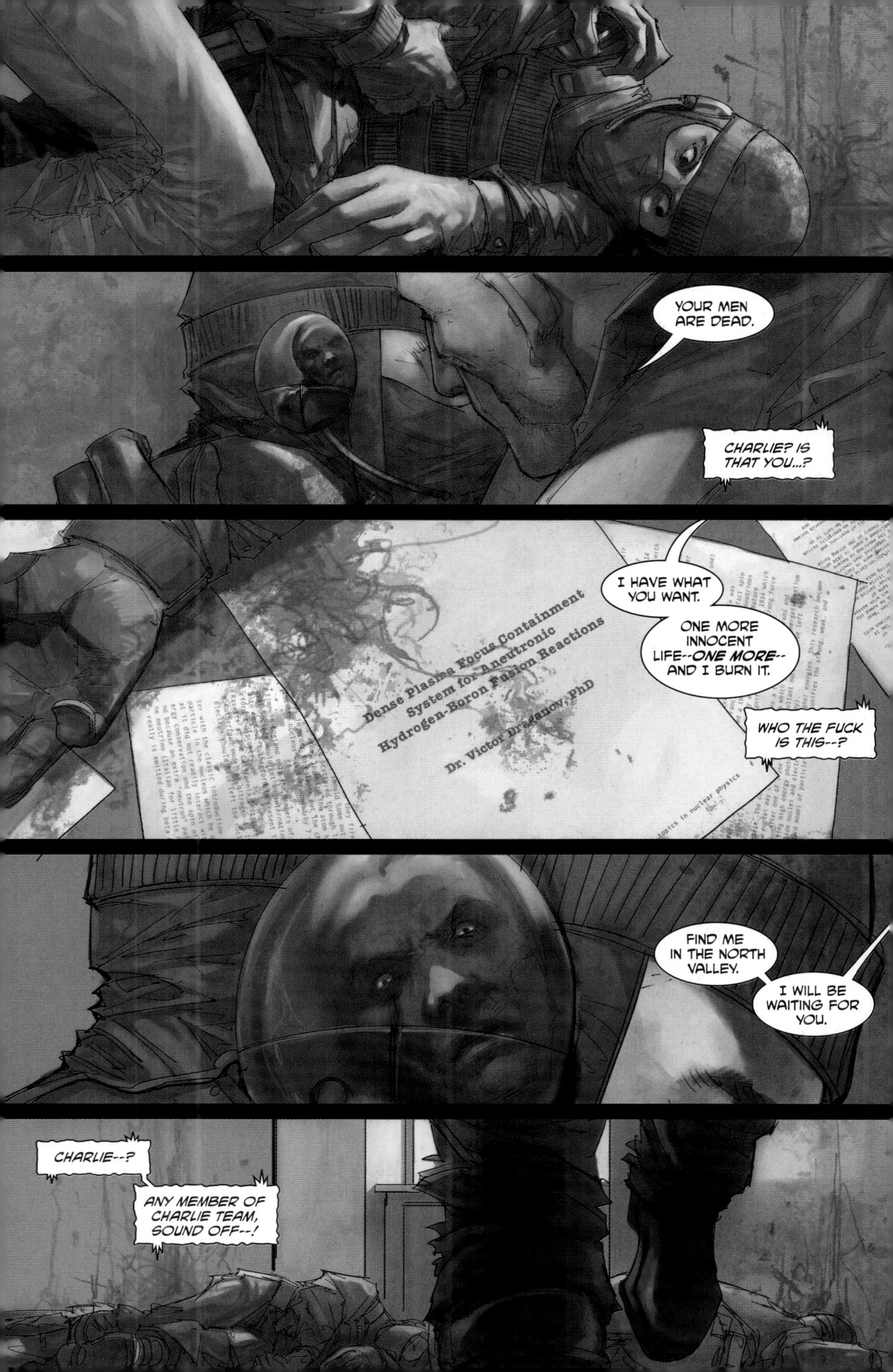
YOUR MEN ARE DEAD.
CHARLIE? IS THAT YOU...?
Dense Plasma Focus Containment System for Aneutronic Hydrogen-Boron Fusion Reactions
Dr. Victor Draganov, PhD
I HAVE WHAT YOU WANT.
ONE MORE INNOCENT LIFE--*ONE MORE*--AND I BURN IT.
WHO THE FUCK IS THIS--?
FIND ME IN THE NORTH VALLEY.
I WILL BE WAITING FOR YOU.
CHARLIE--?
ANY MEMBER OF CHARLIE TEAM, SOUND OFF--!

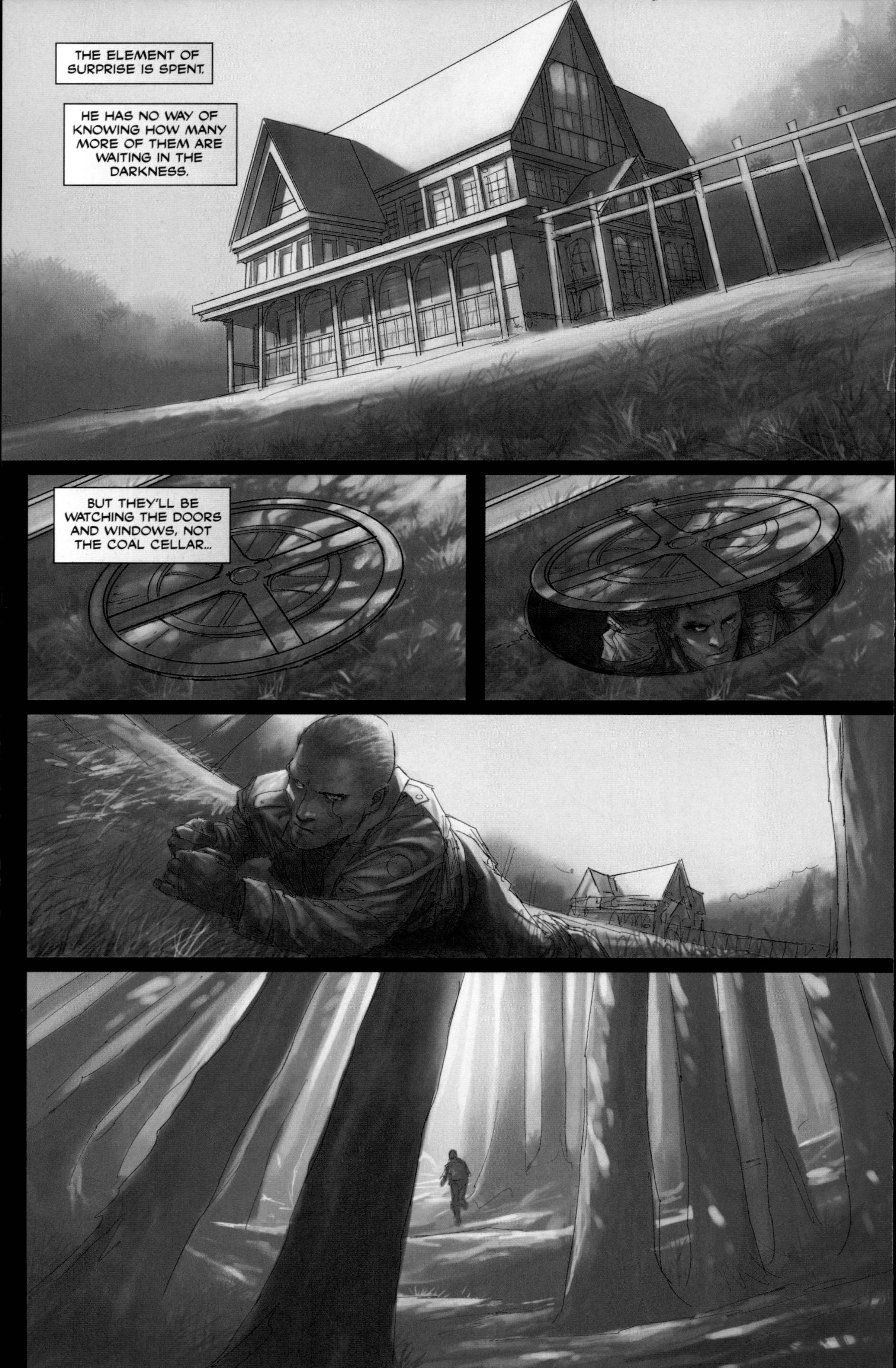
THE ELEMENT OF SURPRISE IS SPENT.
HE HAS NO WAY OF KNOWING HOW MANY MORE OF THEM ARE WAITING IN THE DARKNESS.
BUT THEY'LL BE WATCHING THE DOORS AND WINDOWS, NOT THE COAL CELLAR...

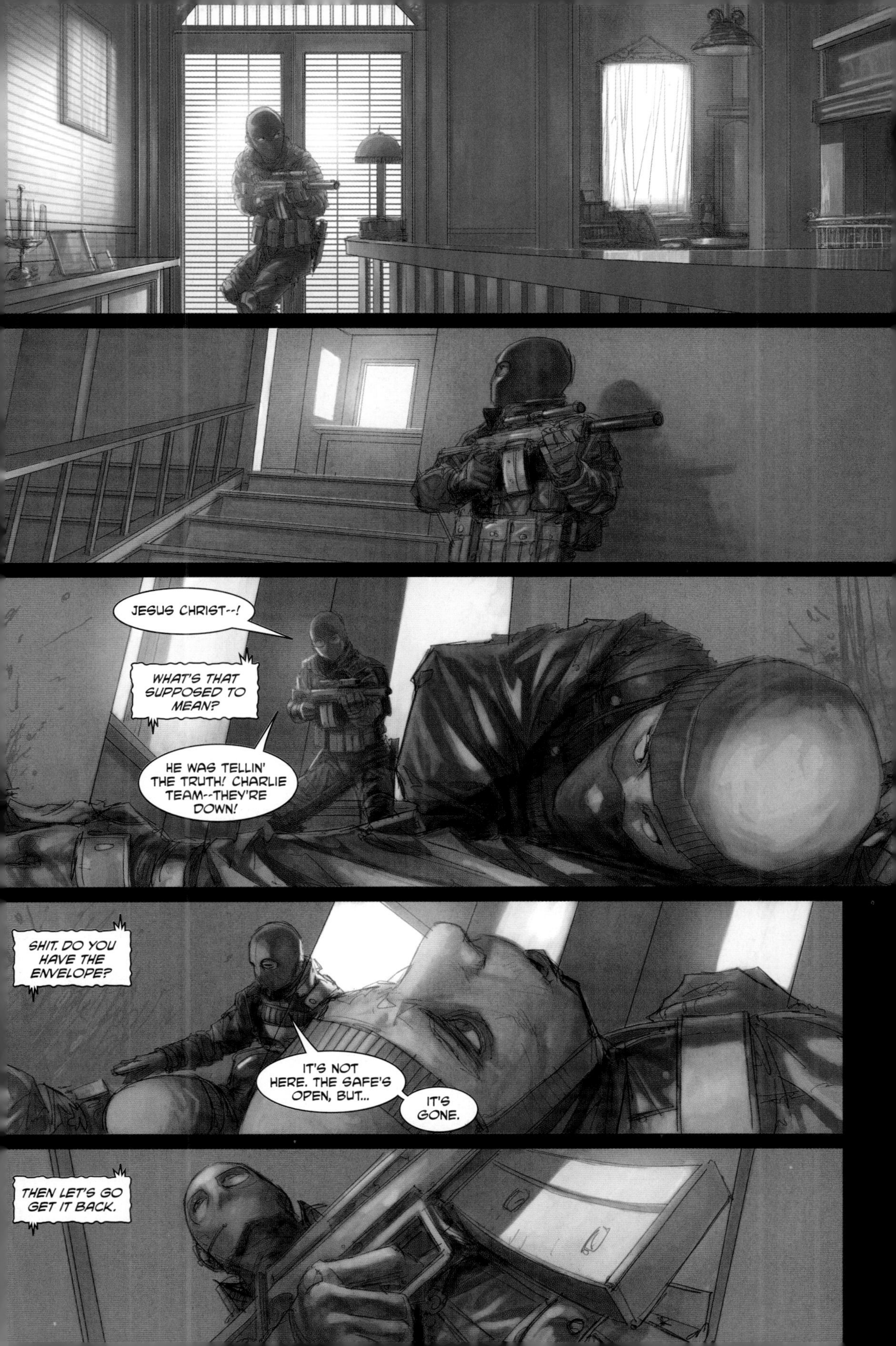
JESUS CHRIST--!
WHAT'S THAT SUPPOSED TO MEAN?
HE WAS TELLIN' THE TRUTH! CHARLIE TEAM--THEY'RE DOWN!
SHIT. DO YOU HAVE THE ENVELOPE?
IT'S NOT HERE. THE SAFE'S OPEN, BUT...
IT'S GONE.
THEN LET'S GO GET IT BACK.

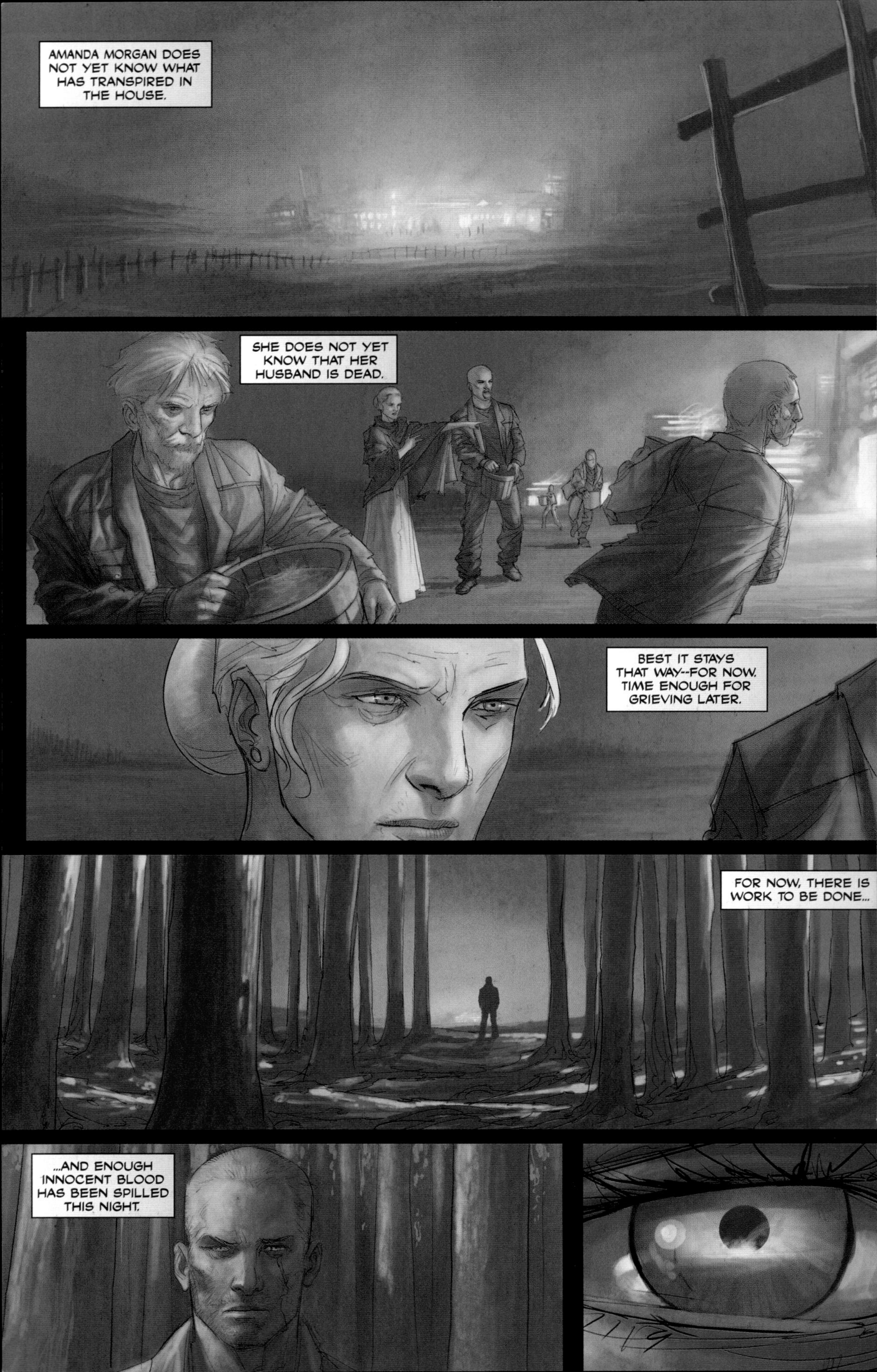
AMANDA MORGAN DOES NOT YET KNOW WHAT HAS TRANSPIRED IN THE HOUSE.
SHE DOES NOT YET KNOW THAT HER HUSBAND IS DEAD.
BEST IT STAYS THAT WAY--FOR NOW. TIME ENOUGH FOR GRIEVING LATER.
FOR NOW, THERE IS WORK TO BE DONE...
...AND ENOUGH INNOCENT BLOOD HAS BEEN SPILLED THIS NIGHT.

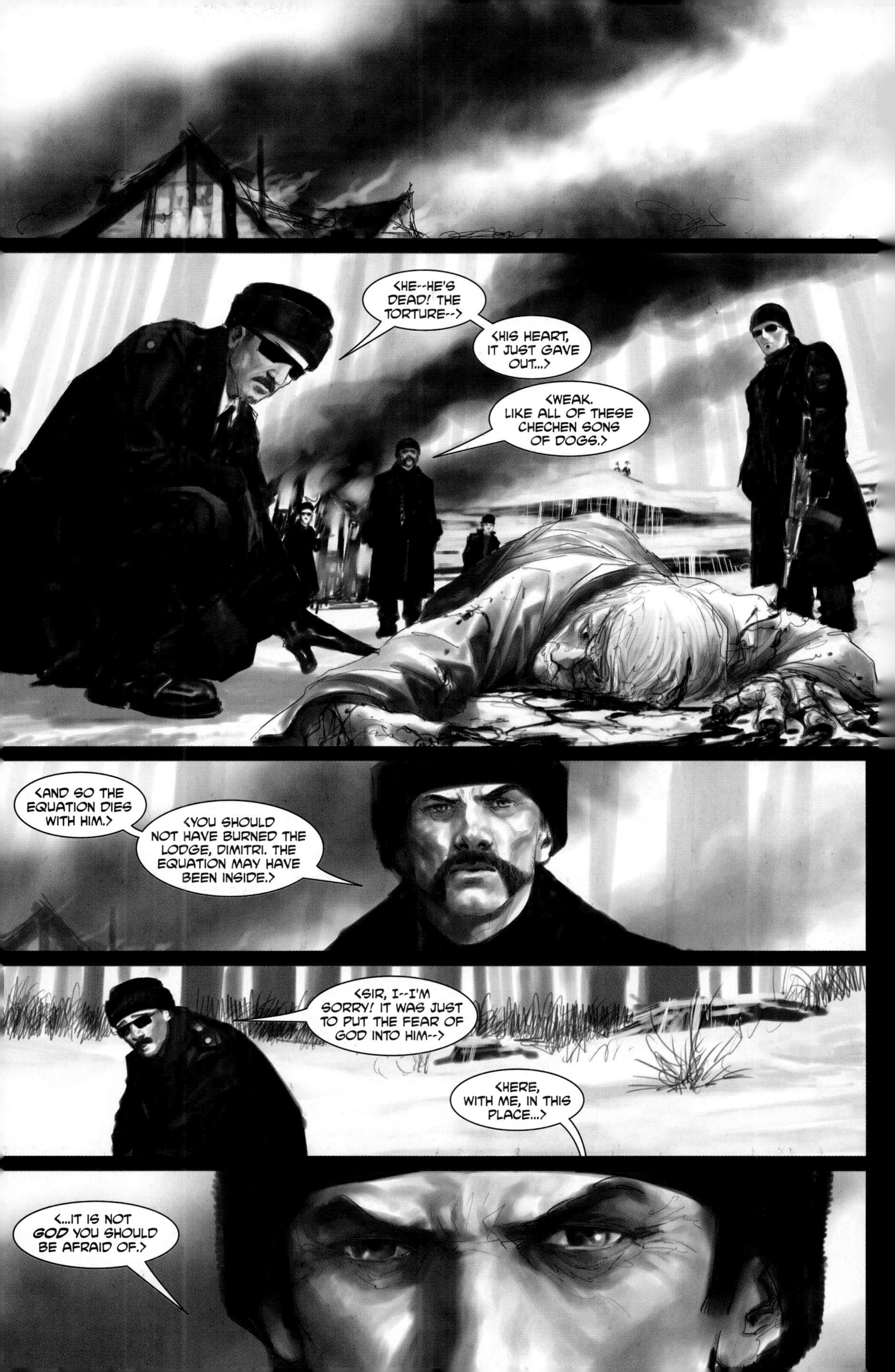
<HE--HE'S DEAD! THE TORTURE-->
<HIS HEART, IT JUST GAVE OUT...>
<WEAK. LIKE ALL OF THESE CHECHEN SONS OF DOGS.>
<AND SO THE EQUATION DIES WITH HIM.>
<YOU SHOULD NOT HAVE BURNED THE LODGE, DIMITRI. THE EQUATION MAY HAVE BEEN INSIDE.>
<SIR, I--I'M SORRY! IT WAS JUST TO PUT THE FEAR OF GOD INTO HIM-->
<HERE, WITH ME, IN THIS PLACE...>
<...IT IS NOT GOD YOU SHOULD BE AFRAID OF.>

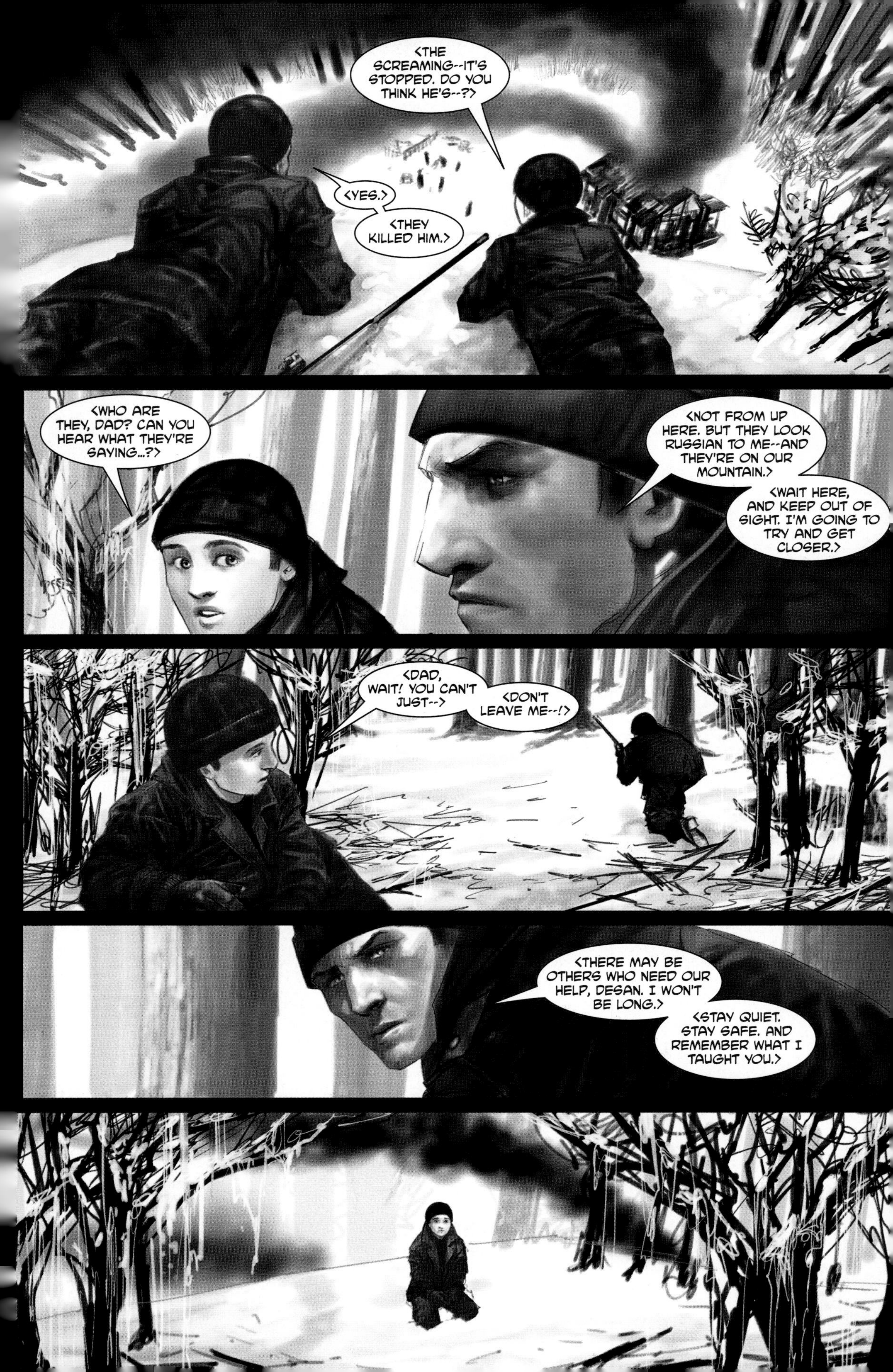
<THE SCREAMING--IT'S STOPPED. DO YOU THINK HE'S--?>
<YES.>
<THEY KILLED HIM.>
<WHO ARE THEY, DAD? CAN YOU HEAR WHAT THEY'RE SAYING...?>
<NOT FROM UP HERE. BUT THEY LOOK RUSSIAN TO ME--AND THEY'RE ON OUR MOUNTAIN.>
<WAIT HERE, AND KEEP OUT OF SIGHT. I'M GOING TO TRY AND GET CLOSER.>
<DAD, WAIT! YOU CAN'T JUST-->
<DON'T LEAVE ME--!>
<THERE MAY BE OTHERS WHO NEED OUR HELP, DESAN. I WON'T BE LONG.>
<STAY QUIET. STAY SAFE. AND REMEMBER WHAT I TAUGHT YOU.>

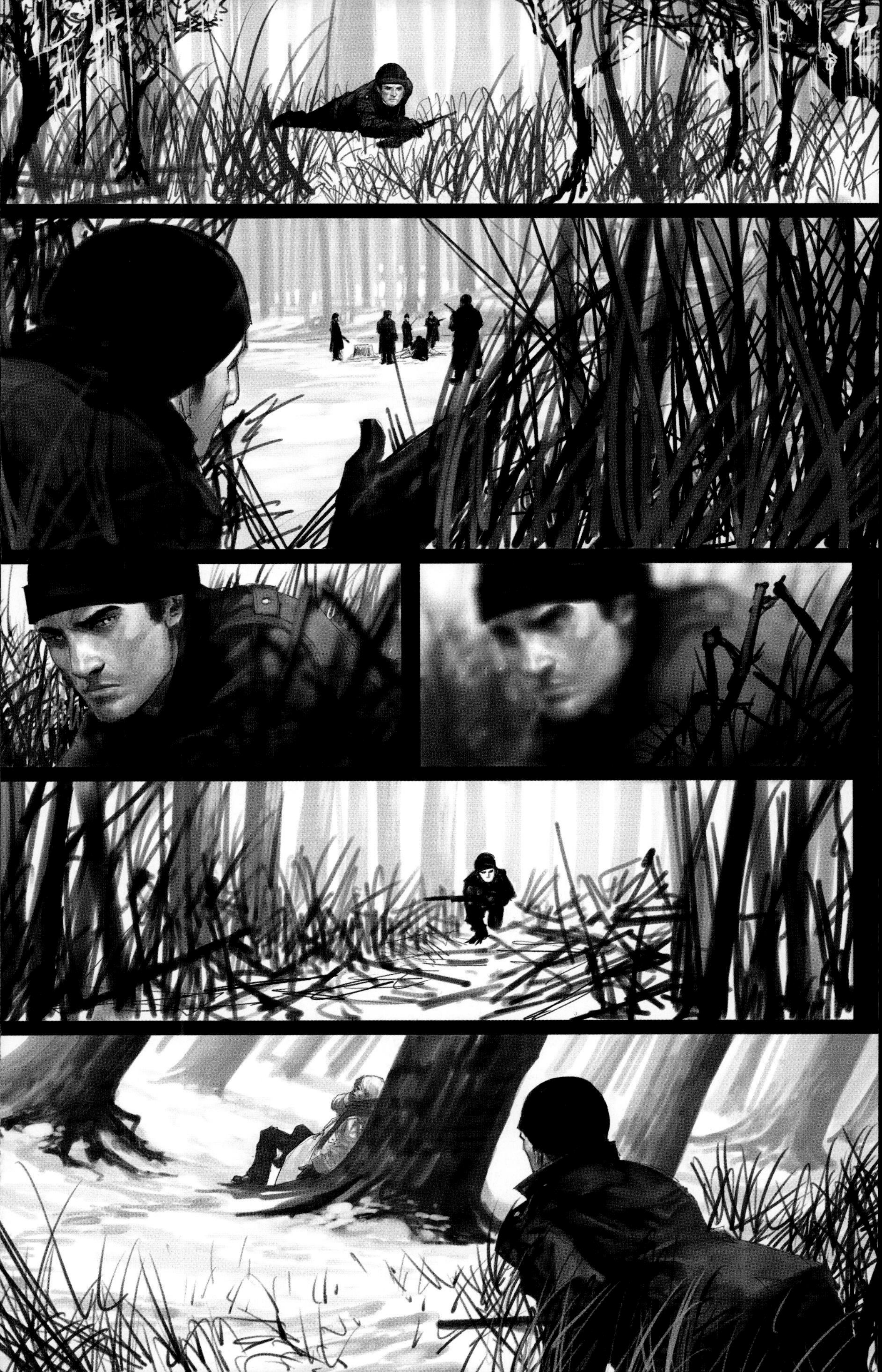

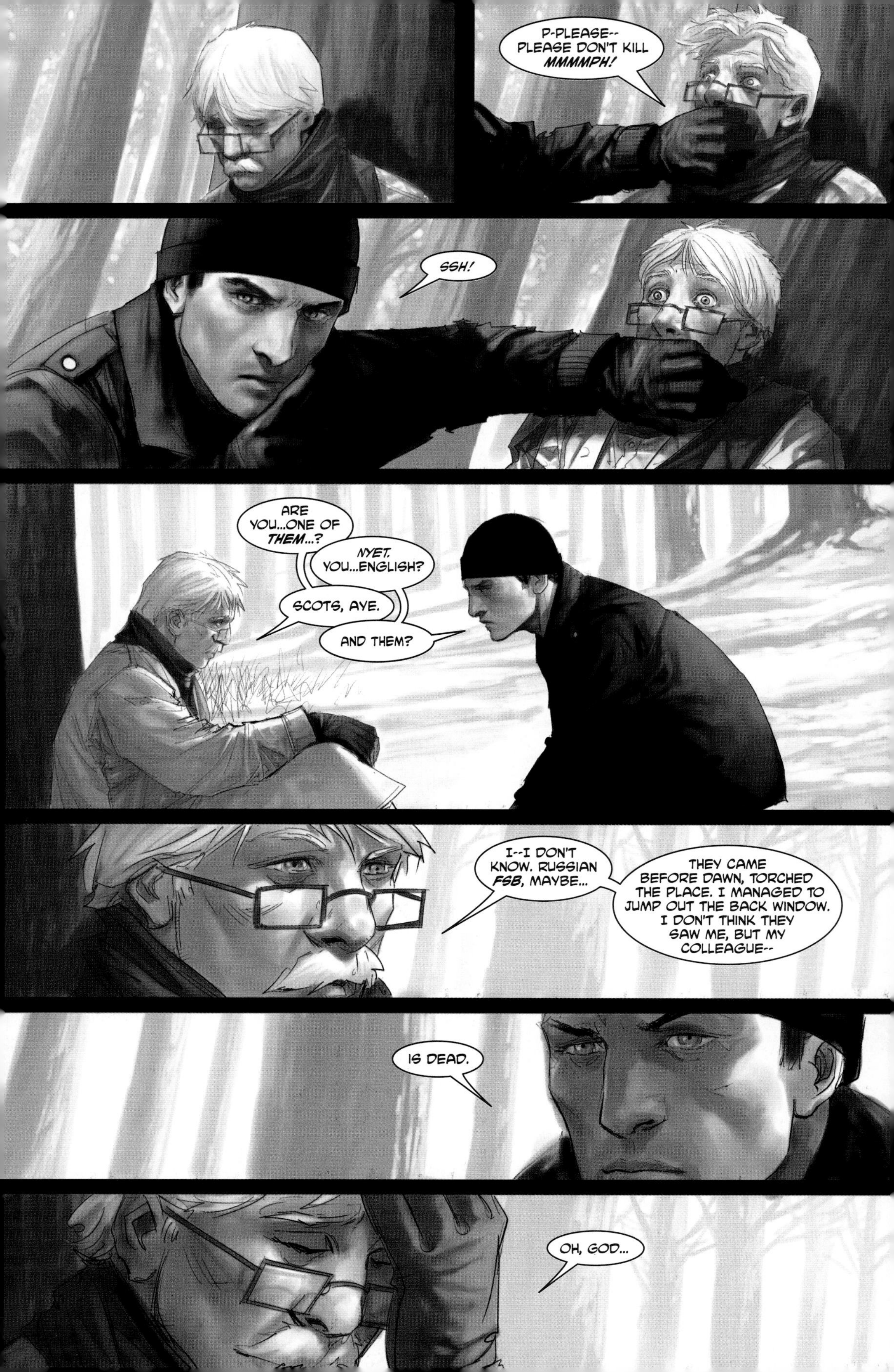
P-PLEASE-- PLEASE DON'T KILL *MMMMPH!*
SSH!
ARE YOU...ONE OF *THEM*...?
NYET. YOU...ENGLISH?
SCOTS, AYE.
AND THEM?
I--I DON'T KNOW. RUSSIAN *FSB*, MAYBE...
THEY CAME BEFORE DAWN, TORCHED THE PLACE. I MANAGED TO JUMP OUT THE BACK WINDOW. I DON'T THINK THEY SAW ME, BUT MY COLLEAGUE--
IS DEAD.
OH, GOD...

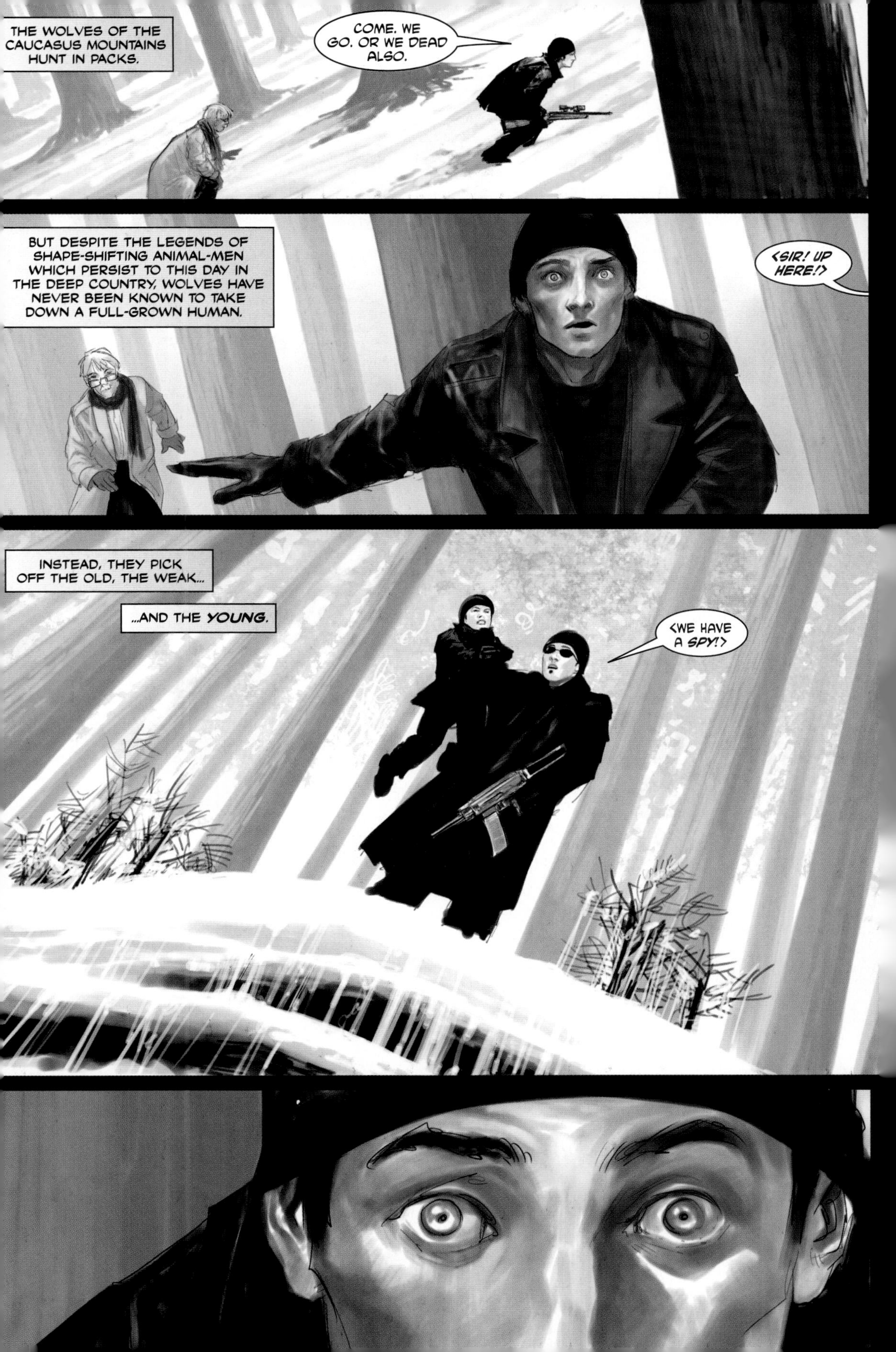
THE WOLVES OF THE CAUCASUS MOUNTAINS HUNT IN PACKS.
COME. WE GO. OR WE DEAD ALSO.
BUT DESPITE THE LEGENDS OF SHAPE-SHIFTING ANIMAL-MEN WHICH PERSIST TO THIS DAY IN THE DEEP COUNTRY, WOLVES HAVE NEVER BEEN KNOWN TO TAKE DOWN A FULL-GROWN HUMAN.
<SIR! UP HERE!>
INSTEAD, THEY PICK OFF THE OLD, THE WEAK...
...AND THE *YOUNG*.
<WE HAVE A *SPY*!>

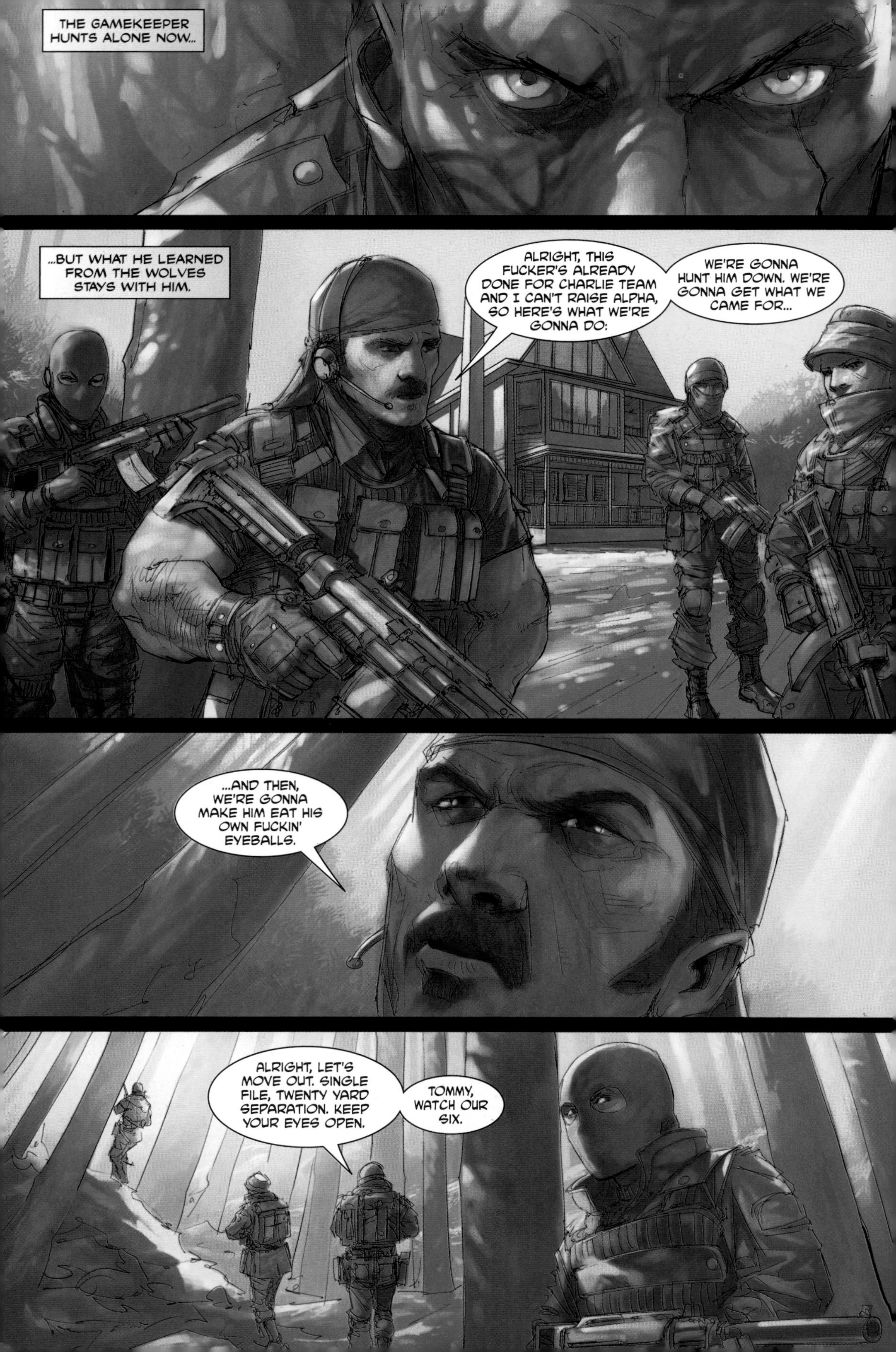
THE GAMEKEEPER HUNTS ALONE NOW...
...BUT WHAT HE LEARNED FROM THE WOLVES STAYS WITH HIM.
ALRIGHT, THIS FUCKER'S ALREADY DONE FOR CHARLIE TEAM AND I CAN'T RAISE ALPHA, SO HERE'S WHAT WE'RE GONNA DO:
WE'RE GONNA HUNT HIM DOWN. WE'RE GONNA GET WHAT WE CAME FOR...
...AND THEN, WE'RE GONNA MAKE HIM EAT HIS OWN FUCKIN' EYEBALLS.
ALRIGHT, LET'S MOVE OUT. SINGLE FILE, TWENTY YARD SEPARATION. KEEP YOUR EYES OPEN.
TOMMY, WATCH OUR SIX.

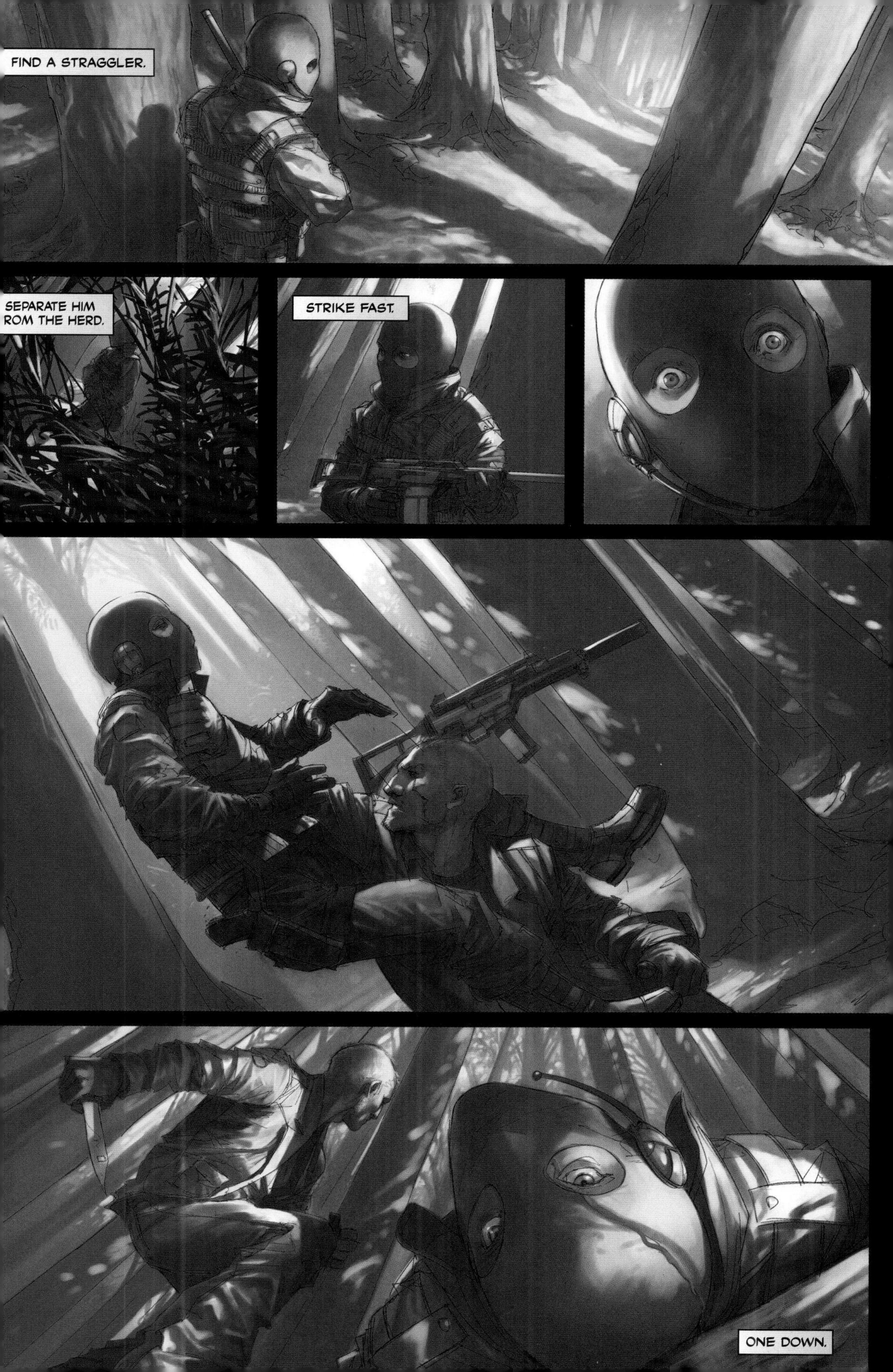
FIND A STRAGGLER.
SEPARATE HIM
ROM THE HERD.
STRIKE FAST.
ONE DOWN.

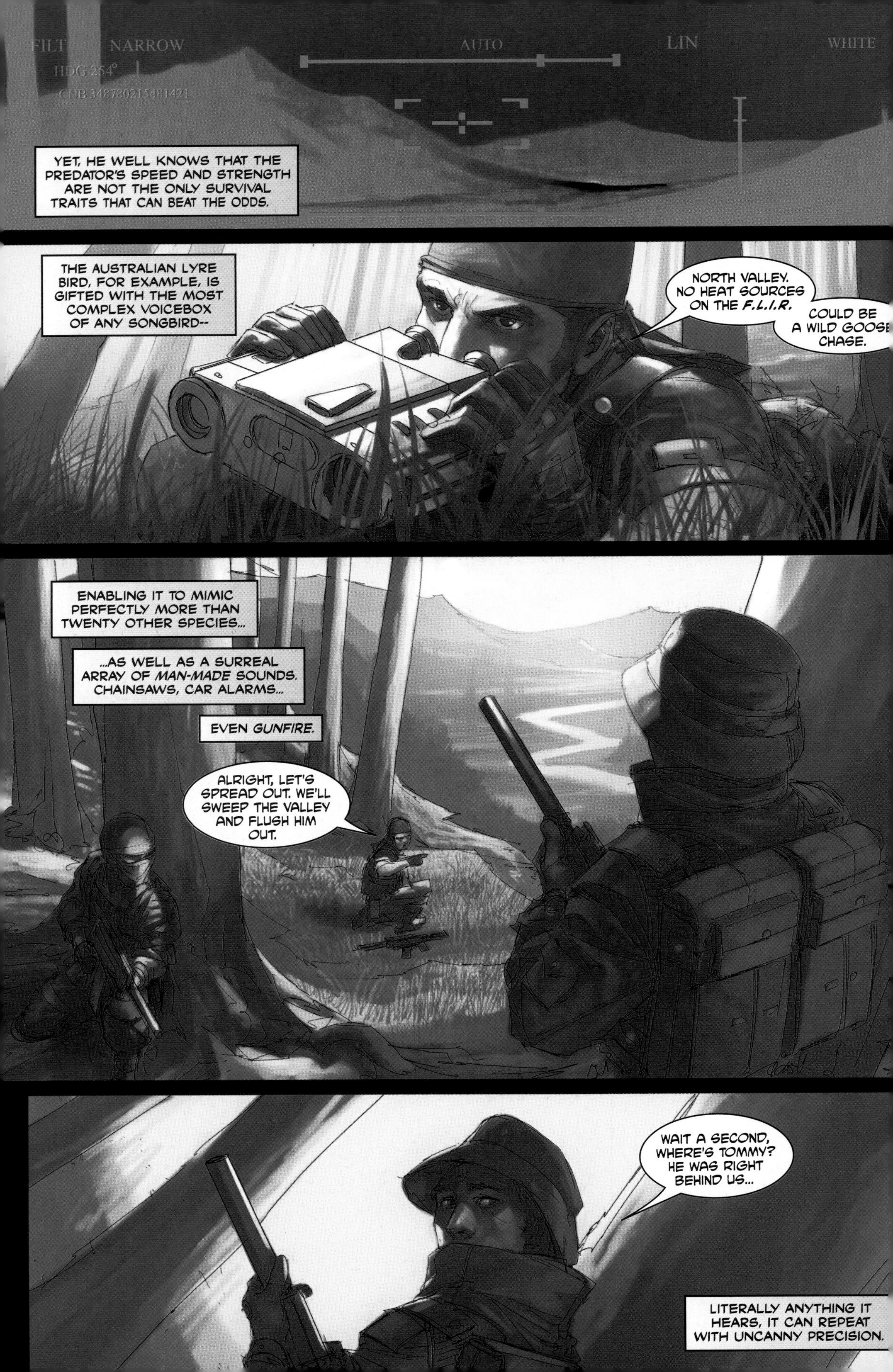
FILT
NARROW
AUTO
LIN
WHITE
HDG 254°
CNB 348780215481421
YET, HE WELL KNOWS THAT THE PREDATOR'S SPEED AND STRENGTH ARE NOT THE ONLY SURVIVAL TRAITS THAT CAN BEAT THE ODDS.
THE AUSTRALIAN LYRE BIRD, FOR EXAMPLE, IS GIFTED WITH THE MOST COMPLEX VOICEBOX OF ANY SONGBIRD--
NORTH VALLEY. NO HEAT SOURCES ON THE *F.L.I.R.*
COULD BE A WILD GOOSE CHASE.
ENABLING IT TO MIMIC PERFECTLY MORE THAN TWENTY OTHER SPECIES...
...AS WELL AS A SURREAL ARRAY OF *MAN-MADE* SOUNDS. CHAINSAWS, CAR ALARMS...
EVEN *GUNFIRE.*
ALRIGHT, LET'S SPREAD OUT. WE'LL SWEEP THE VALLEY AND FLUSH HIM OUT.
WAIT A SECOND, WHERE'S TOMMY? HE WAS RIGHT BEHIND US...
LITERALLY ANYTHING IT HEARS, IT CAN REPEAT WITH UNCANNY PRECISION.

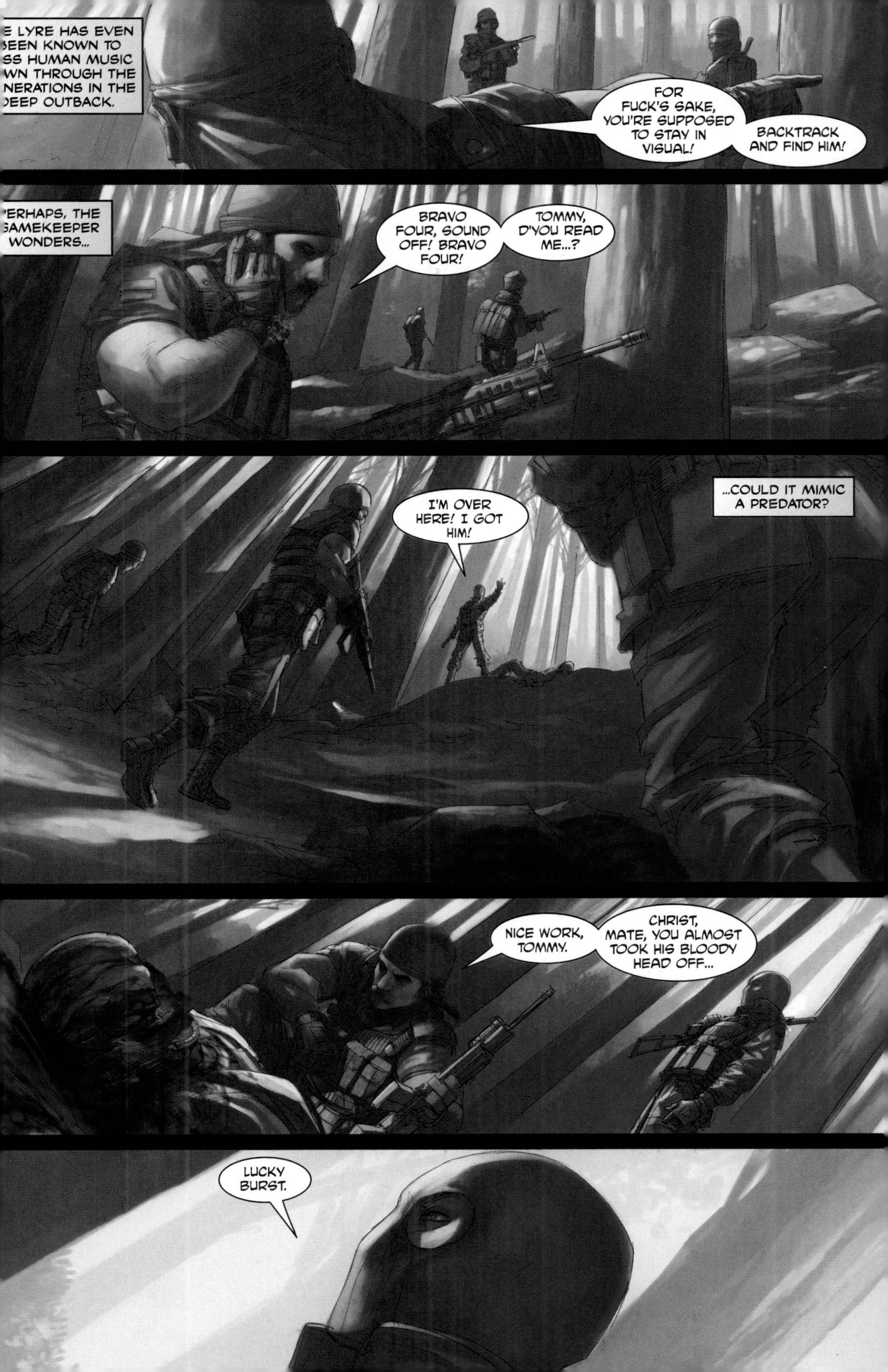
E LYRE HAS EVEN
BEEN KNOWN TO
SS HUMAN MUSIC
WN THROUGH THE
NERATIONS IN THE
DEEP OUTBACK.
FOR FUCK'S SAKE, YOU'RE SUPPOSED TO STAY IN VISUAL!
BACKTRACK AND FIND HIM!
ERHAPS, THE GAMEKEEPER WONDERS...
BRAVO FOUR, SOUND OFF! BRAVO FOUR!
TOMMY, D'YOU READ ME...?
I'M OVER HERE! I GOT HIM!
...COULD IT MIMIC A PREDATOR?
NICE WORK, TOMMY.
CHRIST, MATE, YOU ALMOST TOOK HIS BLOODY HEAD OFF...
LUCKY BURST.

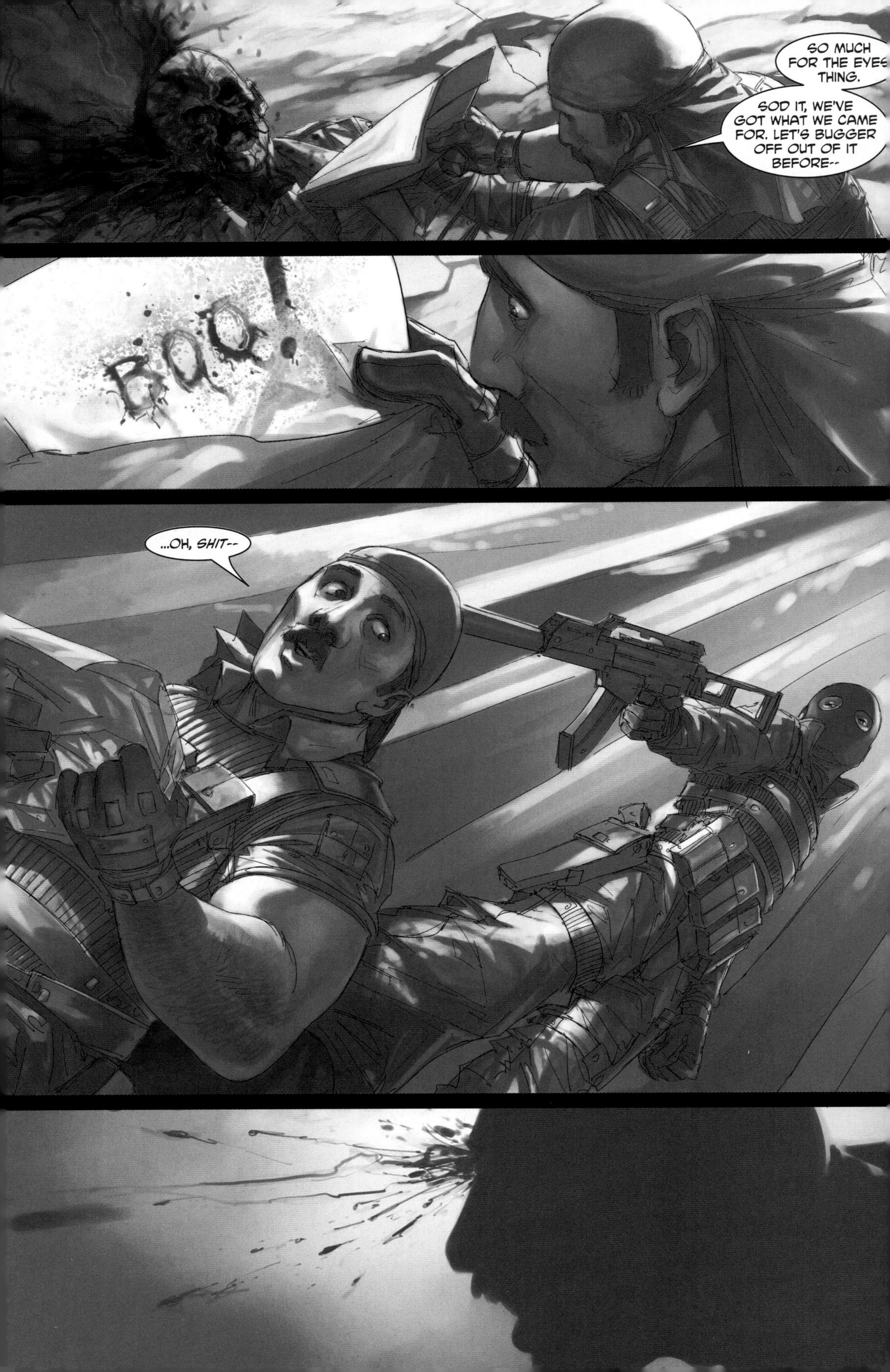
SO MUCH FOR THE EYES THING.
SOD IT, WE'VE GOT WHAT WE CAME FOR. LET'S BUGGER OFF OUT OF IT BEFORE--
BOO!
...OH, SHIT--

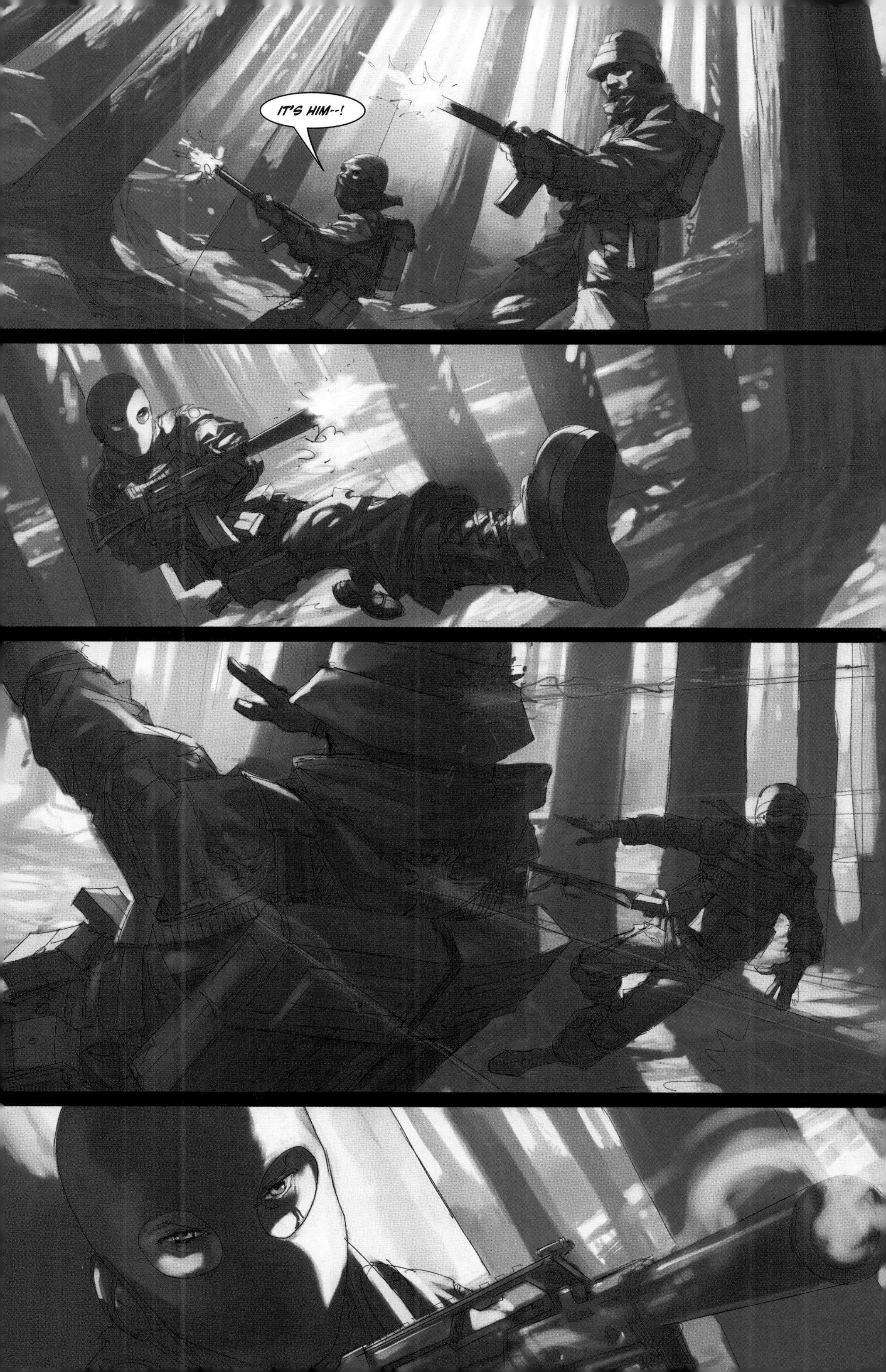
IT'S HIM--!

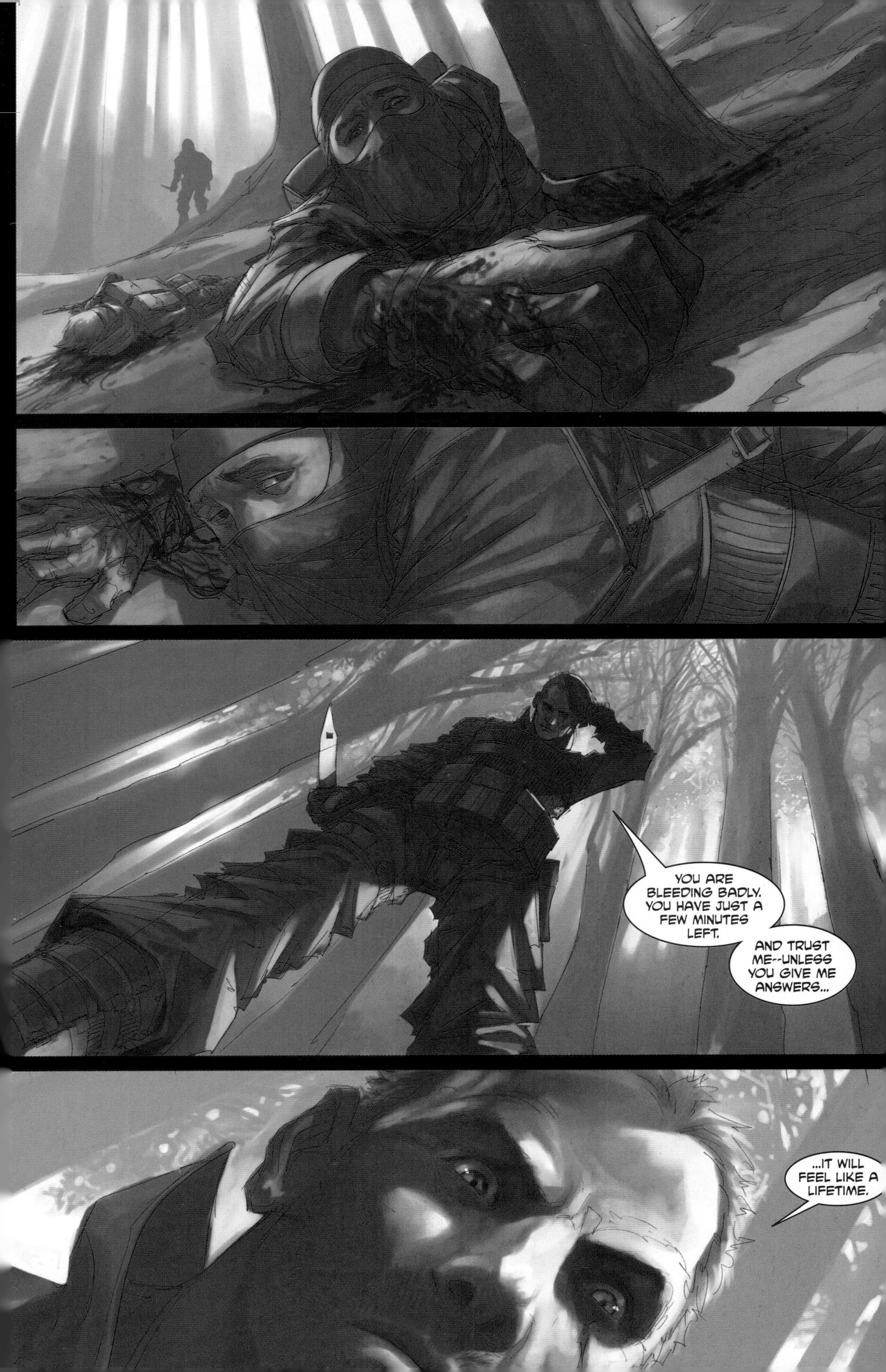
YOU ARE BLEEDING BADLY. YOU HAVE JUST A FEW MINUTES LEFT.
AND TRUST ME--UNLESS YOU GIVE ME ANSWERS...
...IT WILL FEEL LIKE A LIFETIME.

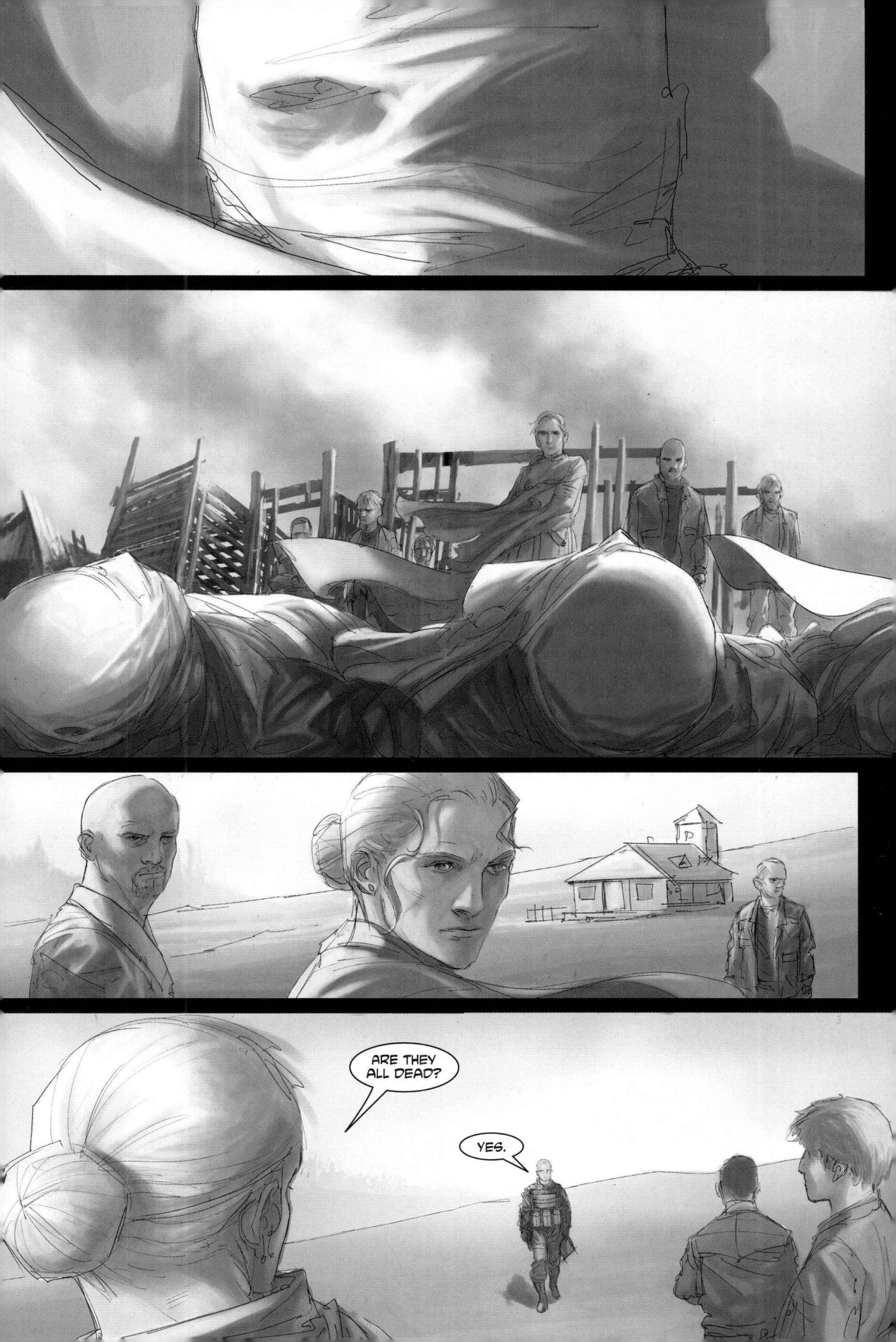
ARE THEY ALL DEAD?
YES.

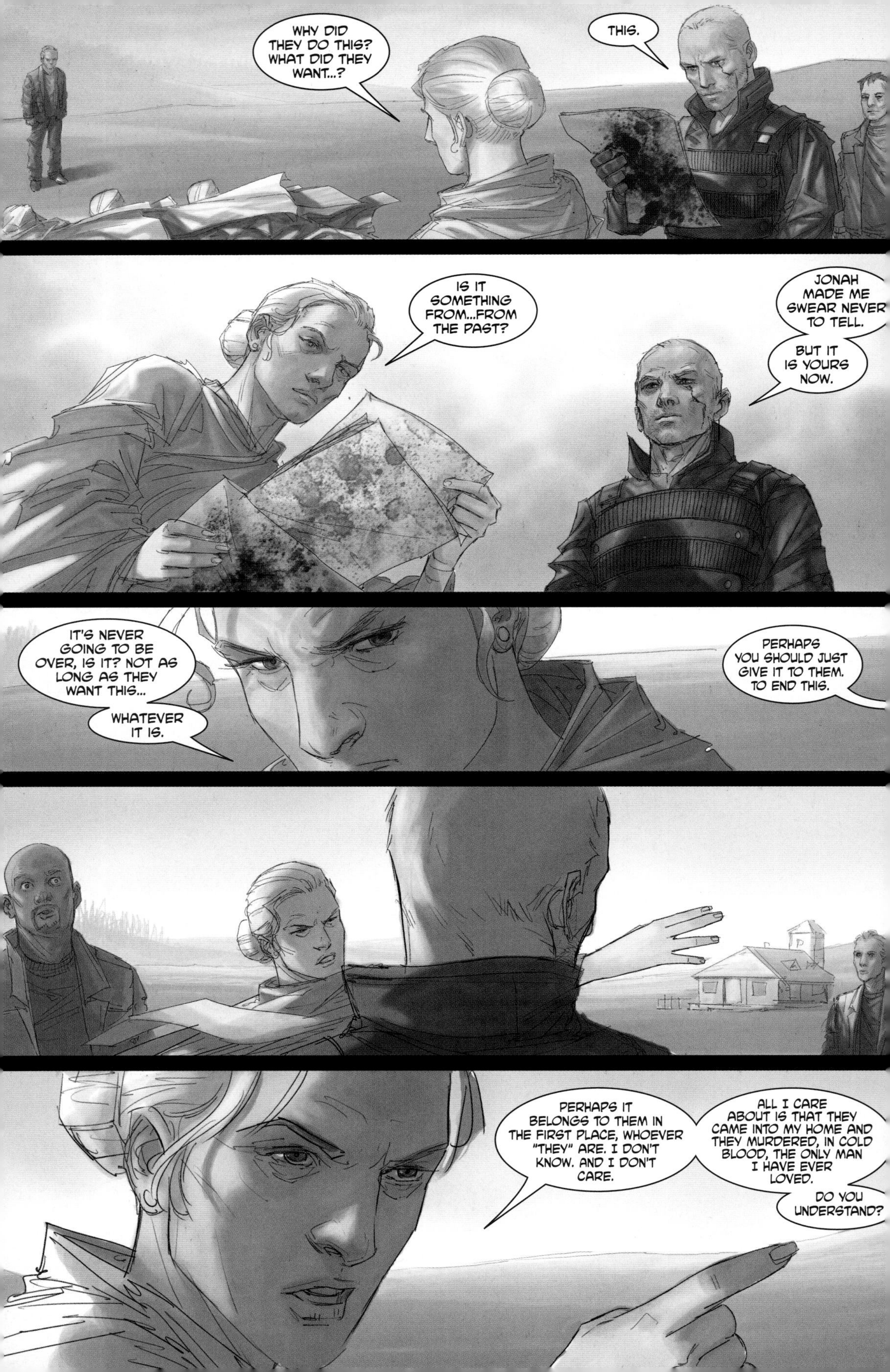
WHY DID THEY DO THIS? WHAT DID THEY WANT...?
THIS.
IS IT SOMETHING FROM...FROM THE PAST?
JONAH MADE ME SWEAR NEVER TO TELL.
BUT IT IS YOURS NOW.
IT'S NEVER GOING TO BE OVER, IS IT? NOT AS LONG AS THEY WANT THIS...
WHATEVER IT IS.
PERHAPS YOU SHOULD JUST GIVE IT TO THEM. TO END THIS.
PERHAPS IT BELONGS TO THEM IN THE FIRST PLACE, WHOEVER "THEY" ARE. I DON'T KNOW. AND I DON'T CARE.
ALL I CARE ABOUT IS THAT THEY CAME INTO MY HOME AND THEY MURDERED, IN COLD BLOOD, THE ONLY MAN I HAVE EVER LOVED.
DO YOU UNDERSTAND?

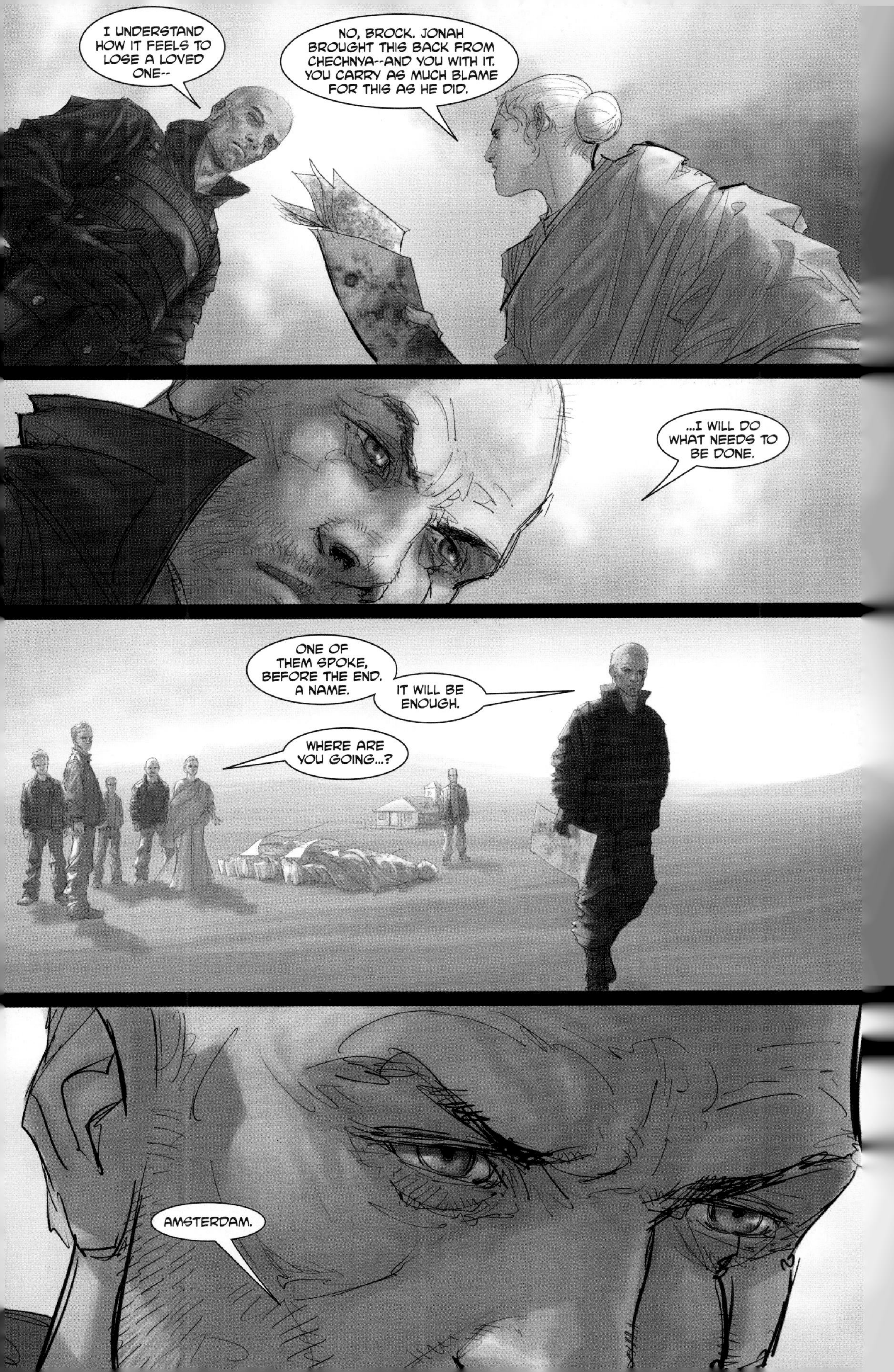
I UNDERSTAND HOW IT FEELS TO LOSE A LOVED ONE--
NO, BROCK. JONAH BROUGHT THIS BACK FROM CHECHNYA--AND YOU WITH IT. YOU CARRY AS MUCH BLAME FOR THIS AS HE DID.
...I WILL DO WHAT NEEDS TO BE DONE.
ONE OF THEM SPOKE, BEFORE THE END. A NAME.
IT WILL BE ENOUGH.
WHERE ARE YOU GOING...?
AMSTERDAM.

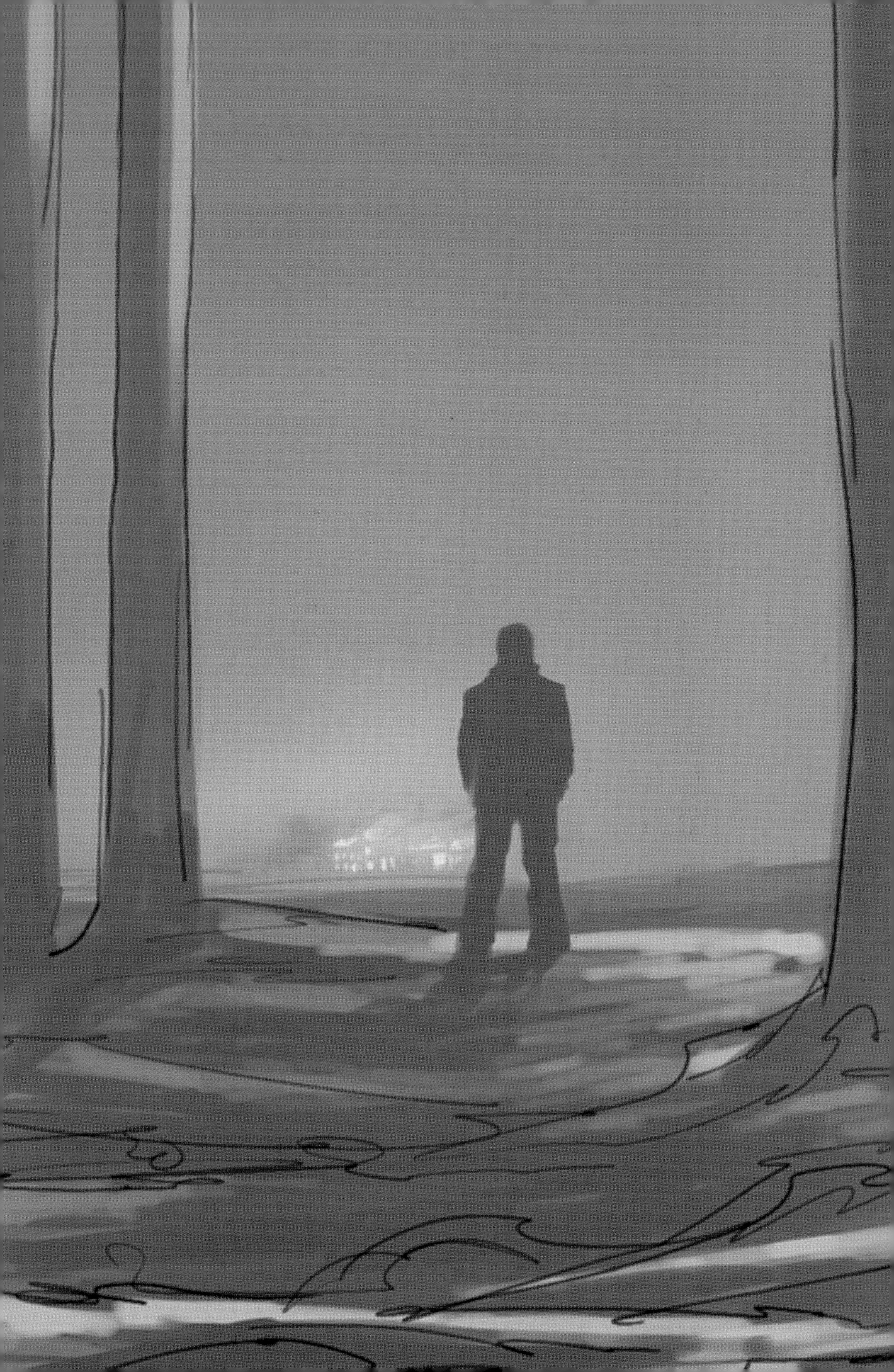

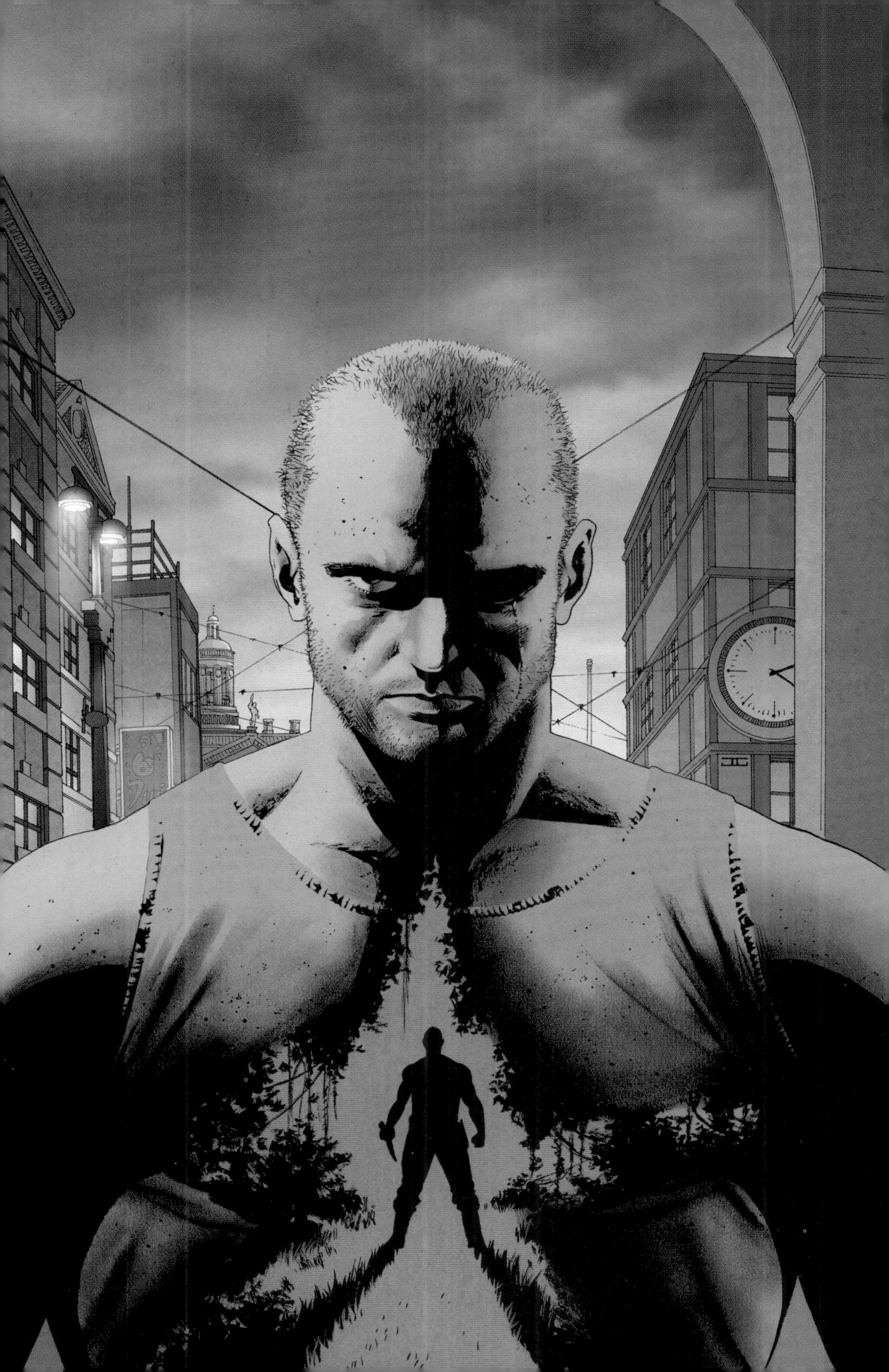

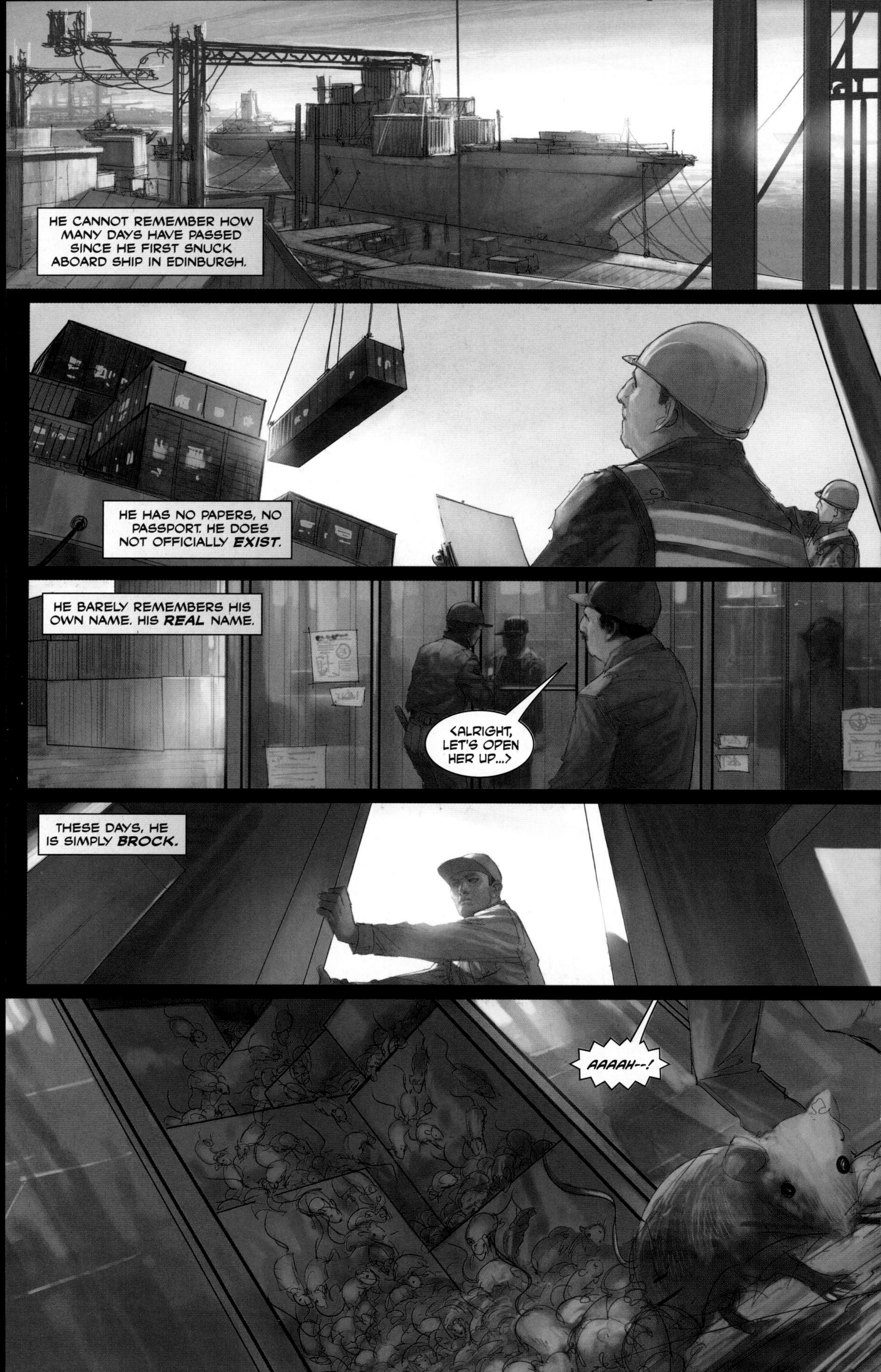

HE CANNOT REMEMBER HOW MANY DAYS HAVE PASSED SINCE HE FIRST SNUCK ABOARD SHIP IN EDINBURGH.
HE HAS NO PAPERS, NO PASSPORT. HE DOES NOT OFFICIALLY EXIST.
HE BARELY REMEMBERS HIS OWN NAME. HIS REAL NAME.
<ALRIGHT, LET'S OPEN HER UP...>
THESE DAYS, HE IS SIMPLY BROCK.
AAAAH--!

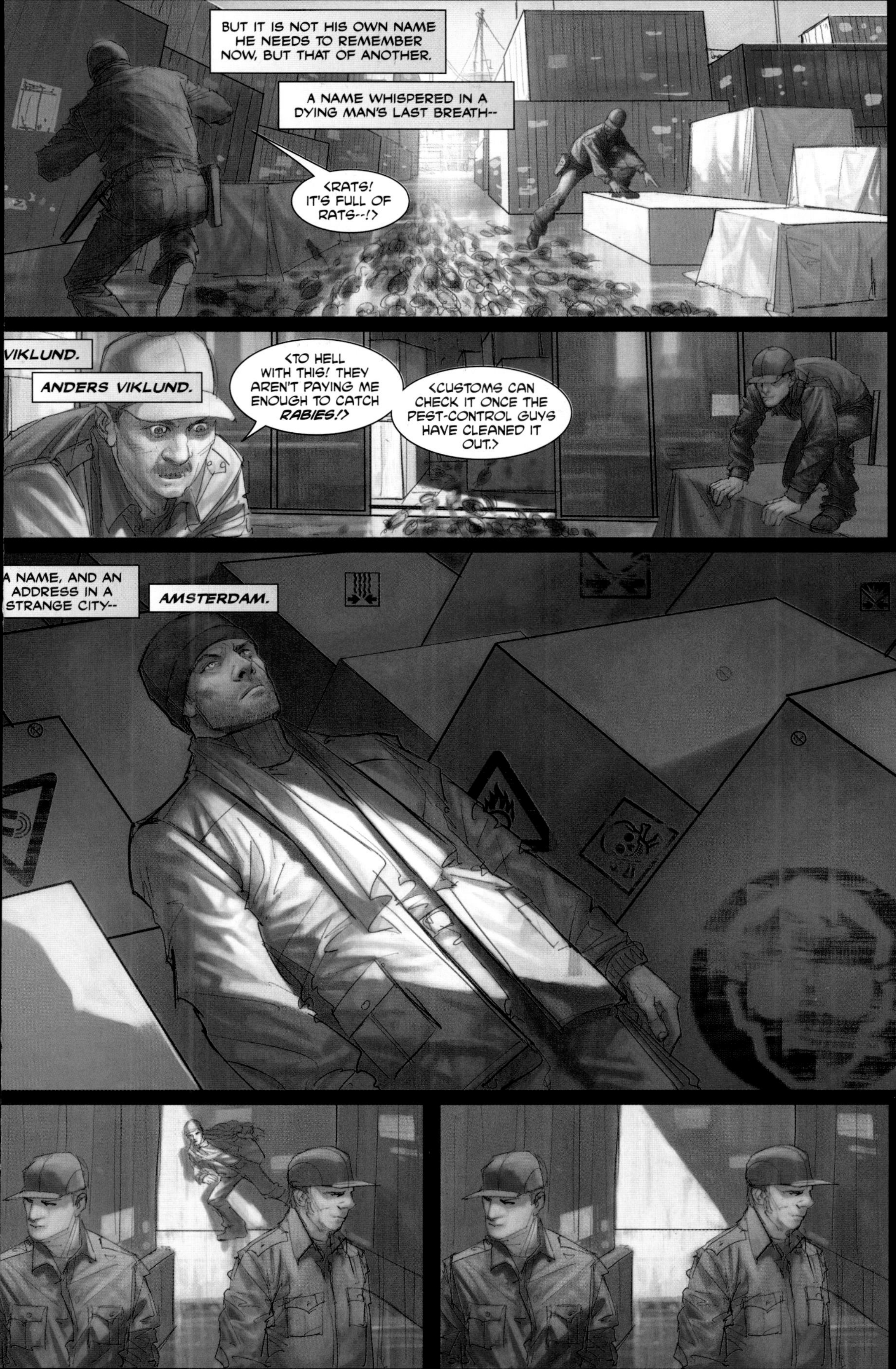
BUT IT IS NOT HIS OWN NAME HE NEEDS TO REMEMBER NOW, BUT THAT OF ANOTHER.
A NAME WHISPERED IN A DYING MAN'S LAST BREATH--
<RATS! IT'S FULL OF RATS--!>
VIKLUND.
ANDERS VIKLUND.
<TO HELL WITH THIS! THEY AREN'T PAYING ME ENOUGH TO CATCH RABIES!>
<CUSTOMS CAN CHECK IT ONCE THE PEST-CONTROL GUYS HAVE CLEANED IT OUT.>
A NAME, AND AN ADDRESS IN A STRANGE CITY--
AMSTERDAM.

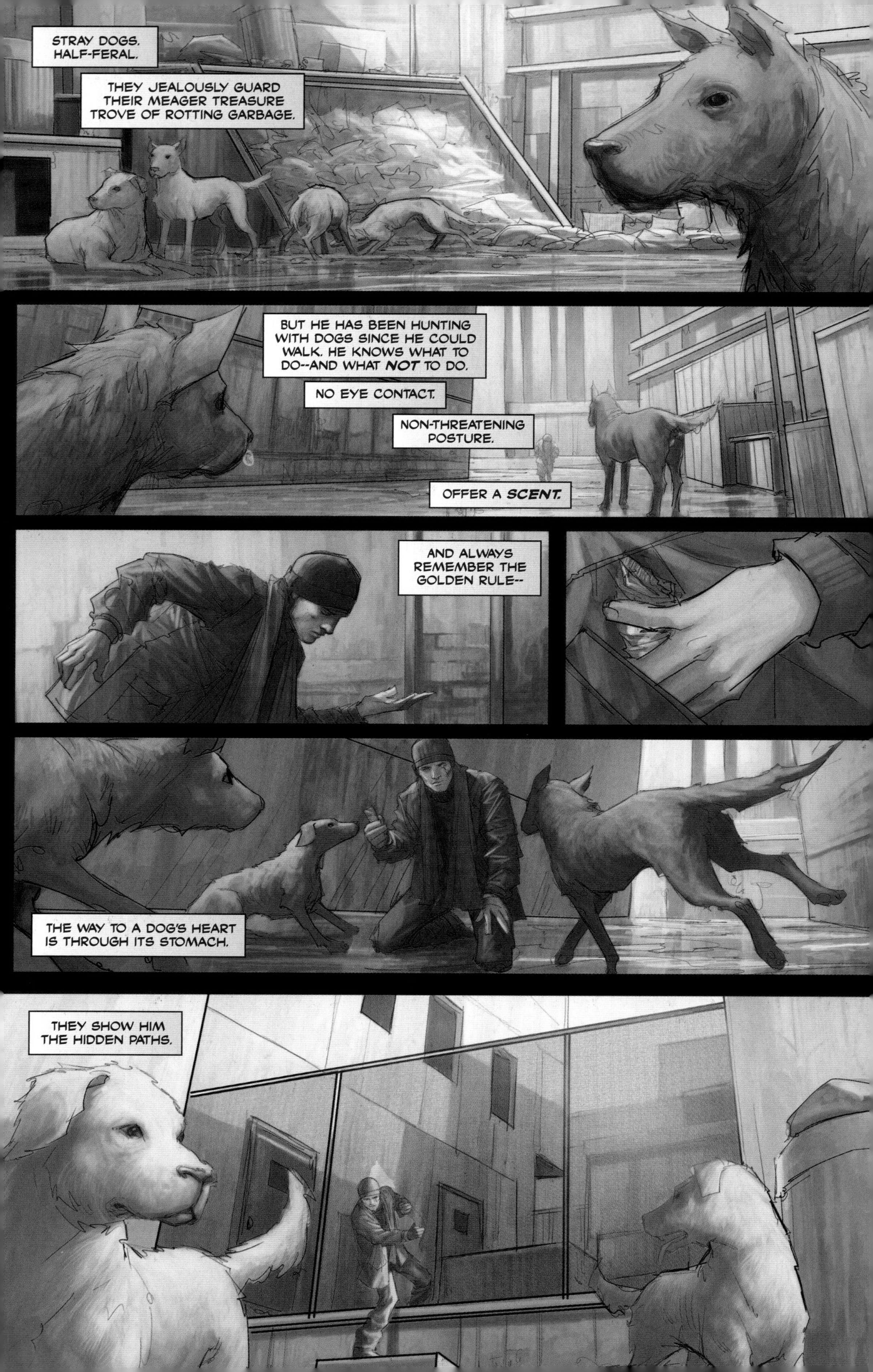
STRAY DOGS. HALF-FERAL.
THEY JEALOUSLY GUARD THEIR MEAGER TREASURE TROVE OF ROTTING GARBAGE.
BUT HE HAS BEEN HUNTING WITH DOGS SINCE HE COULD WALK. HE KNOWS WHAT TO DO--AND WHAT NOT TO DO.
NO EYE CONTACT.
NON-THREATENING POSTURE.
OFFER A SCENT.
AND ALWAYS REMEMBER THE GOLDEN RULE--
THE WAY TO A DOG'S HEART IS THROUGH ITS STOMACH.
THEY SHOW HIM THE HIDDEN PATHS.

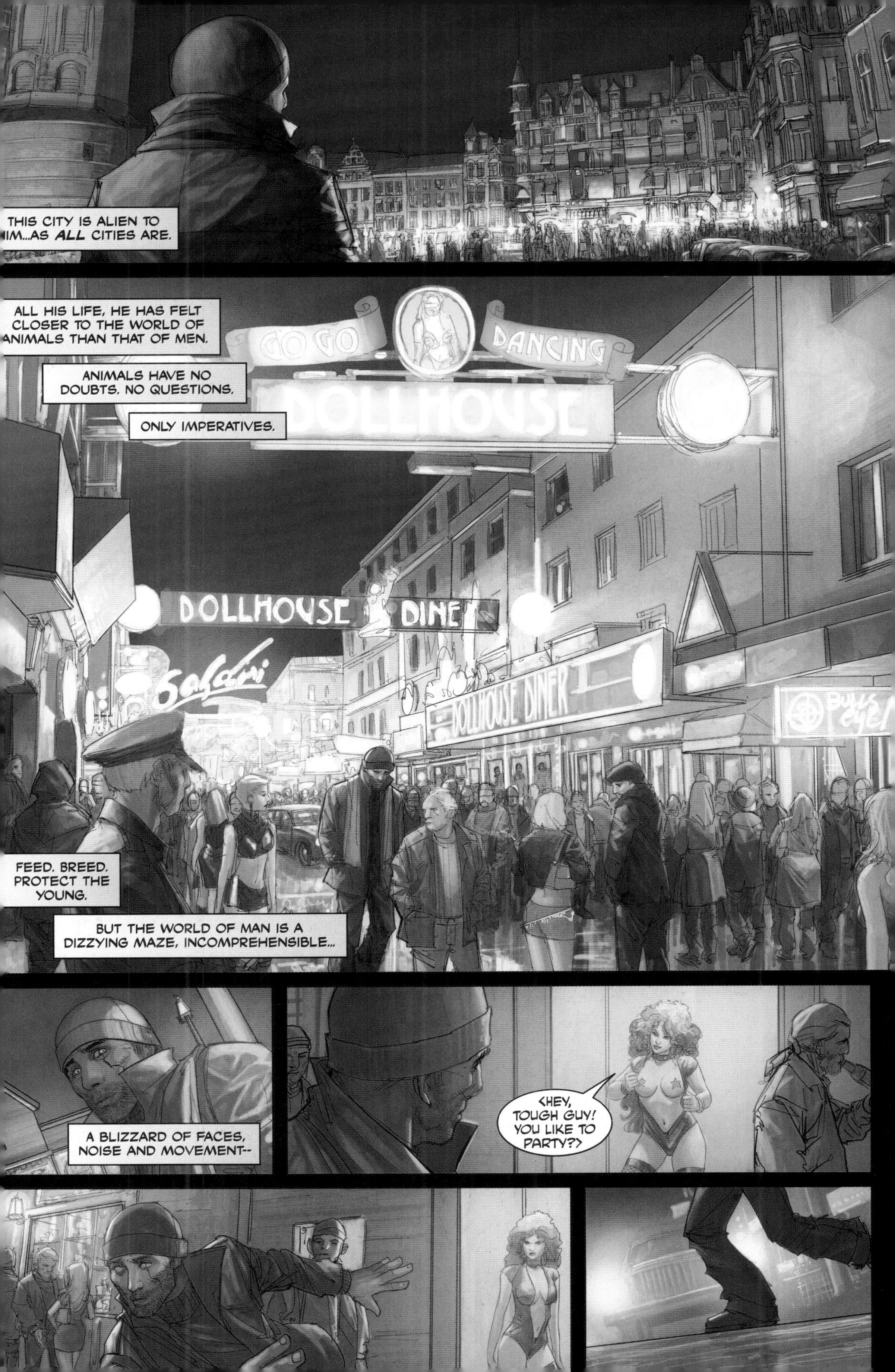
THIS CITY IS ALIEN TO HIM...AS ALL CITIES ARE.
ALL HIS LIFE, HE HAS FELT CLOSER TO THE WORLD OF ANIMALS THAN THAT OF MEN.
ANIMALS HAVE NO DOUBTS. NO QUESTIONS.
ONLY IMPERATIVES.
GO GO DANCING
DOLLHOUSE
DOLLHOUSE DINE
DOLLHOUSE DINER
Safari
FEED. BREED. PROTECT THE YOUNG.
BUT THE WORLD OF MAN IS A DIZZYING MAZE, INCOMPREHENSIBLE...
A BLIZZARD OF FACES, NOISE AND MOVEMENT--
<HEY, TOUGH GUY! YOU LIKE TO PARTY?>

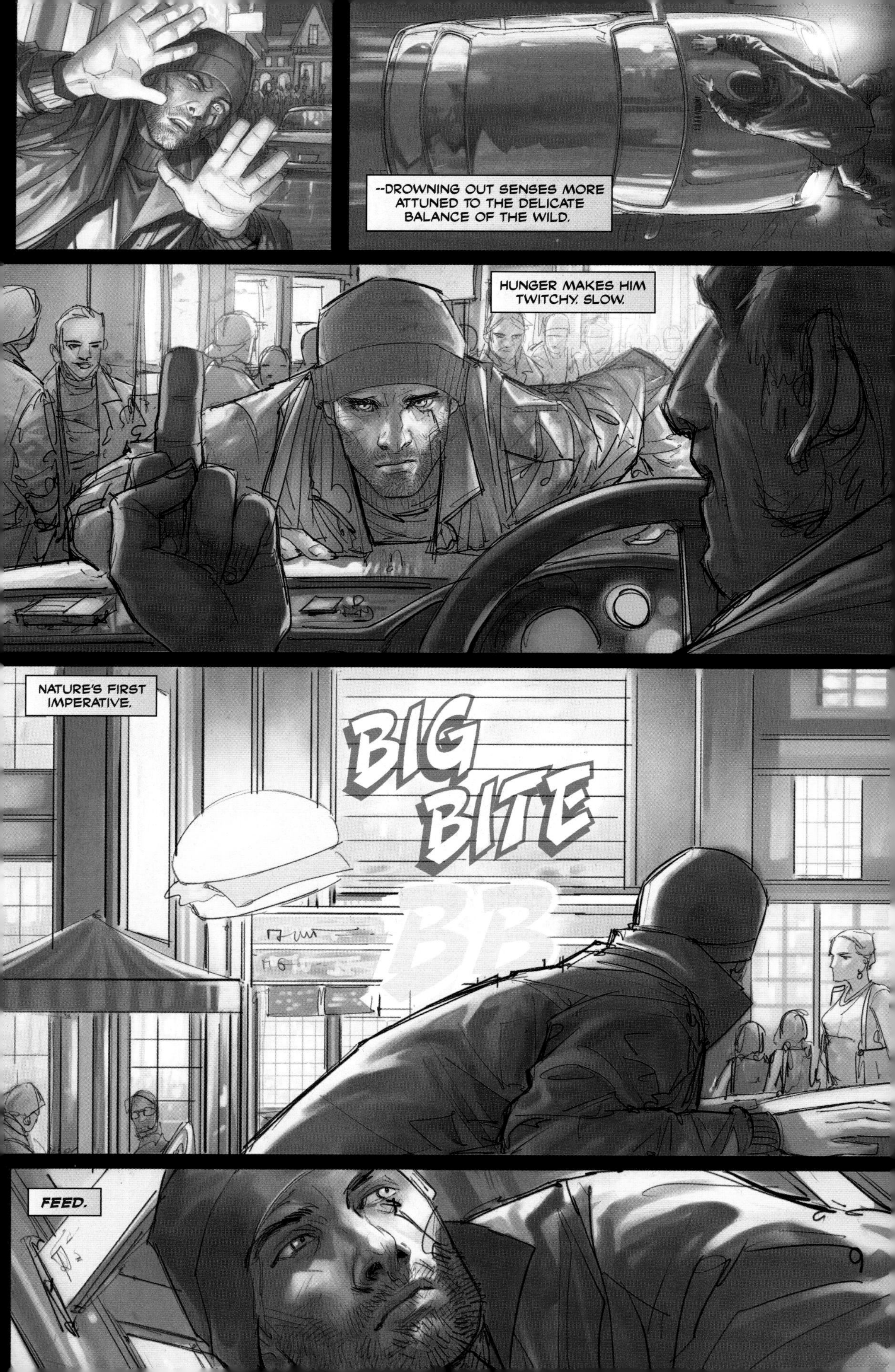
--DROWNING OUT SENSES MORE ATTUNED TO THE DELICATE BALANCE OF THE WILD.
HUNGER MAKES HIM TWITCHY. SLOW.
NATURE'S FIRST IMPERATIVE.
BIG BITE
BB
FEED.

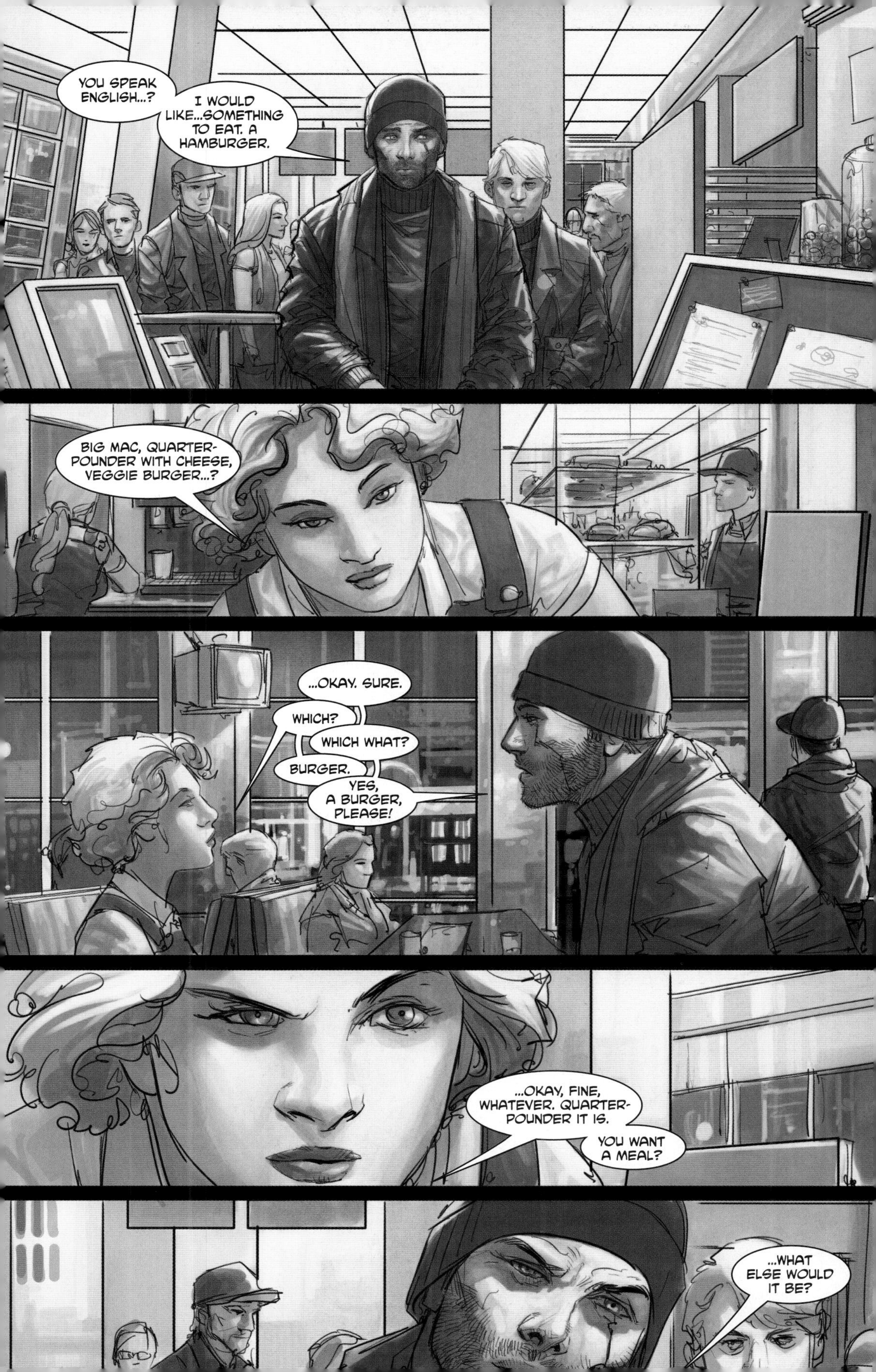
YOU SPEAK ENGLISH...?
I WOULD LIKE...SOMETHING TO EAT. A HAMBURGER.
BIG MAC, QUARTER-POUNDER WITH CHEESE, VEGGIE BURGER...?
...OKAY. SURE.
WHICH?
WHICH WHAT?
BURGER.
YES, A BURGER, PLEASE!
...OKAY, FINE, WHATEVER. QUARTER-POUNDER IT IS.
YOU WANT A MEAL?
...WHAT ELSE WOULD IT BE?

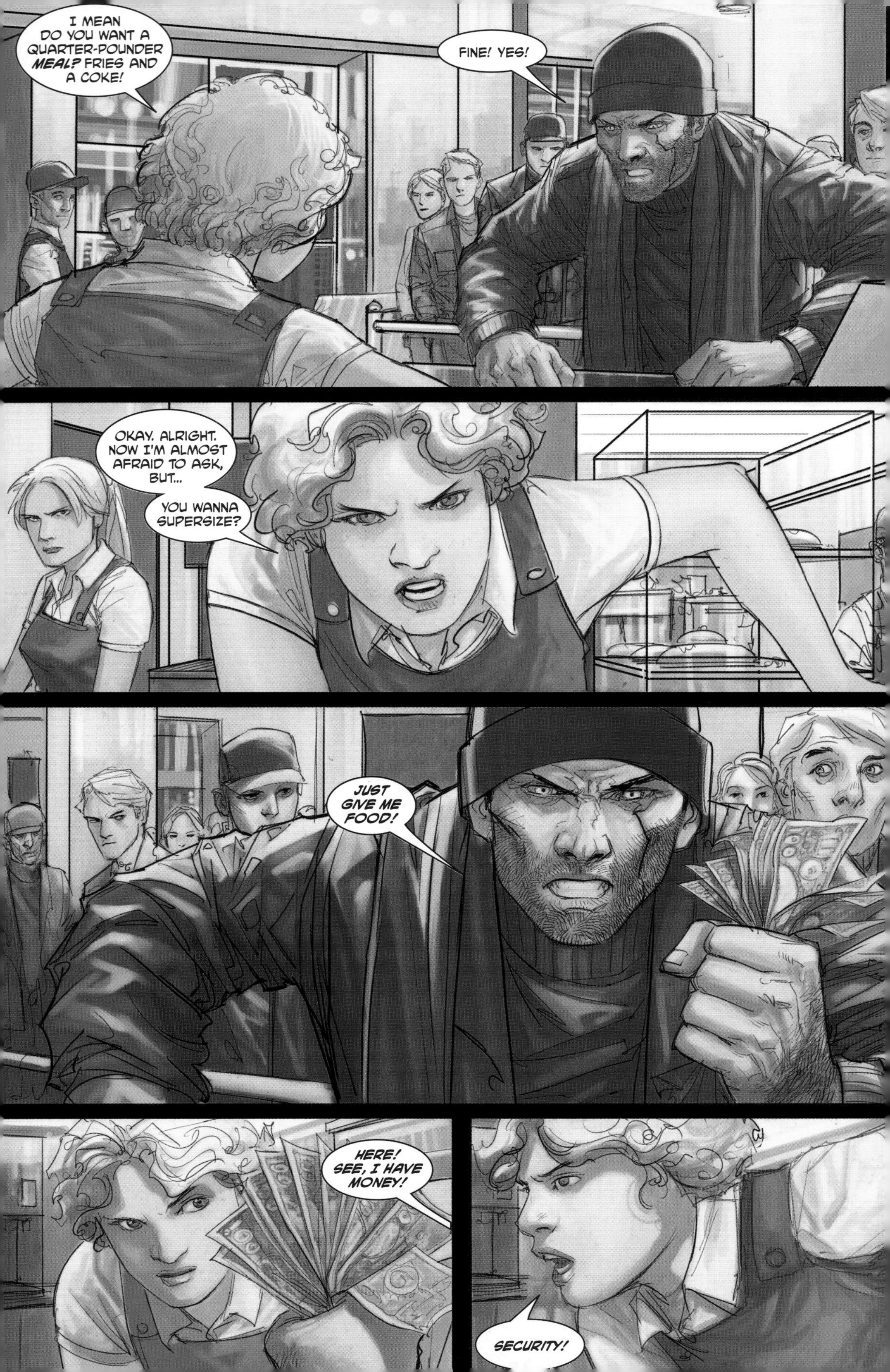
I MEAN DO YOU WANT A QUARTER-POUNDER MEAL? FRIES AND A COKE!
FINE! YES!
OKAY. ALRIGHT. NOW I'M ALMOST AFRAID TO ASK, BUT...
YOU WANNA SUPERSIZE?
JUST GIVE ME FOOD!
HERE! SEE, I HAVE MONEY!
SECURITY!

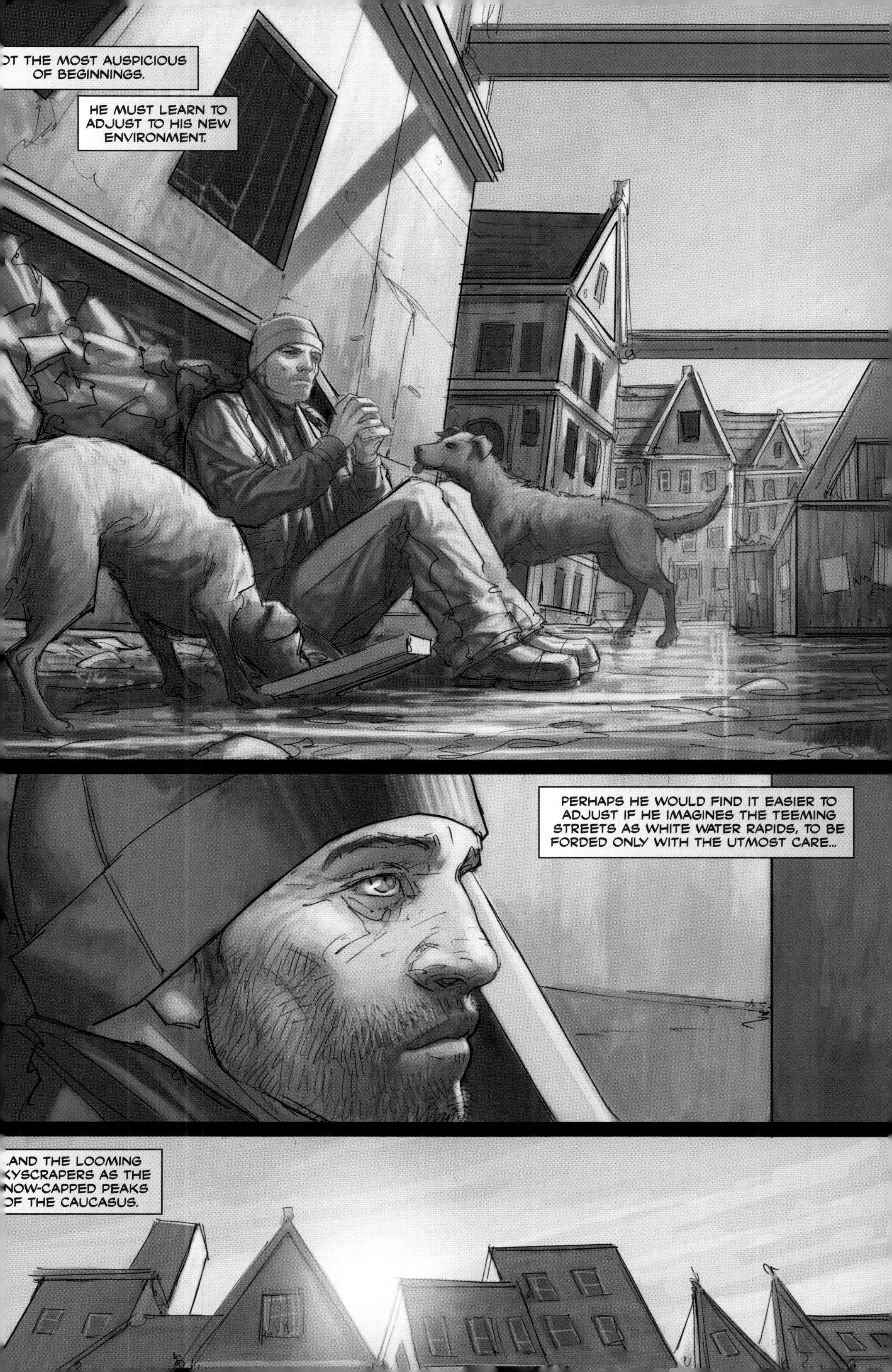
OT THE MOST AUSPICIOUS OF BEGINNINGS.
HE MUST LEARN TO ADJUST TO HIS NEW ENVIRONMENT.
PERHAPS HE WOULD FIND IT EASIER TO ADJUST IF HE IMAGINES THE TEEMING STREETS AS WHITE WATER RAPIDS, TO BE FORDED ONLY WITH THE UTMOST CARE...
..AND THE LOOMING KYSCRAPERS AS THE NOW-CAPPED PEAKS OF THE CAUCASUS.

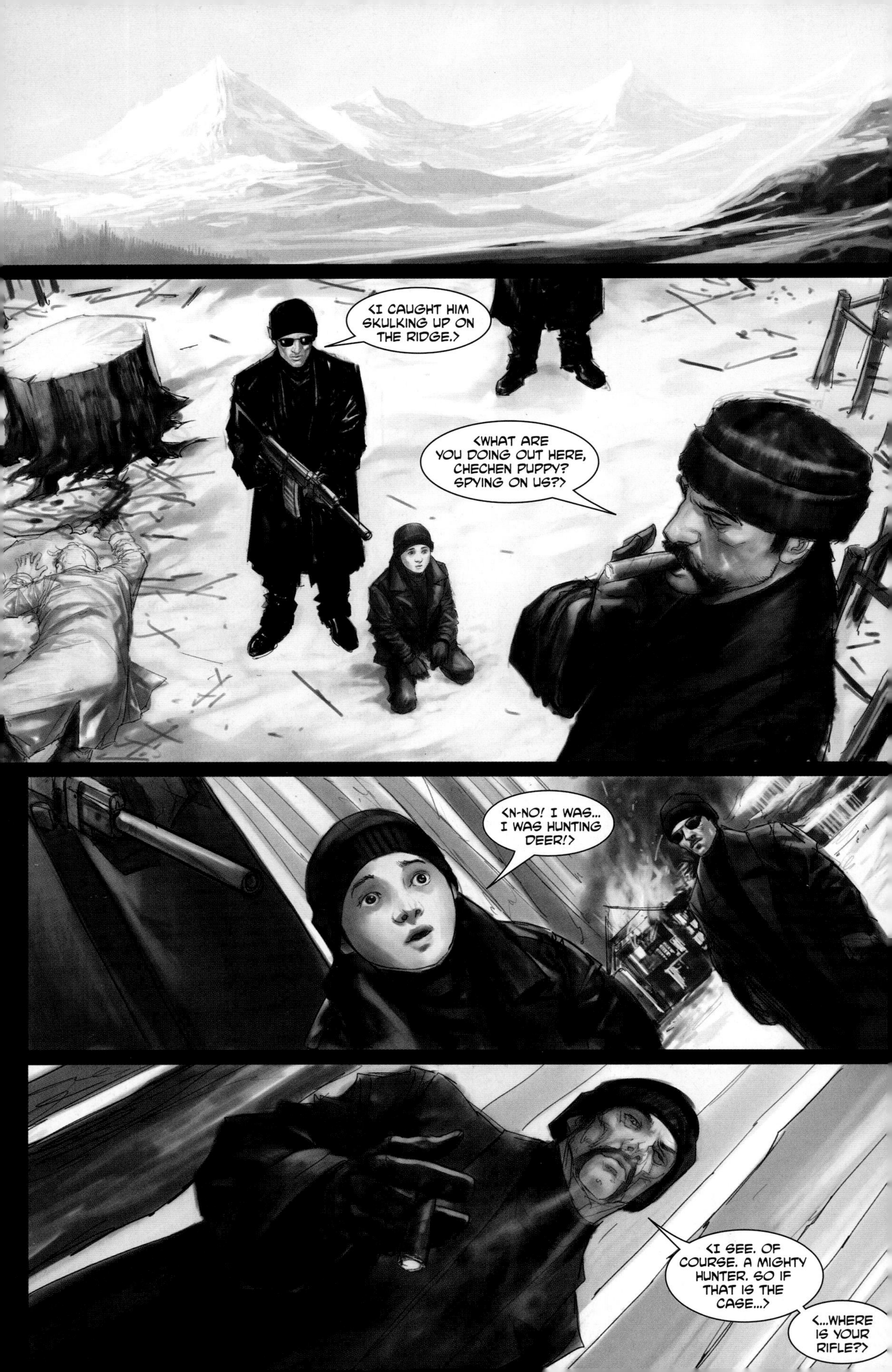
<I CAUGHT HIM SKULKING UP ON THE RIDGE.>
<WHAT ARE YOU DOING OUT HERE, CHECHEN PUPPY? SPYING ON US?>
<N-NO! I WAS... I WAS HUNTING DEER!>
<I SEE. OF COURSE. A MIGHTY HUNTER. SO IF THAT IS THE CASE...>
<...WHERE IS YOUR RIFLE?>

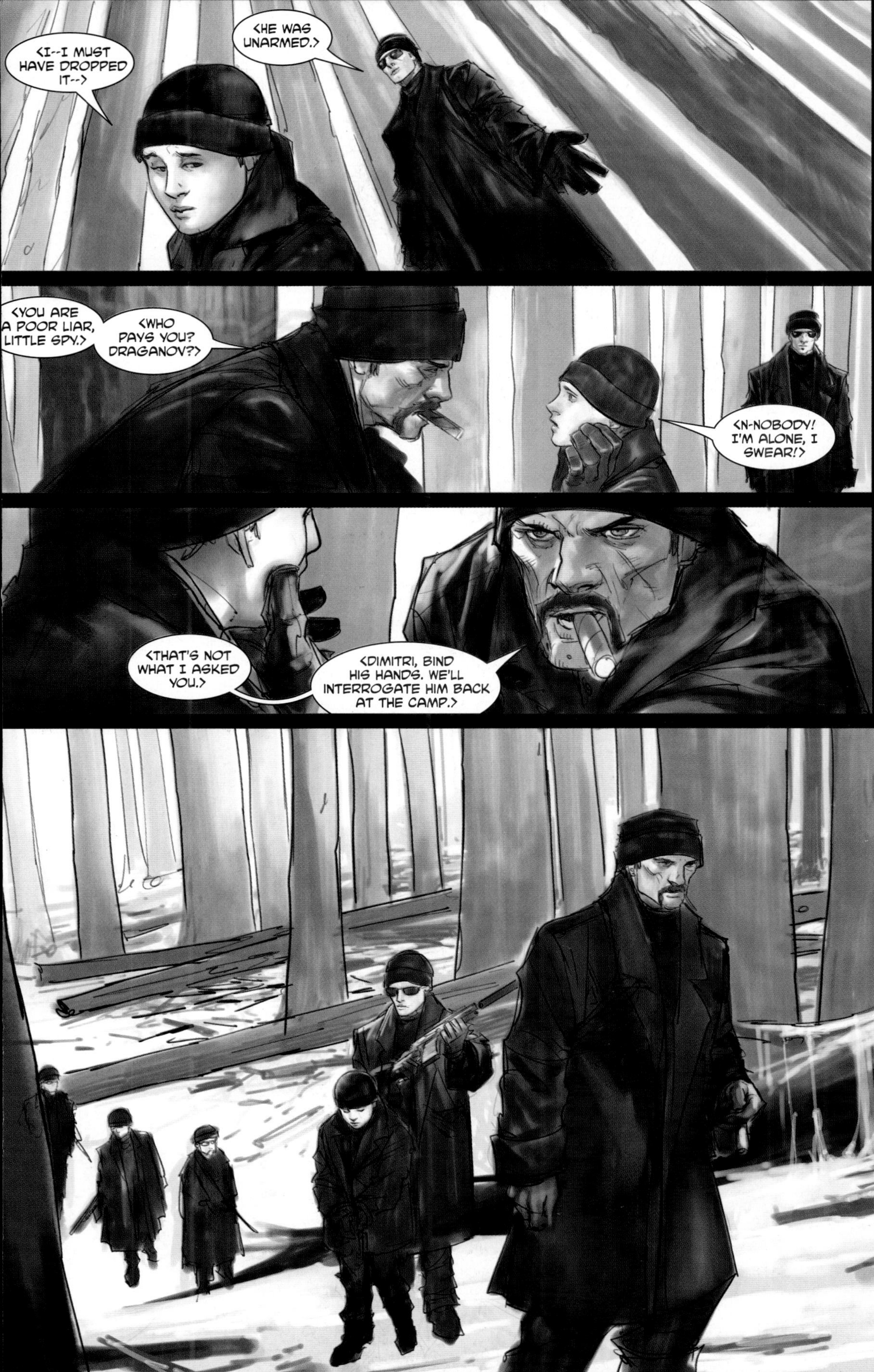
<I--I MUST HAVE DROPPED IT-->
<HE WAS UNARMED.>
<YOU ARE A POOR LIAR, LITTLE SPY.>
<WHO PAYS YOU? DRAGANOV?>
<N-NOBODY! I'M ALONE, I SWEAR!>
<THAT'S NOT WHAT I ASKED YOU.>
<DIMITRI, BIND HIS HANDS. WE'LL INTERROGATE HIM BACK AT THE CAMP.>

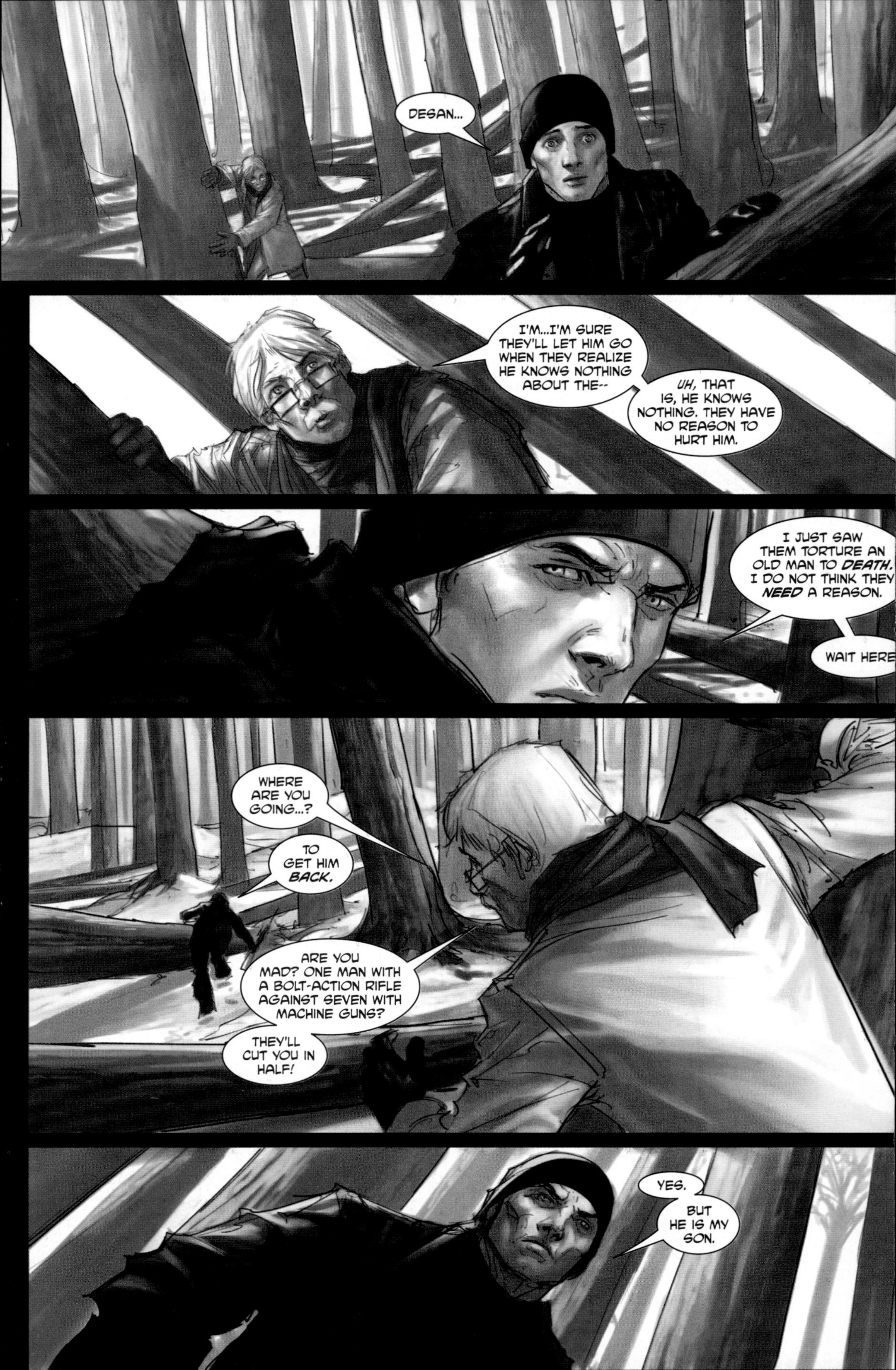
DESAN...
I'M...I'M SURE THEY'LL LET HIM GO WHEN THEY REALIZE HE KNOWS NOTHING ABOUT THE--
UH, THAT IS, HE KNOWS NOTHING. THEY HAVE NO REASON TO HURT HIM.
I JUST SAW THEM TORTURE AN OLD MAN TO DEATH. I DO NOT THINK THEY NEED A REASON.
WAIT HERE
WHERE ARE YOU GOING...?
TO GET HIM BACK.
ARE YOU MAD? ONE MAN WITH A BOLT-ACTION RIFLE AGAINST SEVEN WITH MACHINE GUNS?
THEY'LL CUT YOU IN HALF!
YES.
BUT HE IS MY SON.

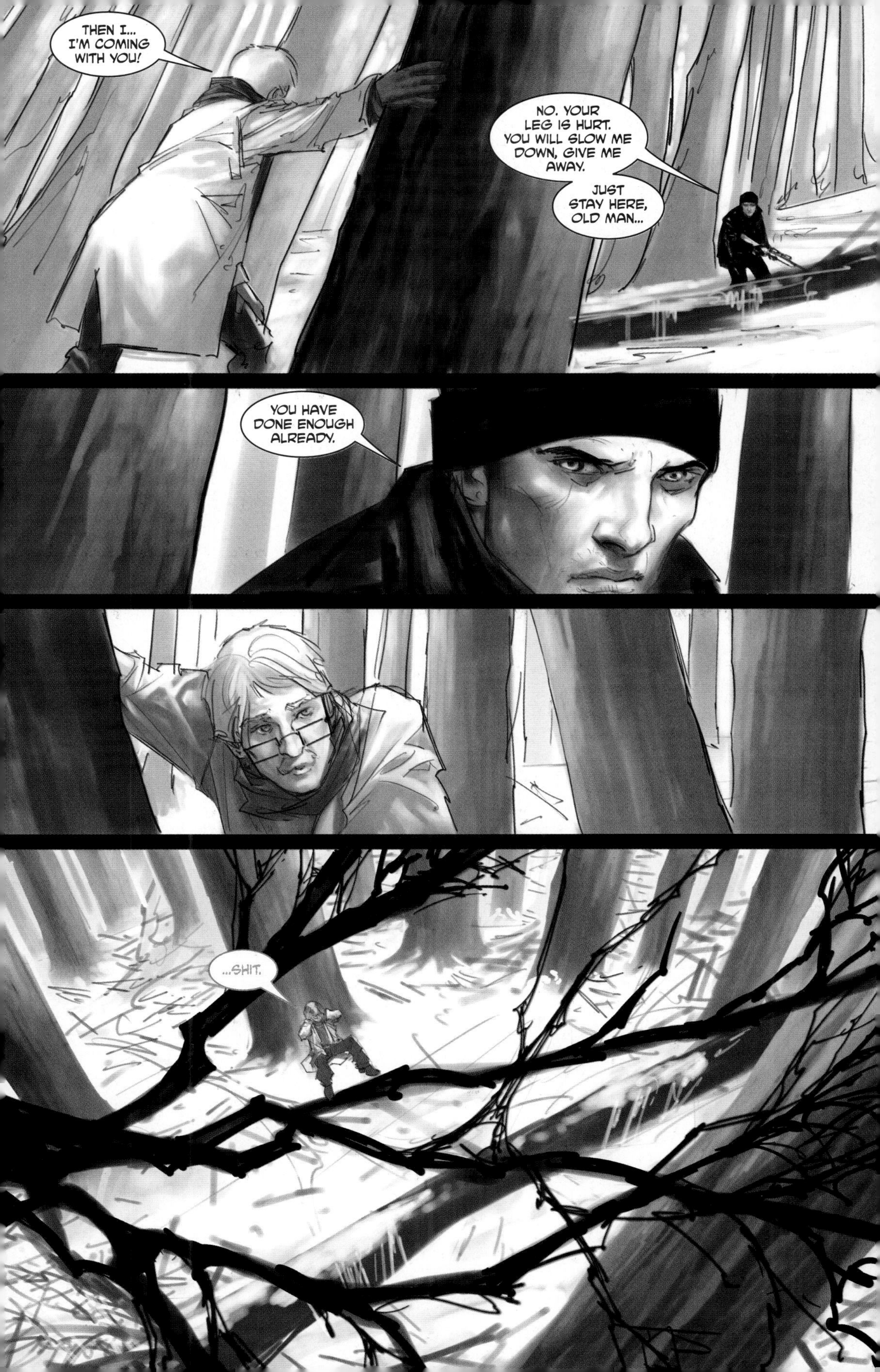
THEN I... I'M COMING WITH YOU!
NO. YOUR LEG IS HURT. YOU WILL SLOW ME DOWN, GIVE ME AWAY.
JUST STAY HERE, OLD MAN...
YOU HAVE DONE ENOUGH ALREADY.
...SHIT.

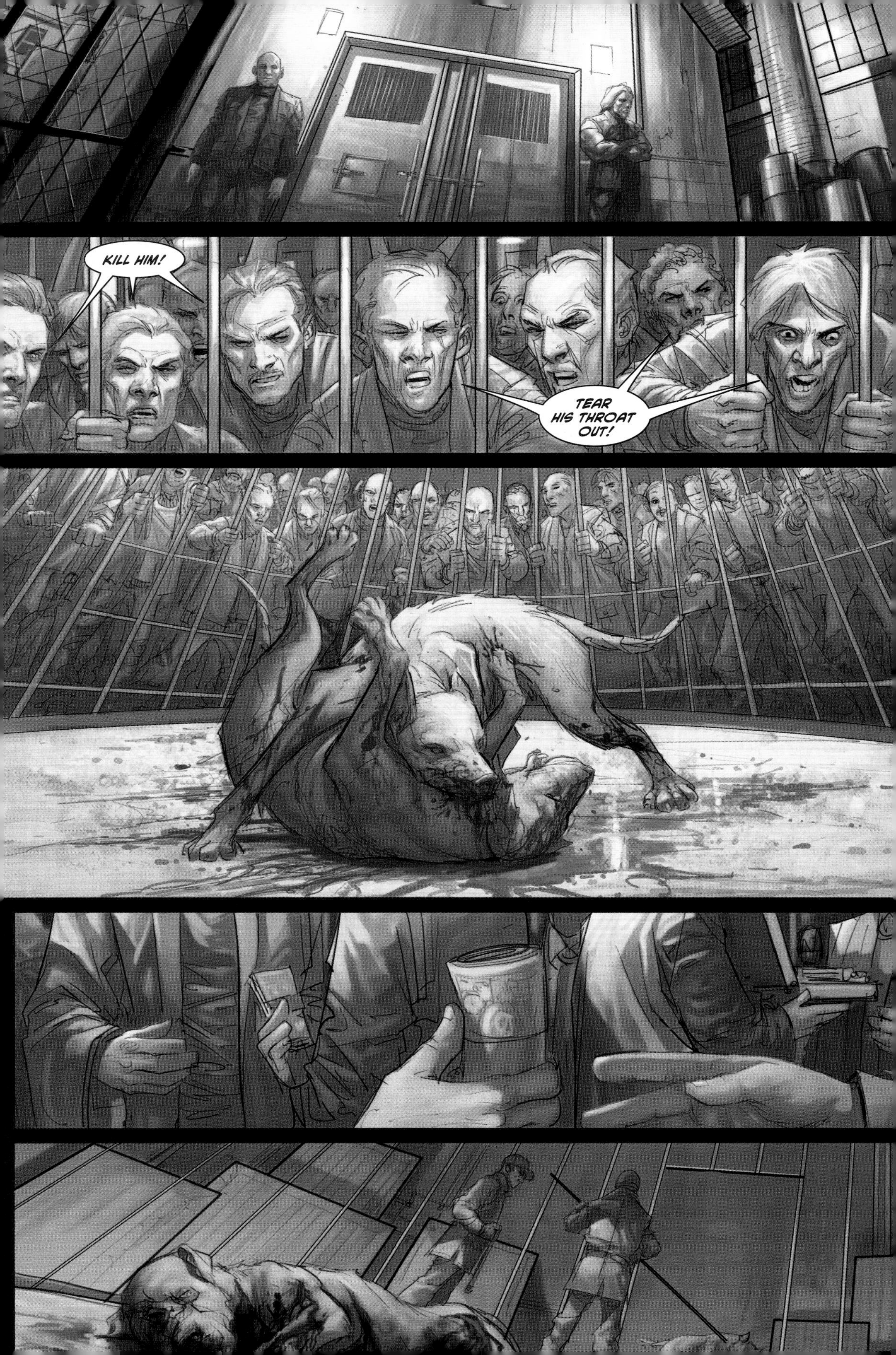
KILL HIM!
TEAR HIS THROAT OUT!

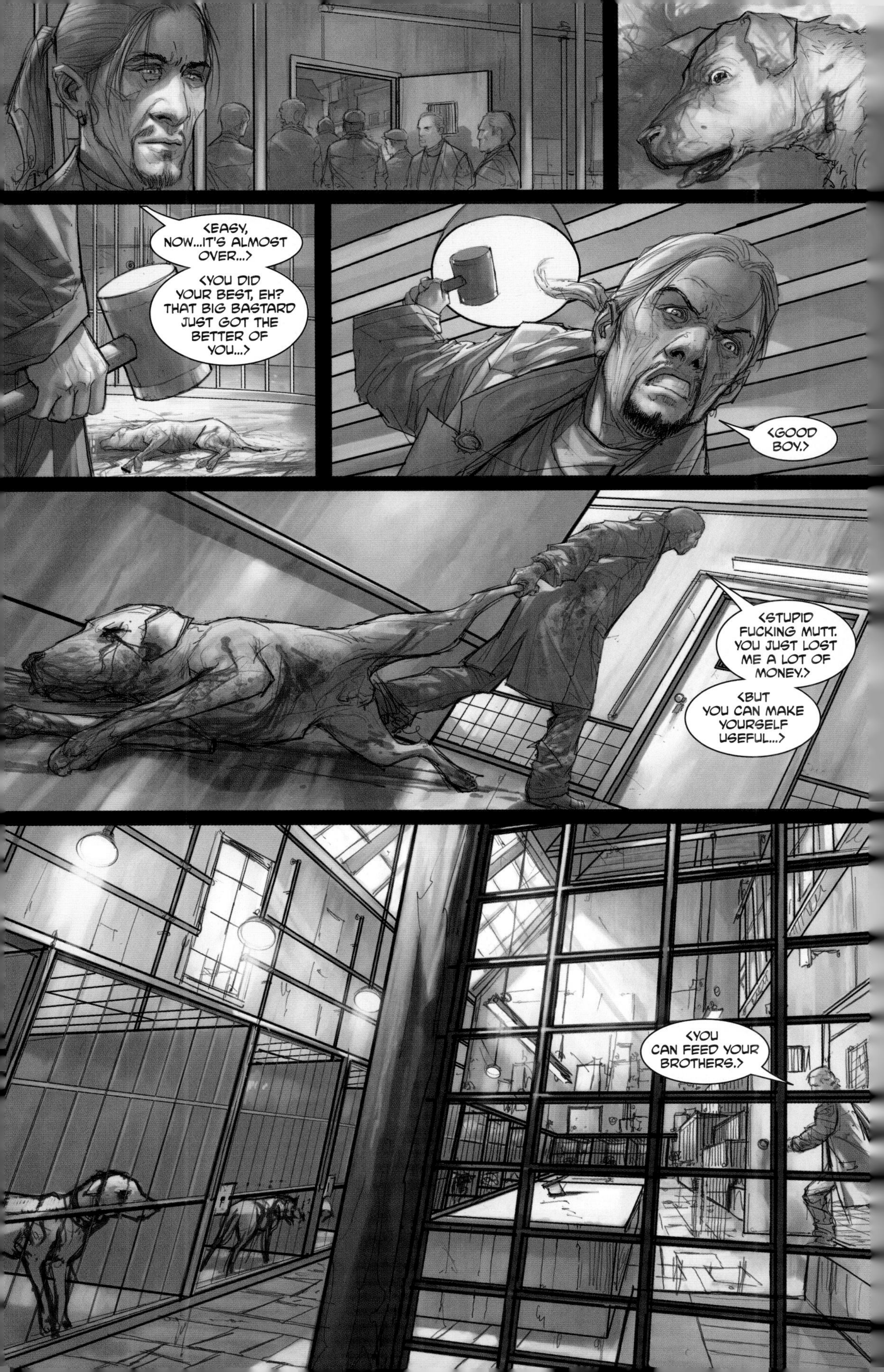
<EASY, NOW...IT'S ALMOST OVER...>
<YOU DID YOUR BEST, EH? THAT BIG BASTARD JUST GOT THE BETTER OF YOU...>
<GOOD BOY.>
<STUPID FUCKING MUTT. YOU JUST LOST ME A LOT OF MONEY.>
<BUT YOU CAN MAKE YOURSELF USEFUL...>
<YOU CAN FEED YOUR BROTHERS.>

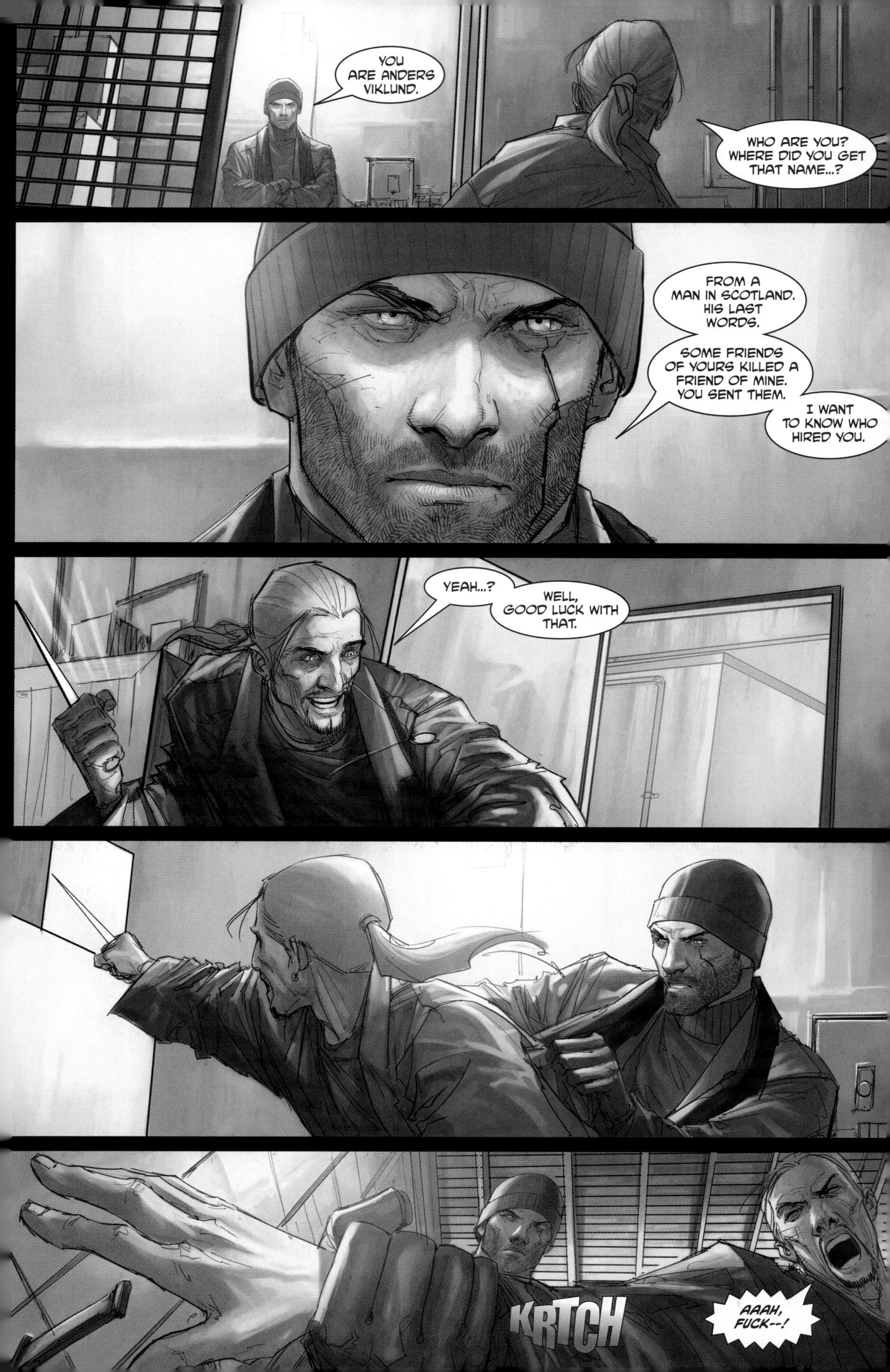
YOU ARE ANDERS VIKLUND.
WHO ARE YOU? WHERE DID YOU GET THAT NAME...?
FROM A MAN IN SCOTLAND. HIS LAST WORDS.
SOME FRIENDS OF YOURS KILLED A FRIEND OF MINE. YOU SENT THEM.
I WANT TO KNOW WHO HIRED YOU.
YEAH...?
WELL, GOOD LUCK WITH THAT.
KRTCH
AAAH, FUCK--!

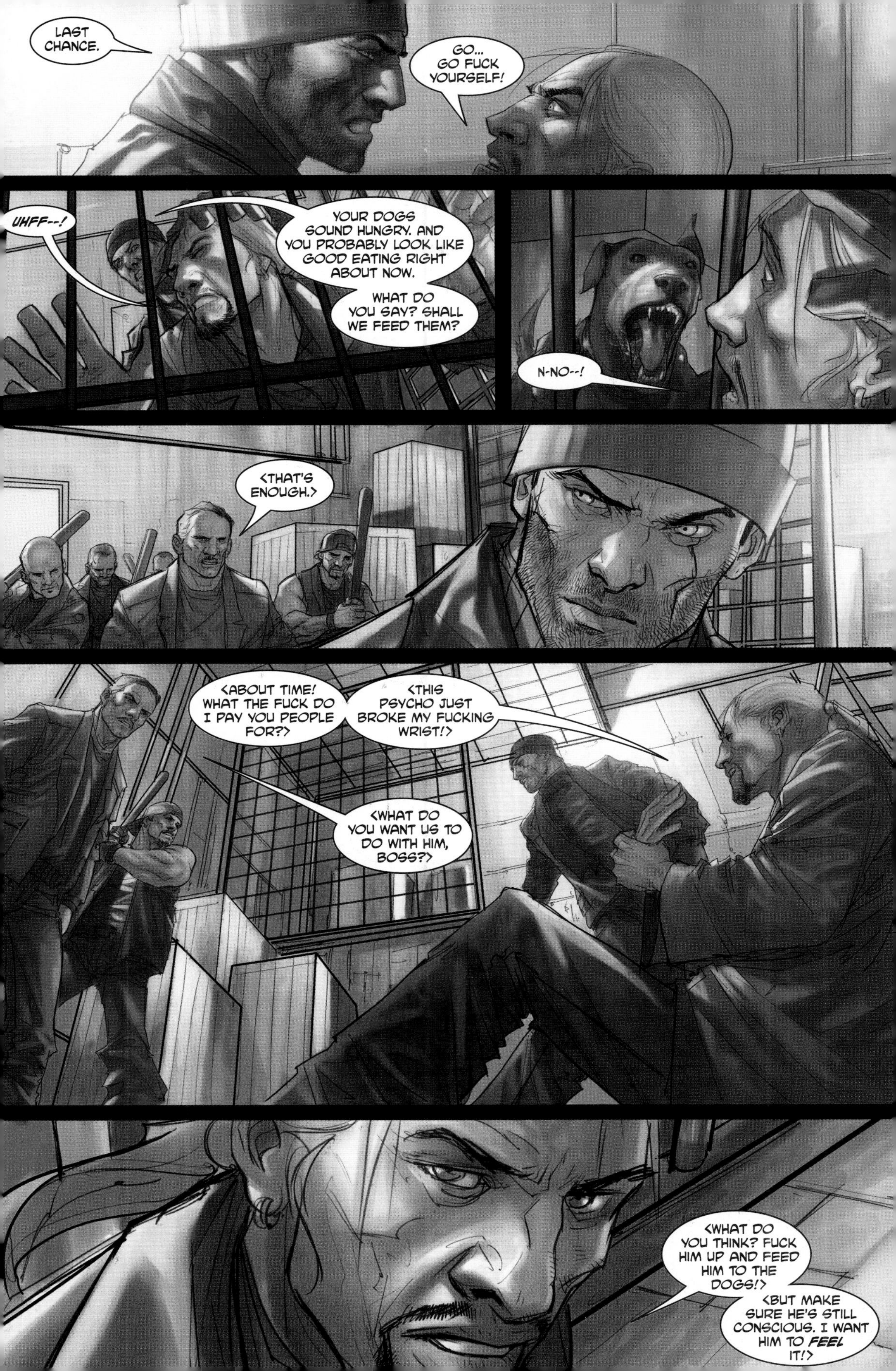
LAST CHANCE.
GO... GO FUCK YOURSELF!
UHFF--!
YOUR DOGS SOUND HUNGRY. AND YOU PROBABLY LOOK LIKE GOOD EATING RIGHT ABOUT NOW.
WHAT DO YOU SAY? SHALL WE FEED THEM?
N-NO--!
<THAT'S ENOUGH.>
<ABOUT TIME! WHAT THE FUCK DO I PAY YOU PEOPLE FOR?>
<THIS PSYCHO JUST BROKE MY FUCKING WRIST!>
<WHAT DO YOU WANT US TO DO WITH HIM, BOSS?>
<WHAT DO YOU THINK? FUCK HIM UP AND FEED HIM TO THE DOGS!>
<BUT MAKE SURE HE'S STILL CONSCIOUS. I WANT HIM TO *FEEL* IT!>

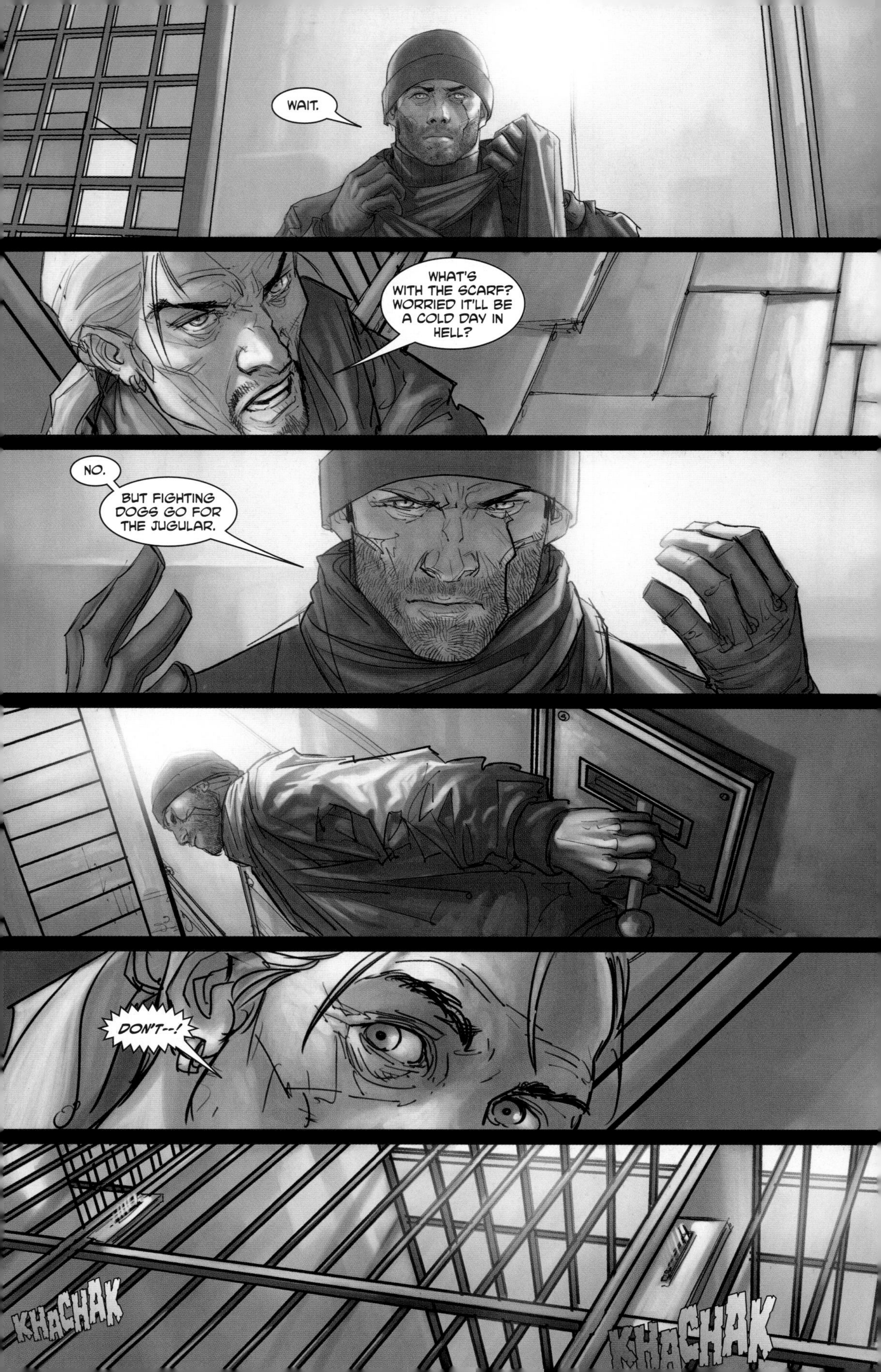
WAIT.
WHAT'S WITH THE SCARF? WORRIED IT'LL BE A COLD DAY IN HELL?
NO.
BUT FIGHTING DOGS GO FOR THE JUGULAR.
DON'T--!
KHACHAK
KHACHAK

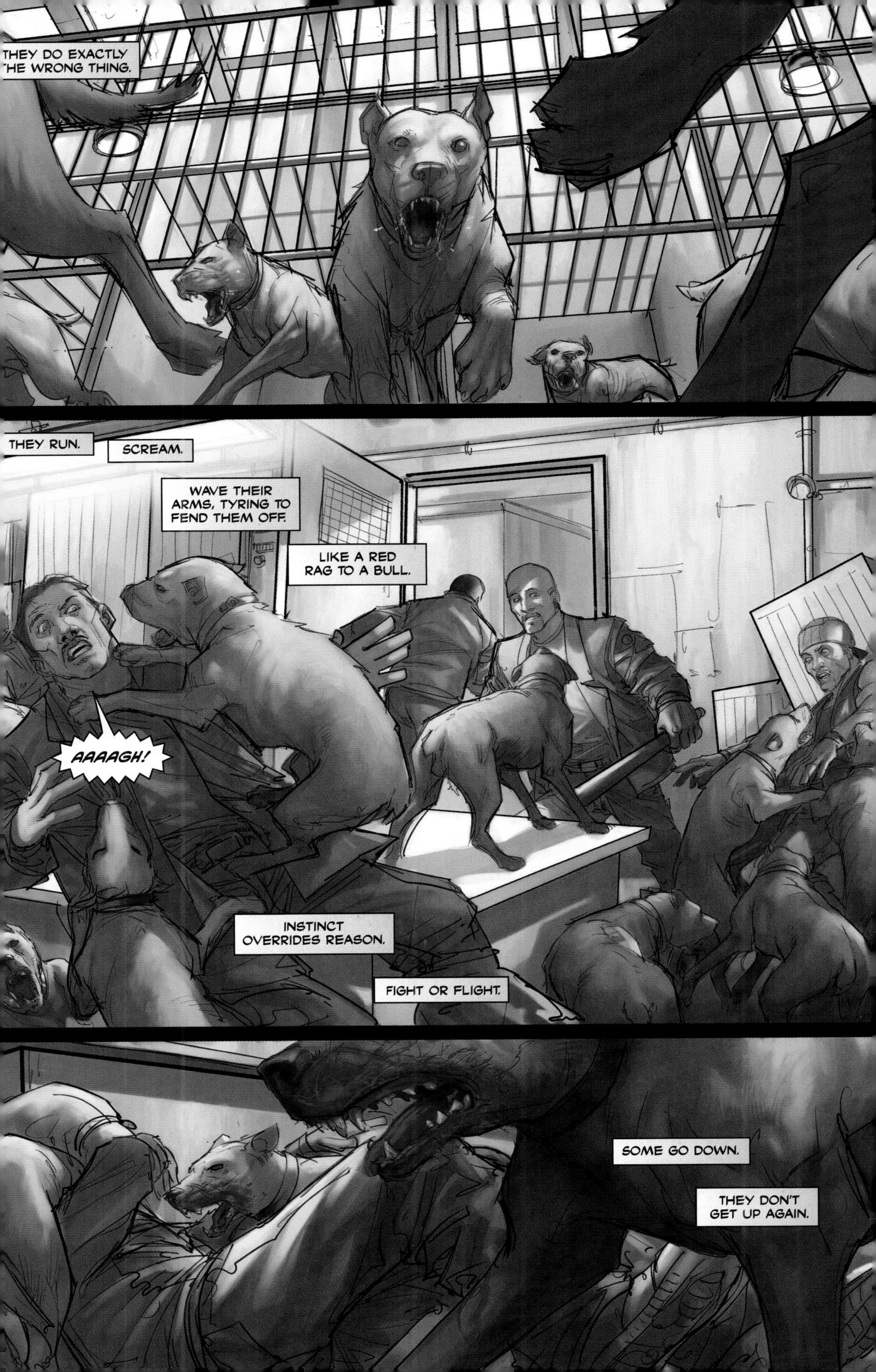
THEY DO EXACTLY THE WRONG THING.
THEY RUN.
SCREAM.
WAVE THEIR ARMS, TYRING TO FEND THEM OFF.
LIKE A RED RAG TO A BULL.
AAAAGH!
INSTINCT OVERRIDES REASON.
FIGHT OR FLIGHT.
SOME GO DOWN.
THEY DON'T GET UP AGAIN.

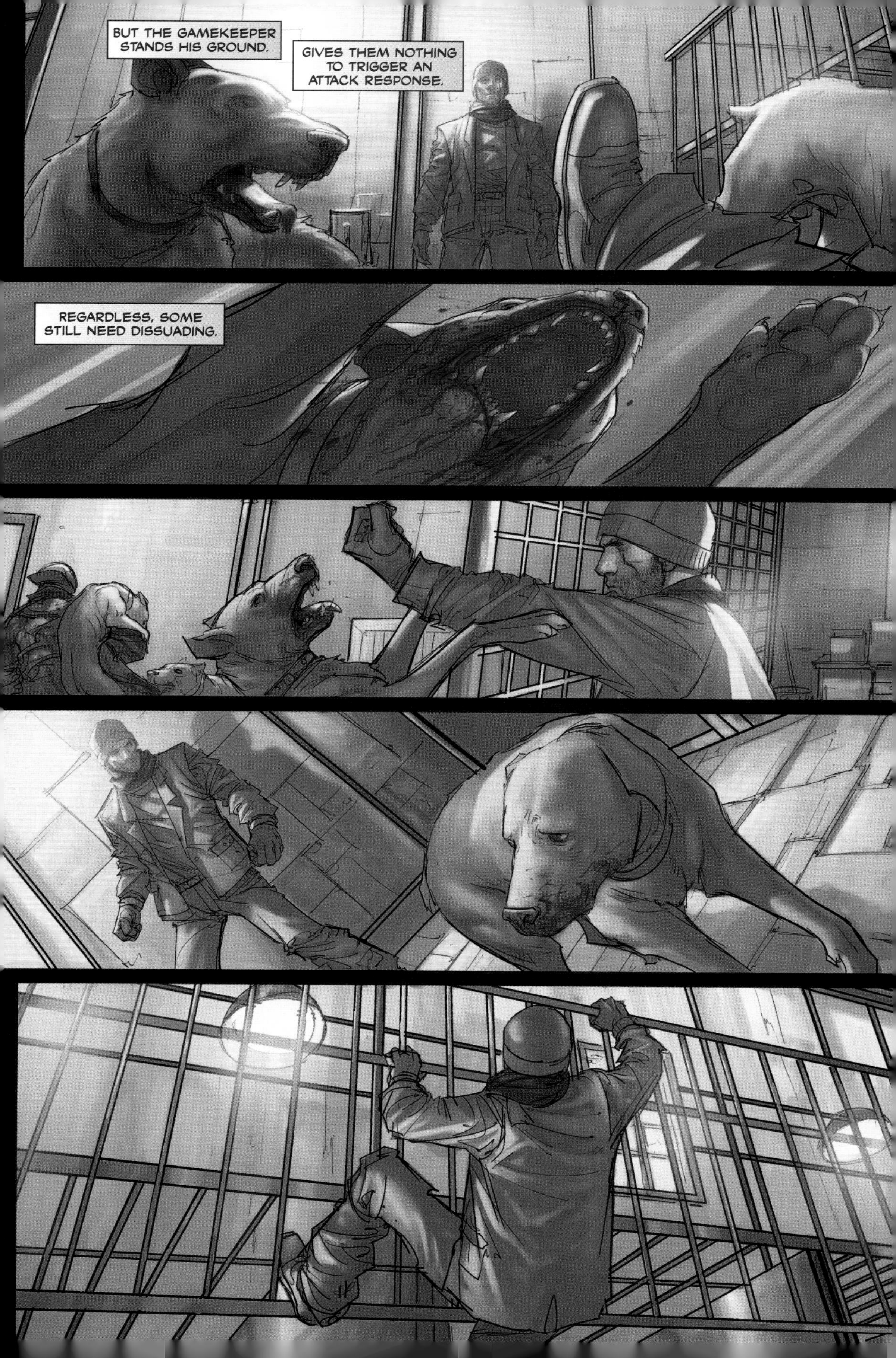
BUT THE GAMEKEEPER STANDS HIS GROUND.
GIVES THEM NOTHING TO TRIGGER AN ATTACK RESPONSE.
REGARDLESS, SOME STILL NEED DISSUADING.

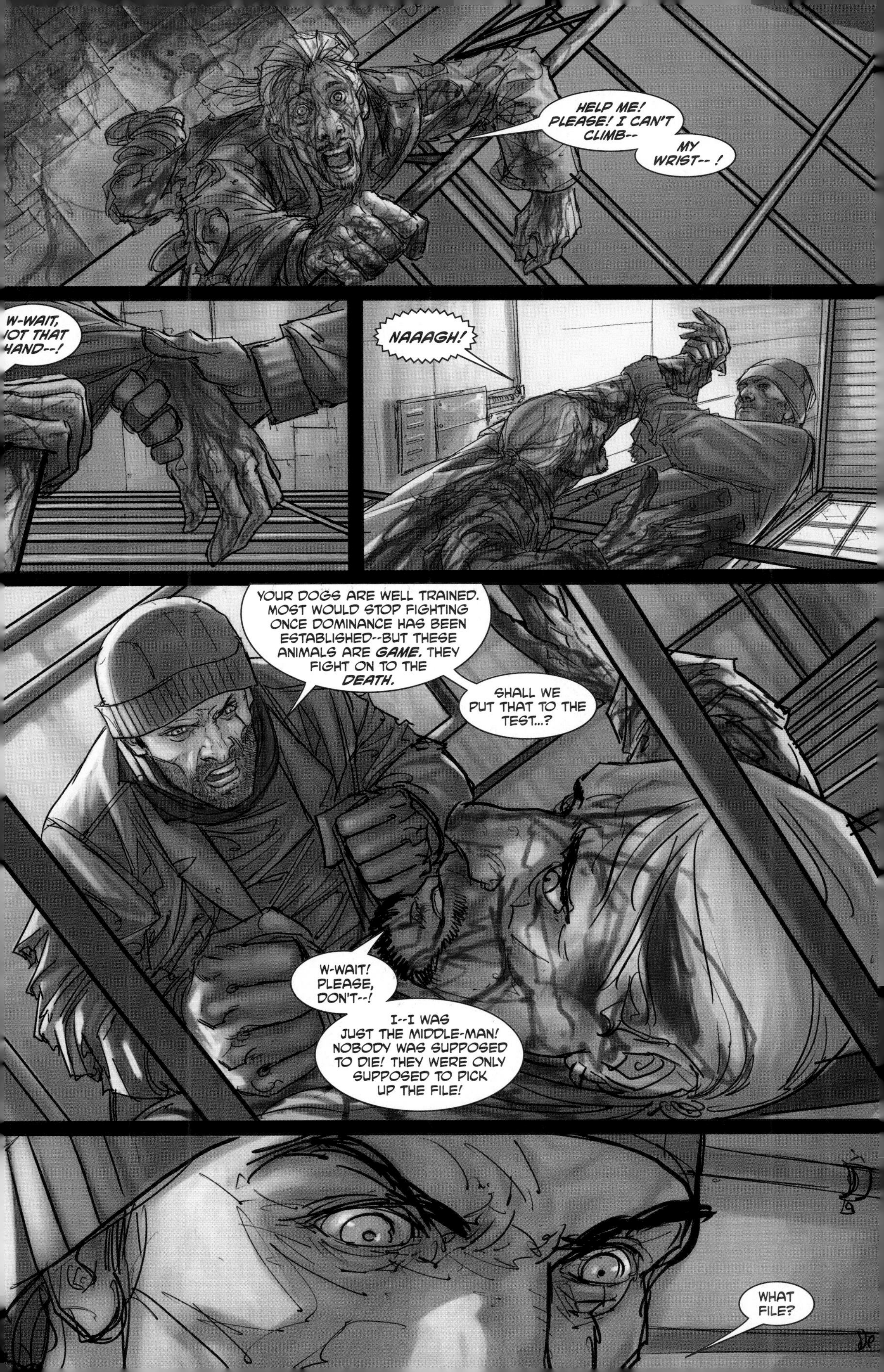
HELP ME! PLEASE! I CAN'T CLIMB--
MY WRIST-- !
W-WAIT, NOT THAT HAND--!
NAAAGH!
YOUR DOGS ARE WELL TRAINED. MOST WOULD STOP FIGHTING ONCE DOMINANCE HAS BEEN ESTABLISHED--BUT THESE ANIMALS ARE GAME. THEY FIGHT ON TO THE DEATH.
SHALL WE PUT THAT TO THE TEST...?
W-WAIT! PLEASE, DON'T--!
I--I WAS JUST THE MIDDLE-MAN! NOBODY WAS SUPPOSED TO DIE! THEY WERE ONLY SUPPOSED TO PICK UP THE FILE!
WHAT FILE?

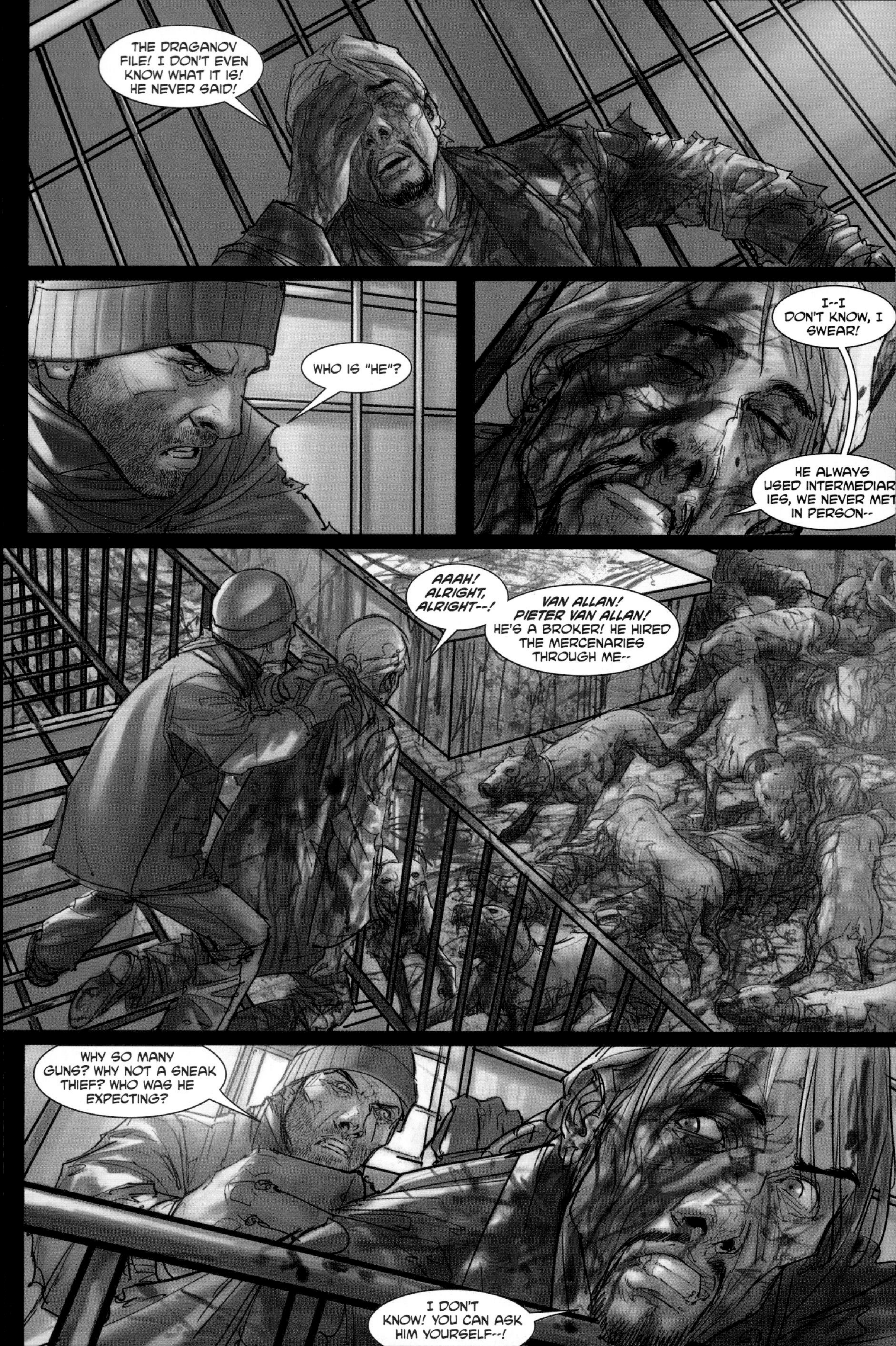
THE DRAGANOV FILE! I DON'T EVEN KNOW WHAT IT IS! HE NEVER SAID!
WHO IS "HE"?
I--I DON'T KNOW, I SWEAR!
HE ALWAYS USED INTERMEDIAR-IES, WE NEVER MET IN PERSON--
AAAH! ALRIGHT, ALRIGHT--!
VAN ALLAN! PIETER VAN ALLAN! HE'S A BROKER! HE HIRED THE MERCENARIES THROUGH ME--
WHY SO MANY GUNS? WHY NOT A SNEAK THIEF? WHO WAS HE EXPECTING?
I DON'T KNOW! YOU CAN ASK HIM YOURSELF--!

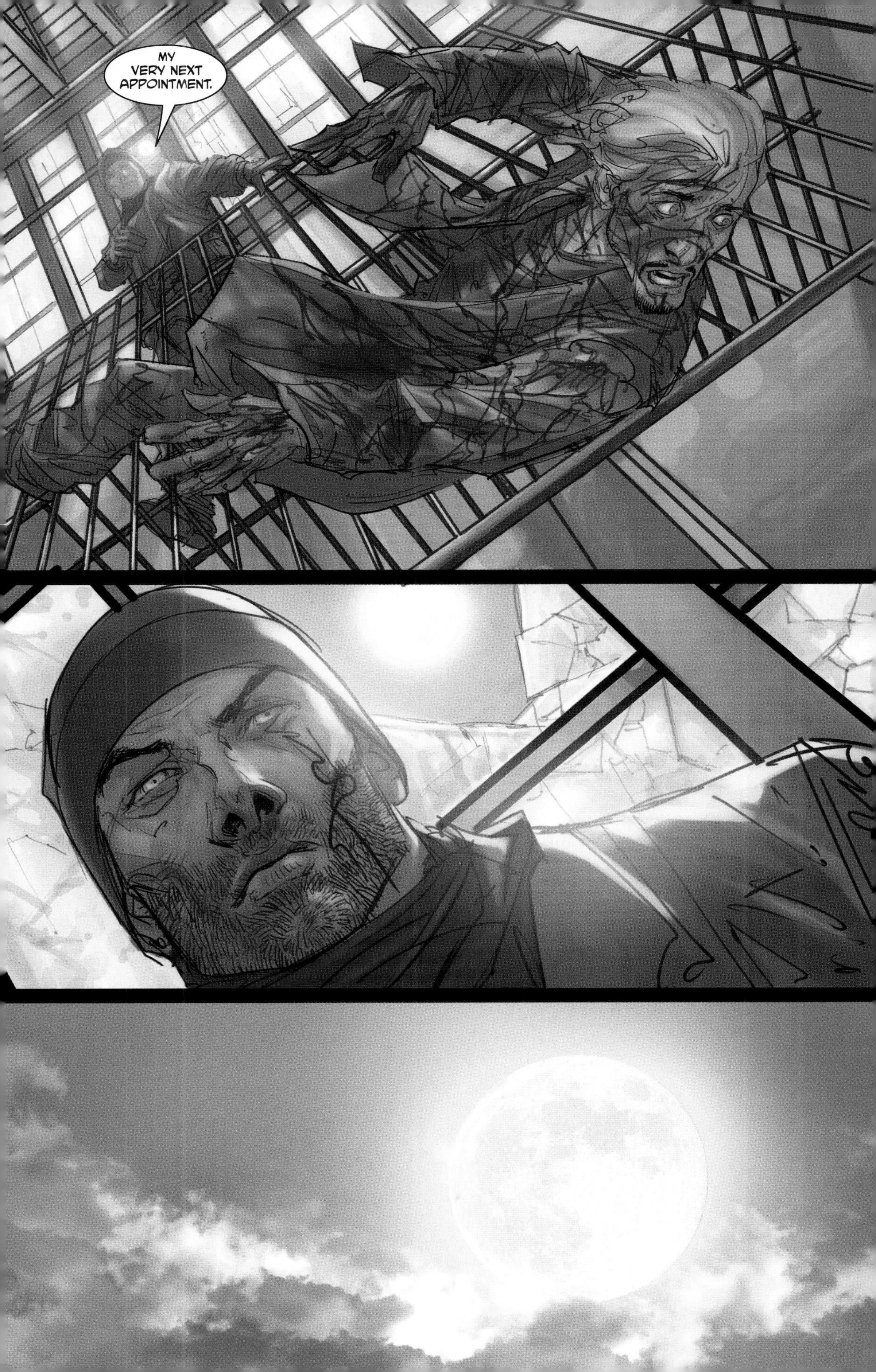
MY VERY NEXT APPOINTMENT.

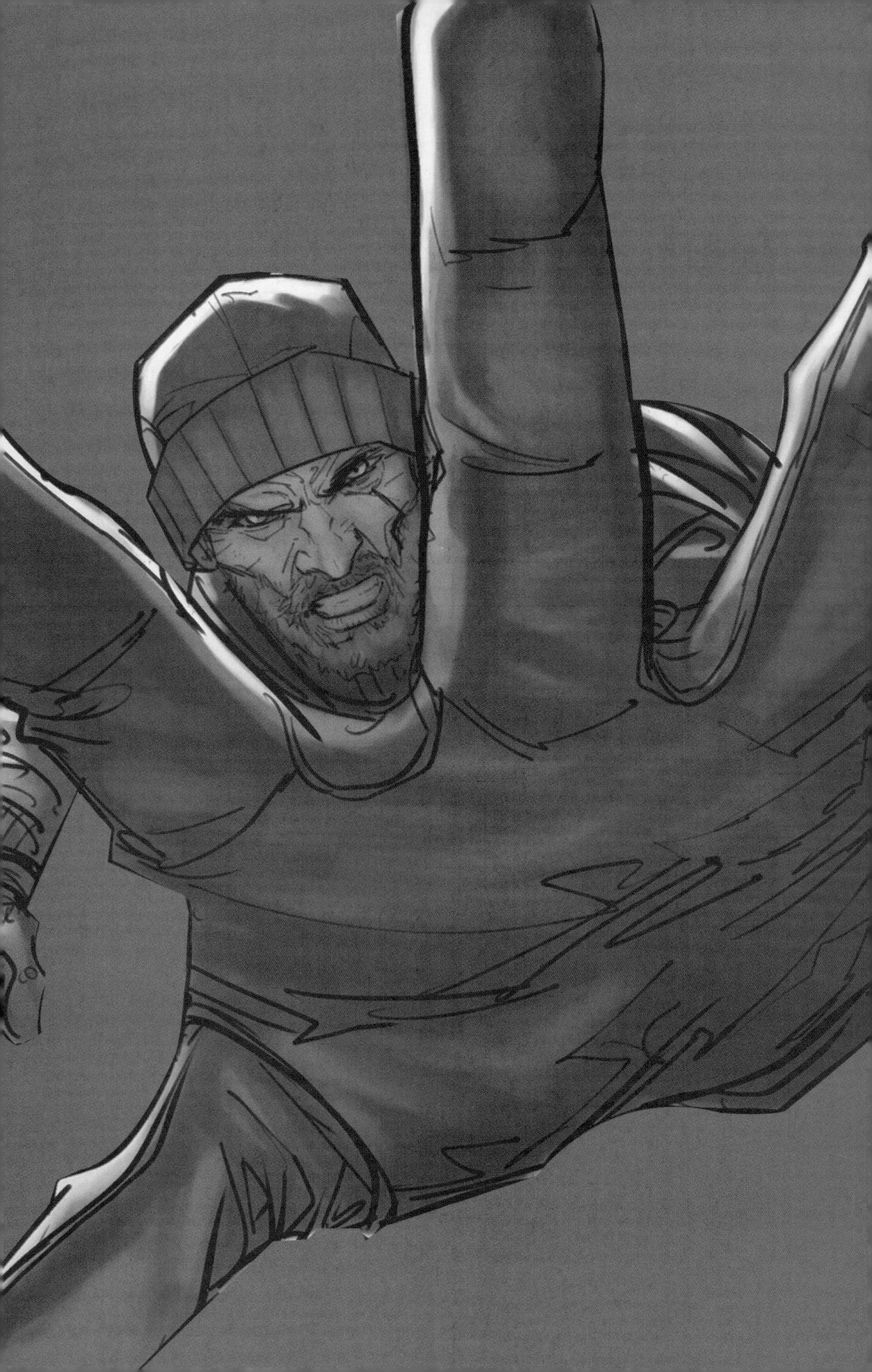

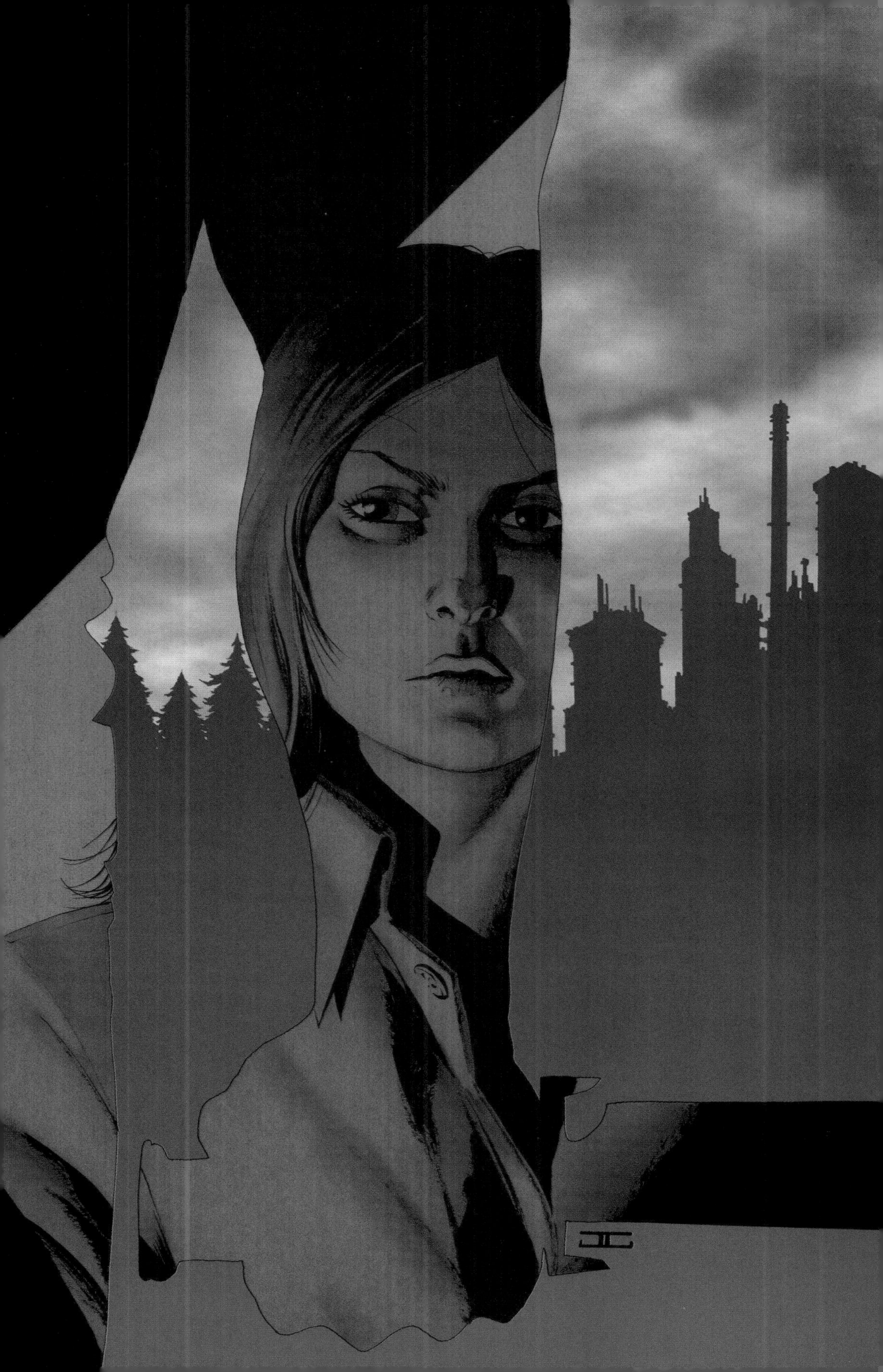

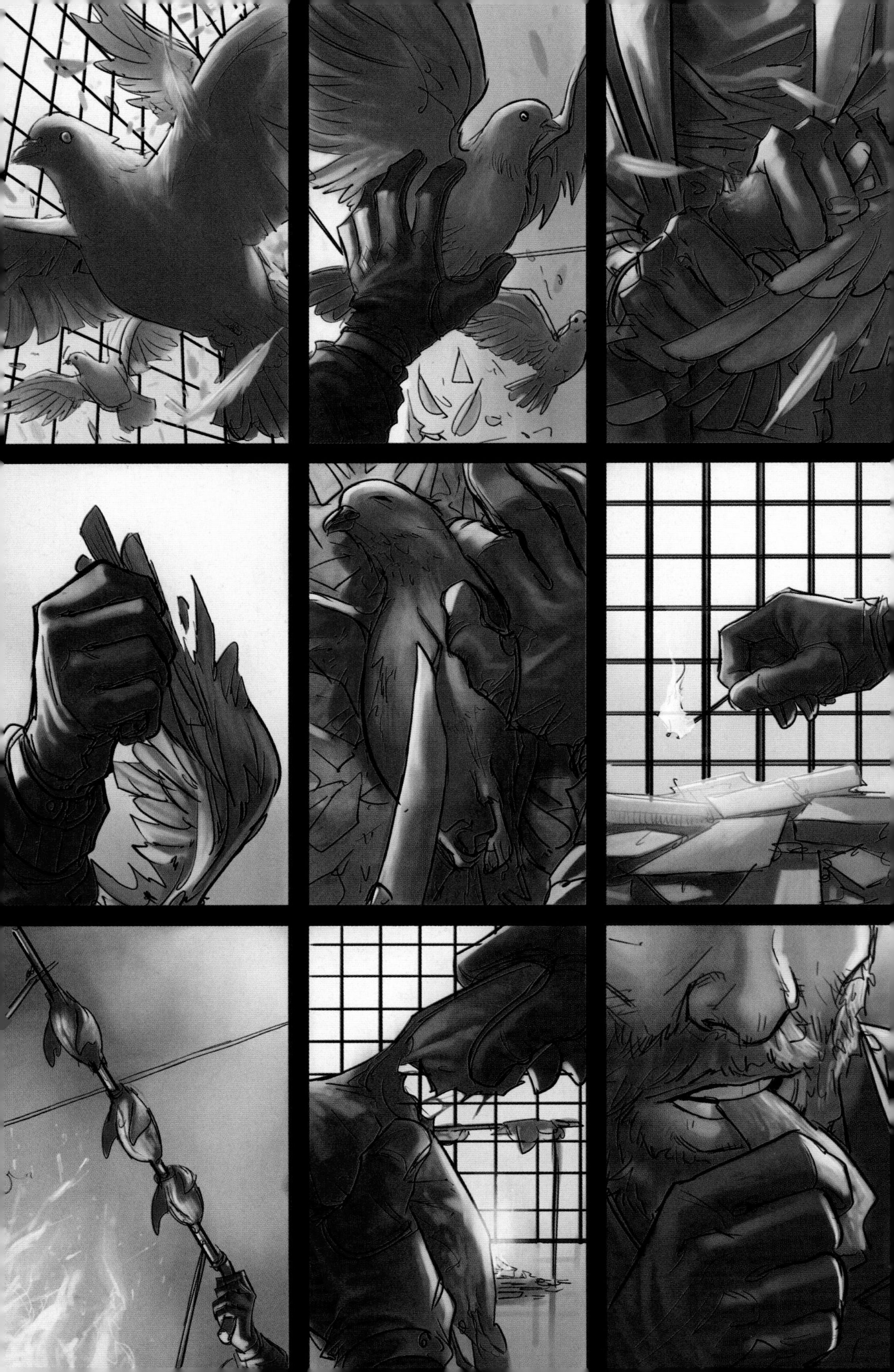

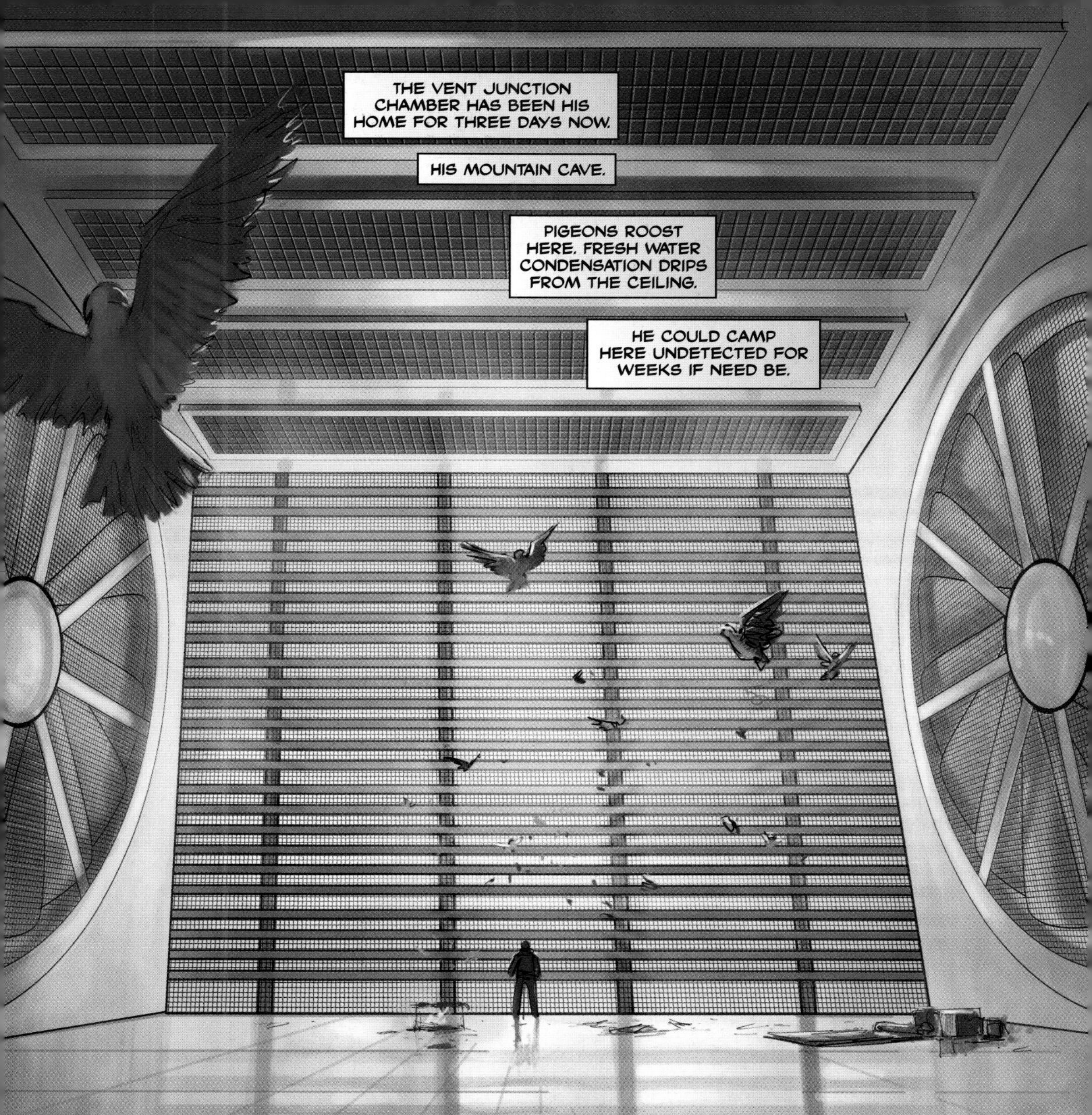
THE VENT JUNCTION CHAMBER HAS BEEN HIS HOME FOR THREE DAYS NOW.
HIS MOUNTAIN CAVE.
PIGEONS ROOST HERE. FRESH WATER CONDENSATION DRIPS FROM THE CEILING.
HE COULD CAMP HERE UNDETECTED FOR WEEKS IF NEED BE.

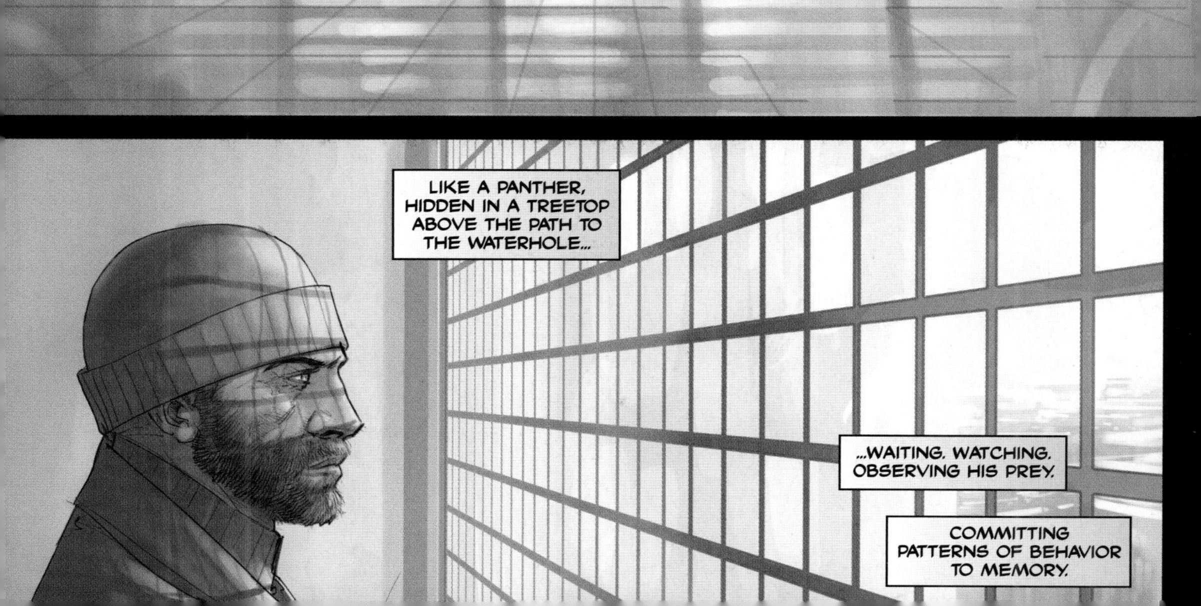
LIKE A PANTHER, HIDDEN IN A TREETOP ABOVE THE PATH TO THE WATERHOLE...
...WAITING, WATCHING, OBSERVING HIS PREY.
COMMITTING PATTERNS OF BEHAVIOR TO MEMORY.

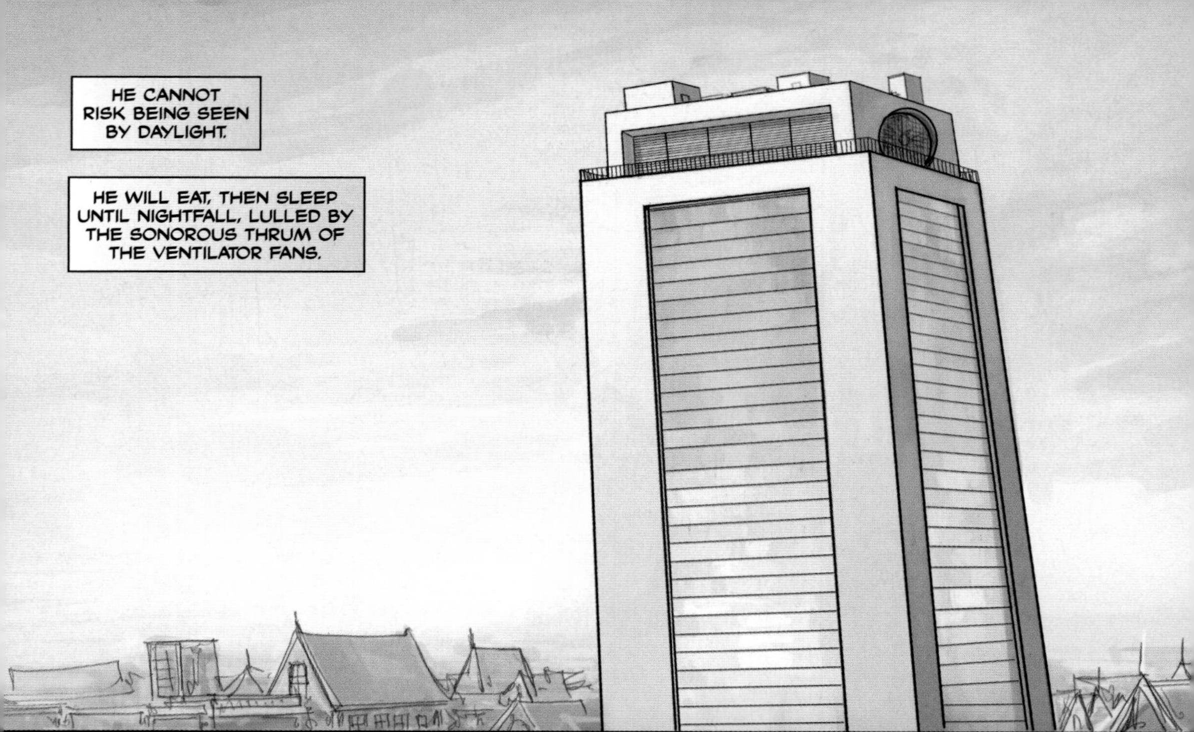
HE CANNOT RISK BEING SEEN BY DAYLIGHT.
HE WILL EAT, THEN SLEEP UNTIL NIGHTFALL, LULLED BY THE SONOROUS THRUM OF THE VENTILATOR FANS.

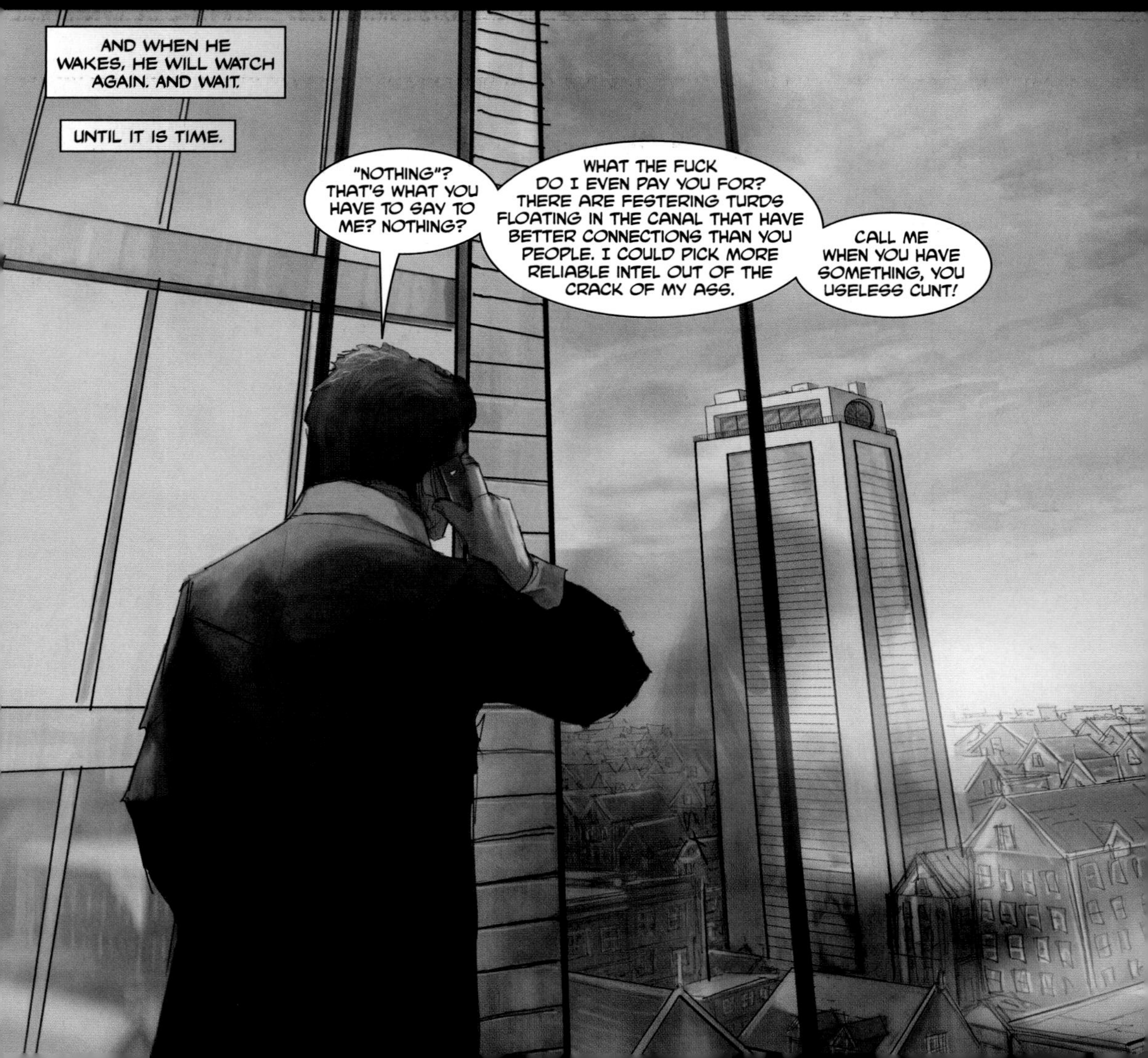
AND WHEN HE WAKES, HE WILL WATCH AGAIN. AND WAIT.
UNTIL IT IS TIME.
"NOTHING"? THAT'S WHAT YOU HAVE TO SAY TO ME? NOTHING?
WHAT THE FUCK DO I EVEN PAY YOU FOR? THERE ARE FESTERING TURDS FLOATING IN THE CANAL THAT HAVE BETTER CONNECTIONS THAN YOU PEOPLE. I COULD PICK MORE RELIABLE INTEL OUT OF THE CRACK OF MY ASS.
CALL ME WHEN YOU HAVE SOMETHING, YOU USELESS CUNT!

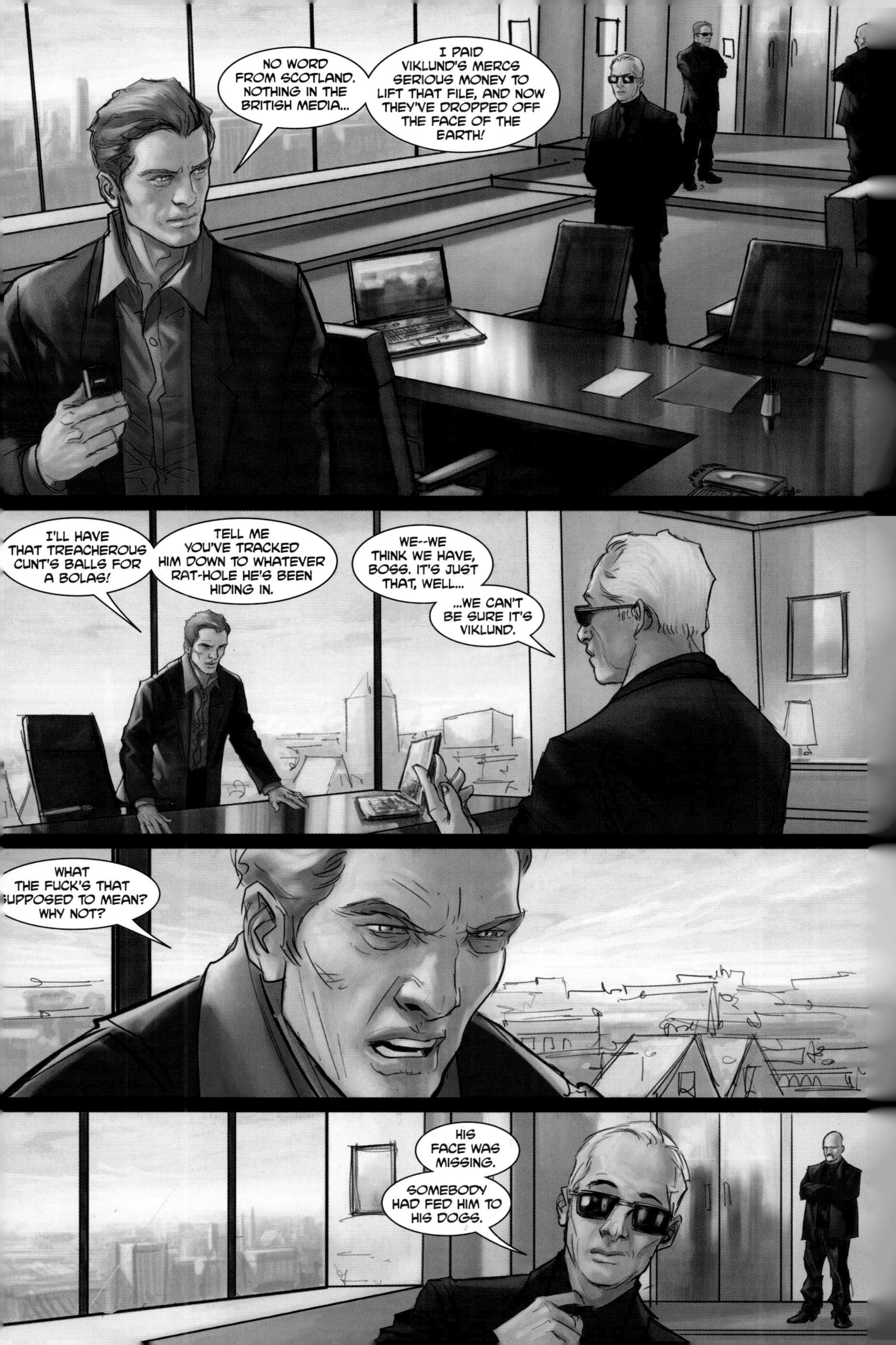
NO WORD FROM SCOTLAND. NOTHING IN THE BRITISH MEDIA...
I PAID VIKLUND'S MERCS SERIOUS MONEY TO LIFT THAT FILE, AND NOW THEY'VE DROPPED OFF THE FACE OF THE EARTH!
I'LL HAVE THAT TREACHEROUS CUNT'S BALLS FOR A BOLAS!
TELL ME YOU'VE TRACKED HIM DOWN TO WHATEVER RAT-HOLE HE'S BEEN HIDING IN.
WE--WE THINK WE HAVE, BOSS. IT'S JUST THAT, WELL...
...WE CAN'T BE SURE IT'S VIKLUND.
WHAT THE FUCK'S THAT SUPPOSED TO MEAN? WHY NOT?
HIS FACE WAS MISSING.
SOMEBODY HAD FED HIM TO HIS DOGS.

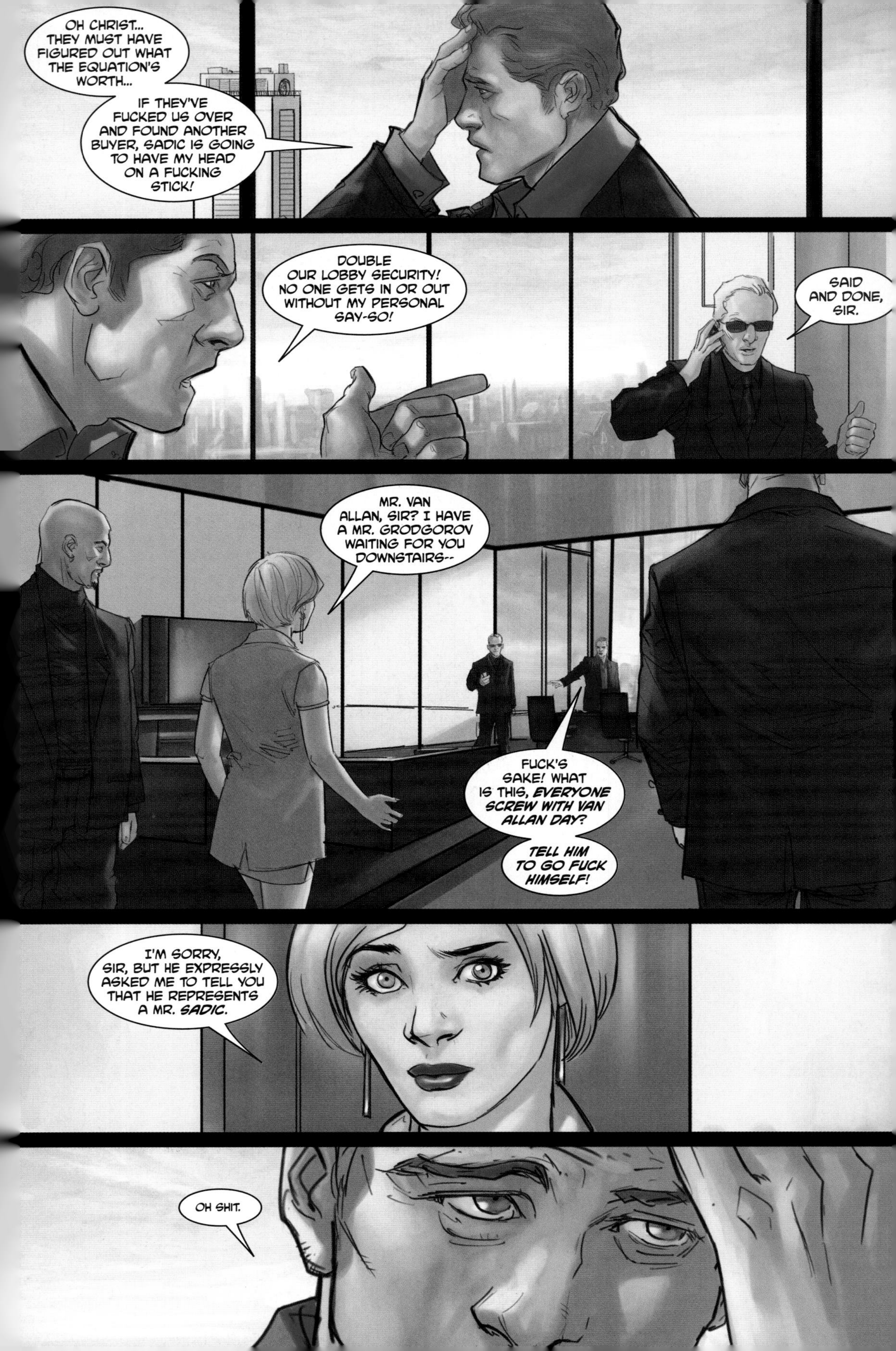
OH CHRIST... THEY MUST HAVE FIGURED OUT WHAT THE EQUATION'S WORTH...
IF THEY'VE FUCKED US OVER AND FOUND ANOTHER BUYER, SADIC IS GOING TO HAVE MY HEAD ON A FUCKING STICK!
DOUBLE OUR LOBBY SECURITY! NO ONE GETS IN OR OUT WITHOUT MY PERSONAL SAY-SO!
SAID AND DONE, SIR.
MR. VAN ALLAN, SIR? I HAVE A MR. GRODGOROV WAITING FOR YOU DOWNSTAIRS--
FUCK'S SAKE! WHAT IS THIS, EVERYONE SCREW WITH VAN ALLAN DAY?
TELL HIM TO GO FUCK HIMSELF!
I'M SORRY, SIR, BUT HE EXPRESSLY ASKED ME TO TELL YOU THAT HE REPRESENTS A MR. SADIC.
OH SHIT.

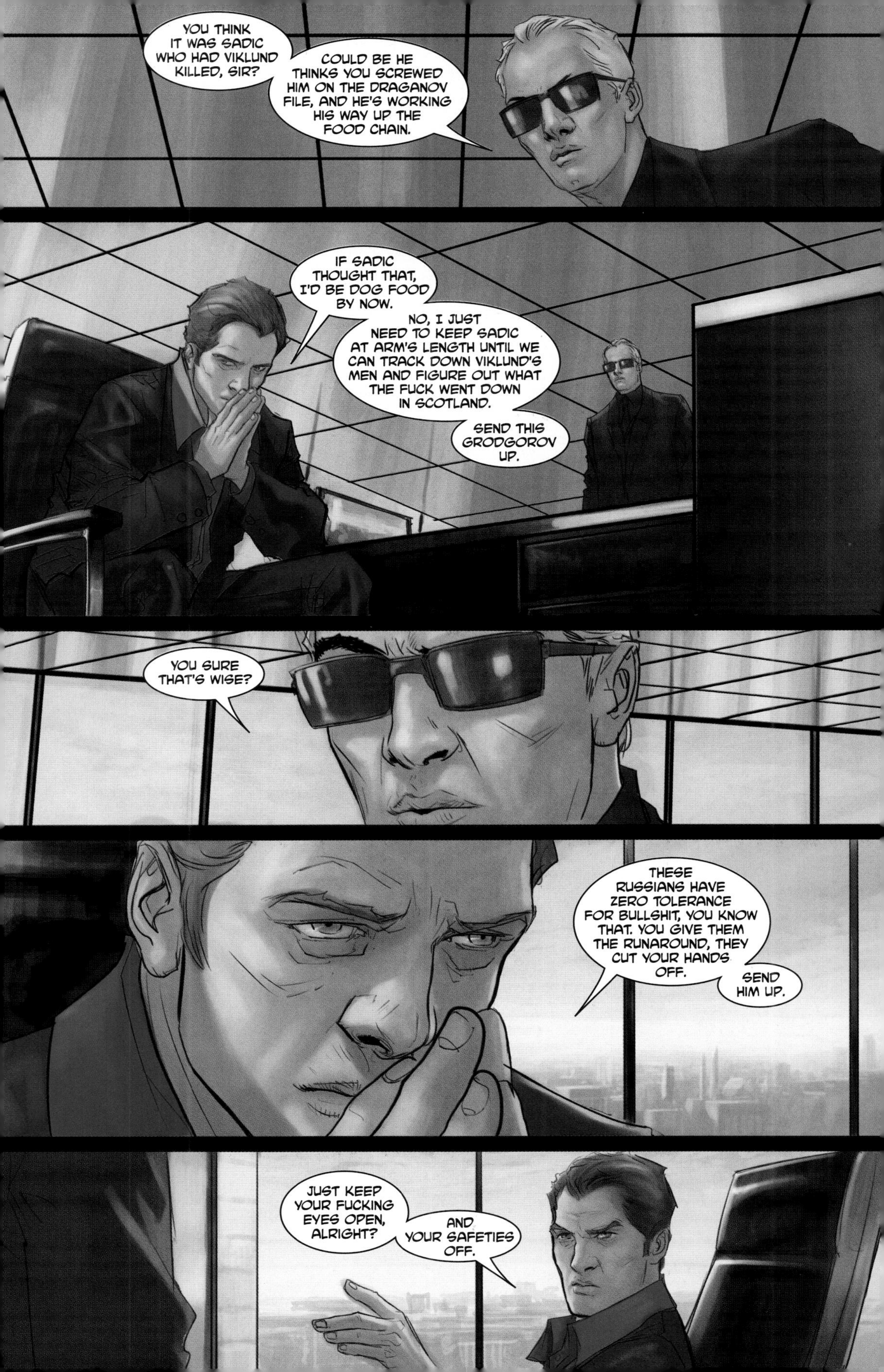
YOU THINK IT WAS SADIC WHO HAD VIKLUND KILLED, SIR?
COULD BE HE THINKS YOU SCREWED HIM ON THE DRAGANOV FILE, AND HE'S WORKING HIS WAY UP THE FOOD CHAIN.
IF SADIC THOUGHT THAT, I'D BE DOG FOOD BY NOW.
NO, I JUST NEED TO KEEP SADIC AT ARM'S LENGTH UNTIL WE CAN TRACK DOWN VIKLUND'S MEN AND FIGURE OUT WHAT THE FUCK WENT DOWN IN SCOTLAND.
SEND THIS GRODGOROV UP.
YOU SURE THAT'S WISE?
THESE RUSSIANS HAVE ZERO TOLERANCE FOR BULLSHIT, YOU KNOW THAT. YOU GIVE THEM THE RUNAROUND, THEY CUT YOUR HANDS OFF.
SEND HIM UP.
JUST KEEP YOUR FUCKING EYES OPEN, ALRIGHT?
AND YOUR SAFETIES OFF.

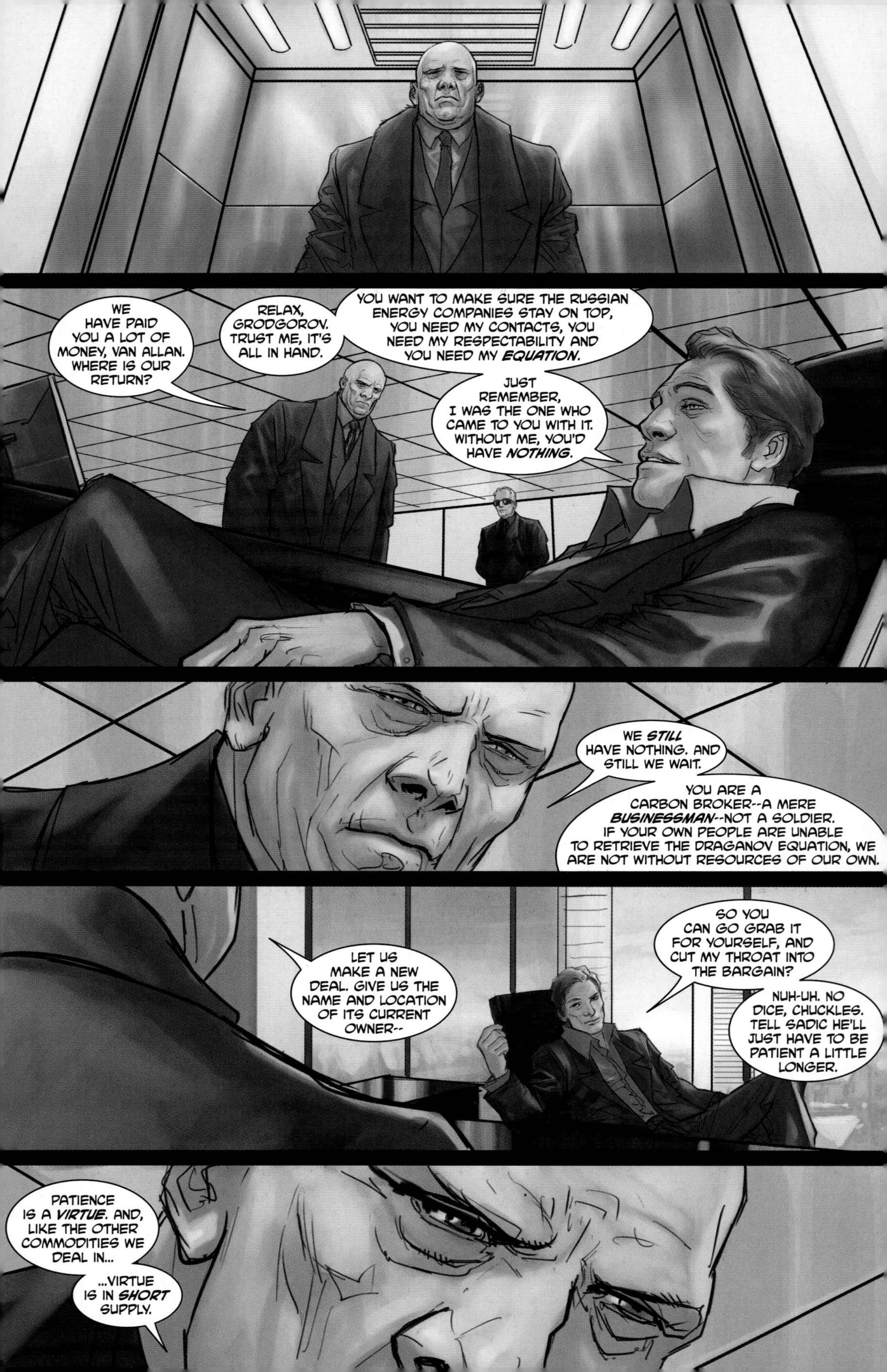
WE HAVE PAID YOU A LOT OF MONEY, VAN ALLAN. WHERE IS OUR RETURN?
RELAX, GRODGOROV. TRUST ME, IT'S ALL IN HAND.
YOU WANT TO MAKE SURE THE RUSSIAN ENERGY COMPANIES STAY ON TOP, YOU NEED MY CONTACTS, YOU NEED MY RESPECTABILITY AND YOU NEED MY *EQUATION*.
JUST REMEMBER, I WAS THE ONE WHO CAME TO YOU WITH IT. WITHOUT ME, YOU'D HAVE *NOTHING*.
WE *STILL* HAVE NOTHING. AND STILL WE WAIT.
YOU ARE A CARBON BROKER--A MERE *BUSINESSMAN*--NOT A SOLDIER. IF YOUR OWN PEOPLE ARE UNABLE TO RETRIEVE THE DRAGANOV EQUATION, WE ARE NOT WITHOUT RESOURCES OF OUR OWN.
LET US MAKE A NEW DEAL. GIVE US THE NAME AND LOCATION OF ITS CURRENT OWNER--
SO YOU CAN GO GRAB IT FOR YOURSELF, AND CUT MY THROAT INTO THE BARGAIN?
NUH-UH. NO DICE, CHUCKLES. TELL SADIC HE'LL JUST HAVE TO BE PATIENT A LITTLE LONGER.
PATIENCE IS A *VIRTUE*. AND, LIKE THE OTHER COMMODITIES WE DEAL IN...
...VIRTUE IS IN *SHORT* SUPPLY.

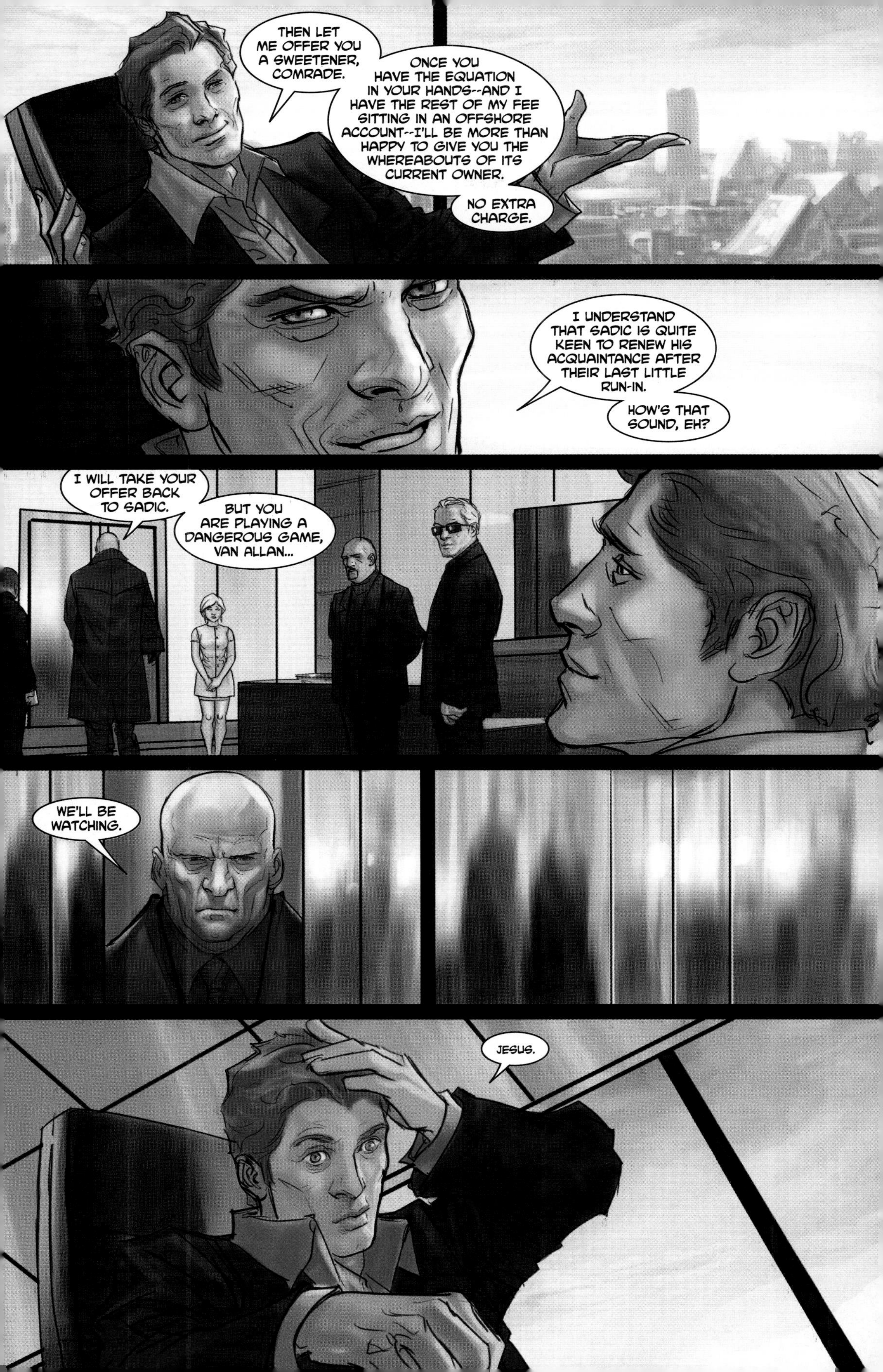
THEN LET ME OFFER YOU A SWEETENER, COMRADE.
ONCE YOU HAVE THE EQUATION IN YOUR HANDS--AND I HAVE THE REST OF MY FEE SITTING IN AN OFFSHORE ACCOUNT--I'LL BE MORE THAN HAPPY TO GIVE YOU THE WHEREABOUTS OF ITS CURRENT OWNER.
NO EXTRA CHARGE.
I UNDERSTAND THAT SADIC IS QUITE KEEN TO RENEW HIS ACQUAINTANCE AFTER THEIR LAST LITTLE RUN-IN.
HOW'S THAT SOUND, EH?
I WILL TAKE YOUR OFFER BACK TO SADIC.
BUT YOU ARE PLAYING A DANGEROUS GAME, VAN ALLAN...
WE'LL BE WATCHING.
JESUS.

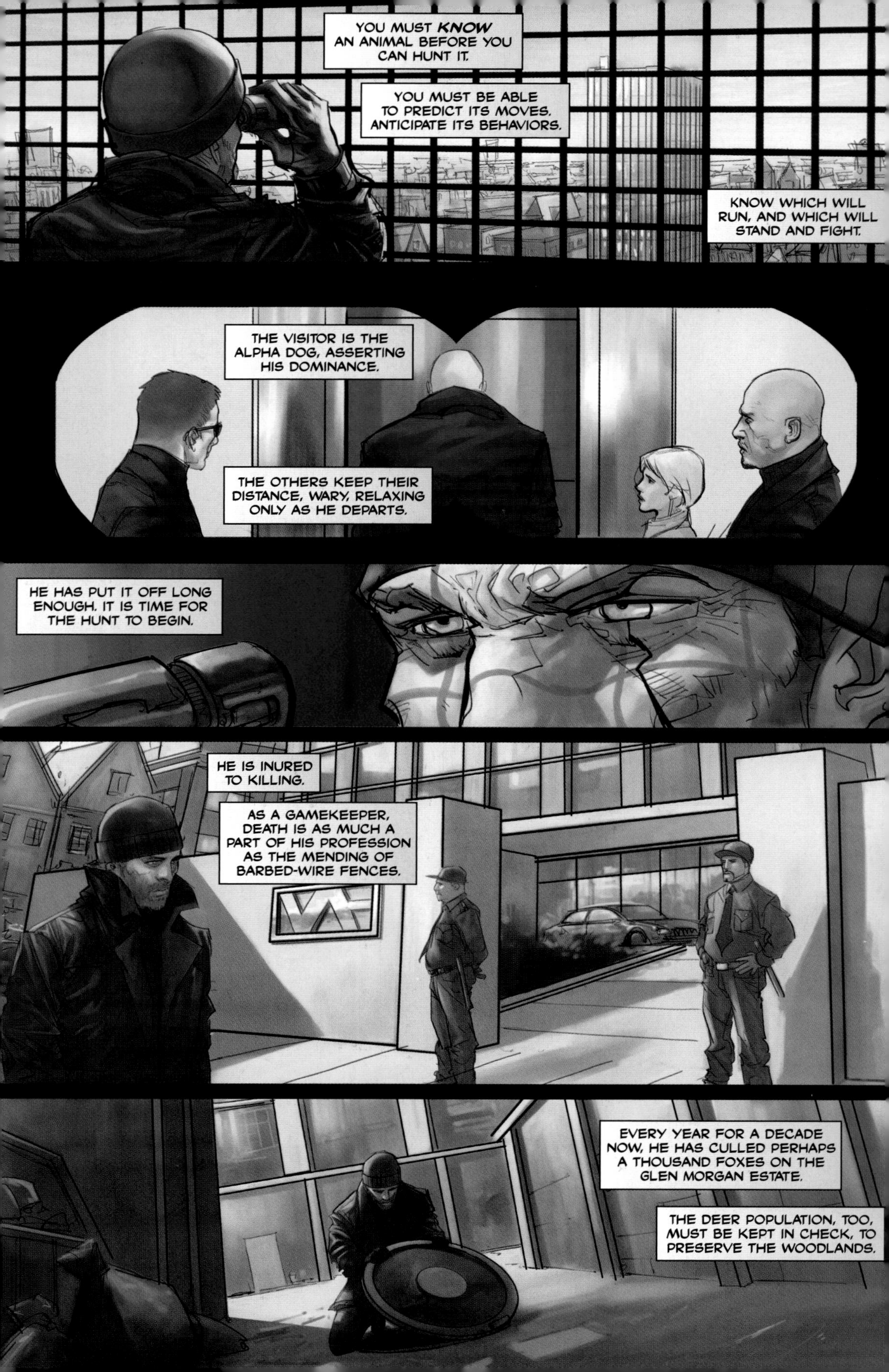
YOU MUST *KNOW* AN ANIMAL BEFORE YOU CAN HUNT IT.
YOU MUST BE ABLE TO PREDICT ITS MOVES, ANTICIPATE ITS BEHAVIORS.
KNOW WHICH WILL RUN, AND WHICH WILL STAND AND FIGHT.
THE VISITOR IS THE ALPHA DOG, ASSERTING HIS DOMINANCE.
THE OTHERS KEEP THEIR DISTANCE, WARY, RELAXING ONLY AS HE DEPARTS.
HE HAS PUT IT OFF LONG ENOUGH. IT IS TIME FOR THE HUNT TO BEGIN.
HE IS INURED TO KILLING.
AS A GAMEKEEPER, DEATH IS AS MUCH A PART OF HIS PROFESSION AS THE MENDING OF BARBED-WIRE FENCES.
EVERY YEAR FOR A DECADE NOW, HE HAS CULLED PERHAPS A THOUSAND FOXES ON THE GLEN MORGAN ESTATE.
THE DEER POPULATION, TOO, MUST BE KEPT IN CHECK, TO PRESERVE THE WOODLANDS.

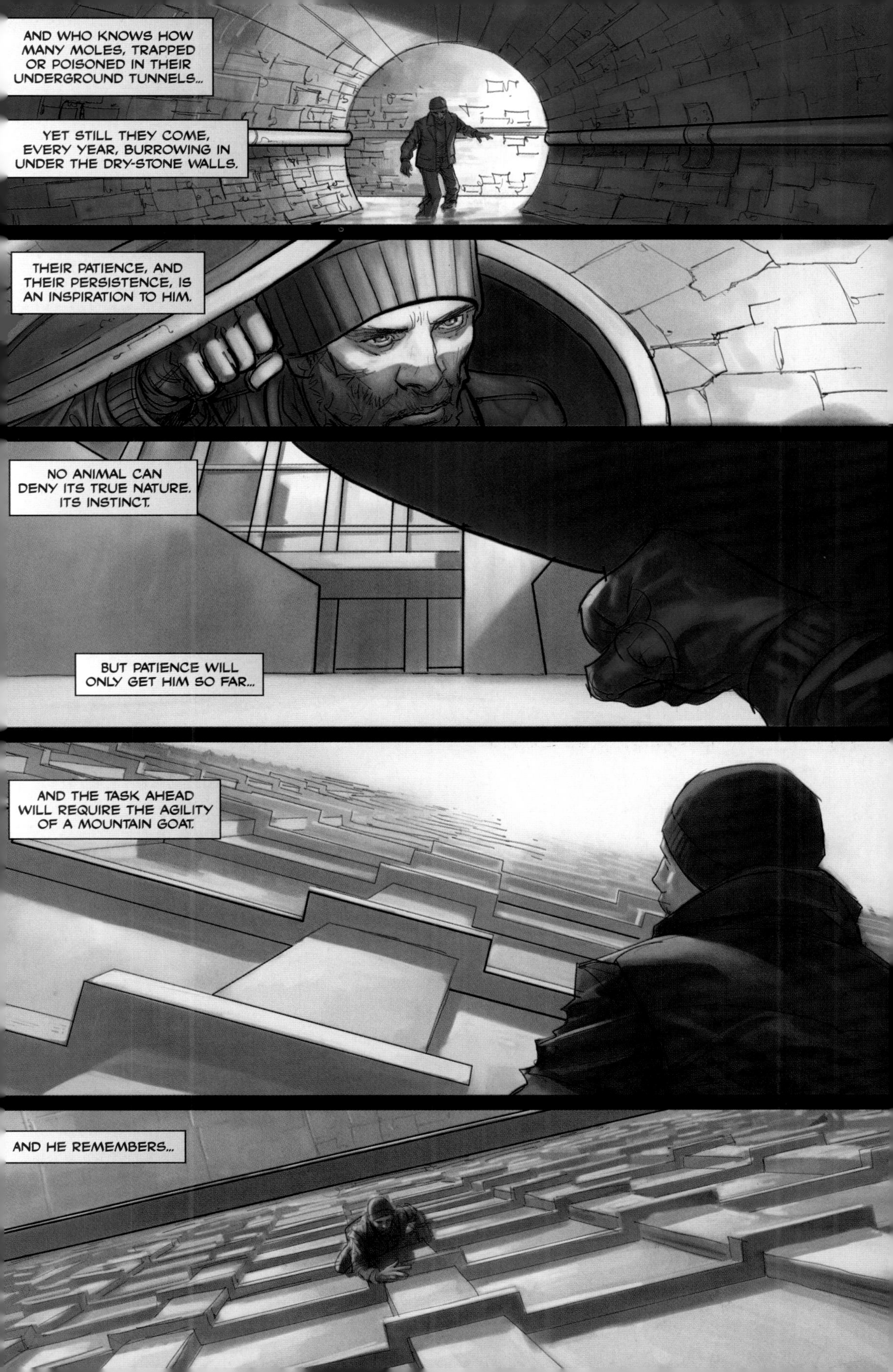
AND WHO KNOWS HOW MANY MOLES, TRAPPED OR POISONED IN THEIR UNDERGROUND TUNNELS...
YET STILL THEY COME, EVERY YEAR, BURROWING IN UNDER THE DRY-STONE WALLS.
THEIR PATIENCE, AND THEIR PERSISTENCE, IS AN INSPIRATION TO HIM.
NO ANIMAL CAN DENY ITS TRUE NATURE. ITS INSTINCT.
BUT PATIENCE WILL ONLY GET HIM SO FAR...
AND THE TASK AHEAD WILL REQUIRE THE AGILITY OF A MOUNTAIN GOAT.
AND HE REMEMBERS...

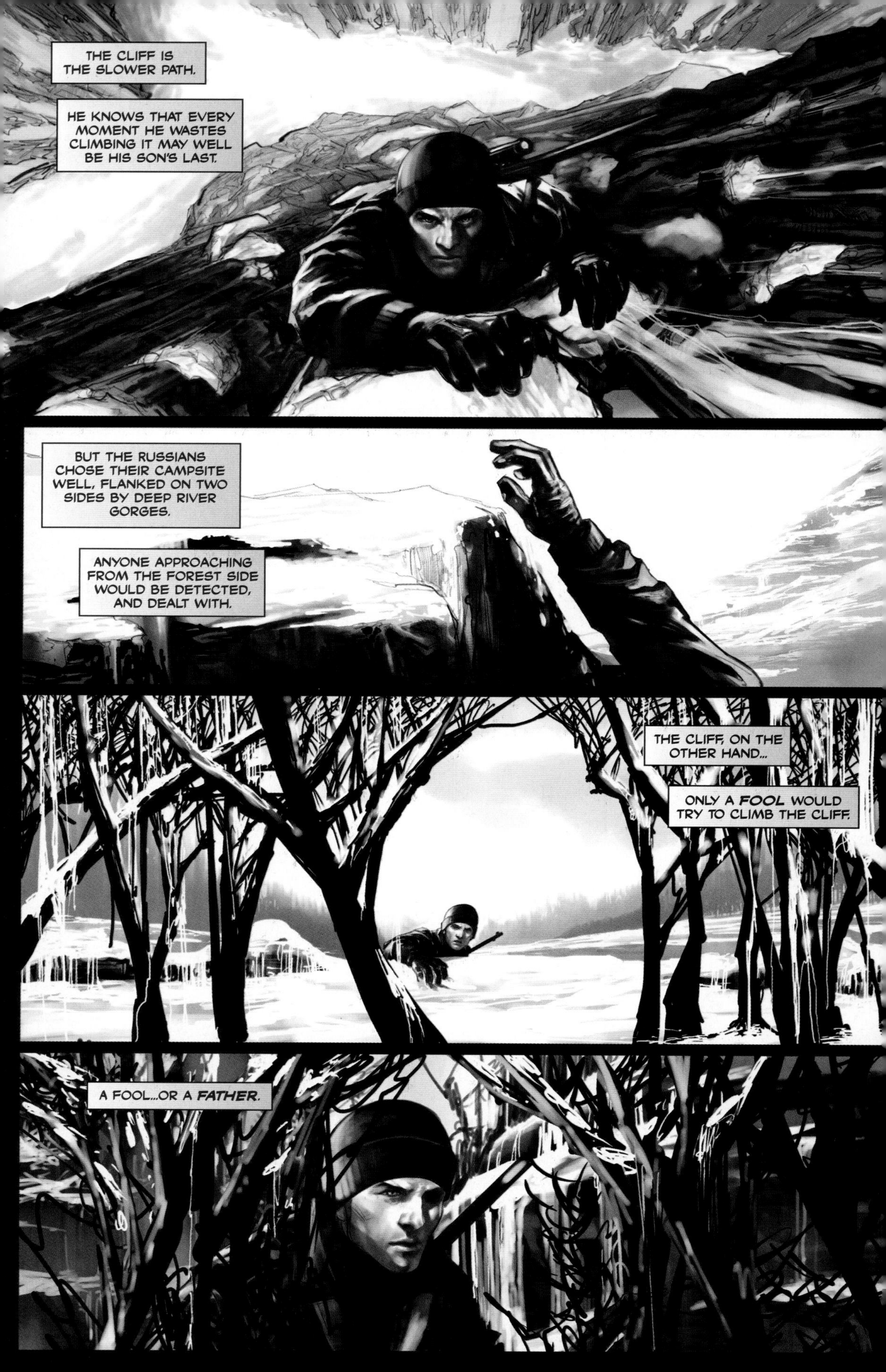
THE CLIFF IS THE SLOWER PATH.
HE KNOWS THAT EVERY MOMENT HE WASTES CLIMBING IT MAY WELL BE HIS SON'S LAST.
BUT THE RUSSIANS CHOSE THEIR CAMPSITE WELL, FLANKED ON TWO SIDES BY DEEP RIVER GORGES.
ANYONE APPROACHING FROM THE FOREST SIDE WOULD BE DETECTED, AND DEALT WITH.
THE CLIFF, ON THE OTHER HAND...
ONLY A *FOOL* WOULD TRY TO CLIMB THE CLIFF.
A FOOL...OR A *FATHER*.

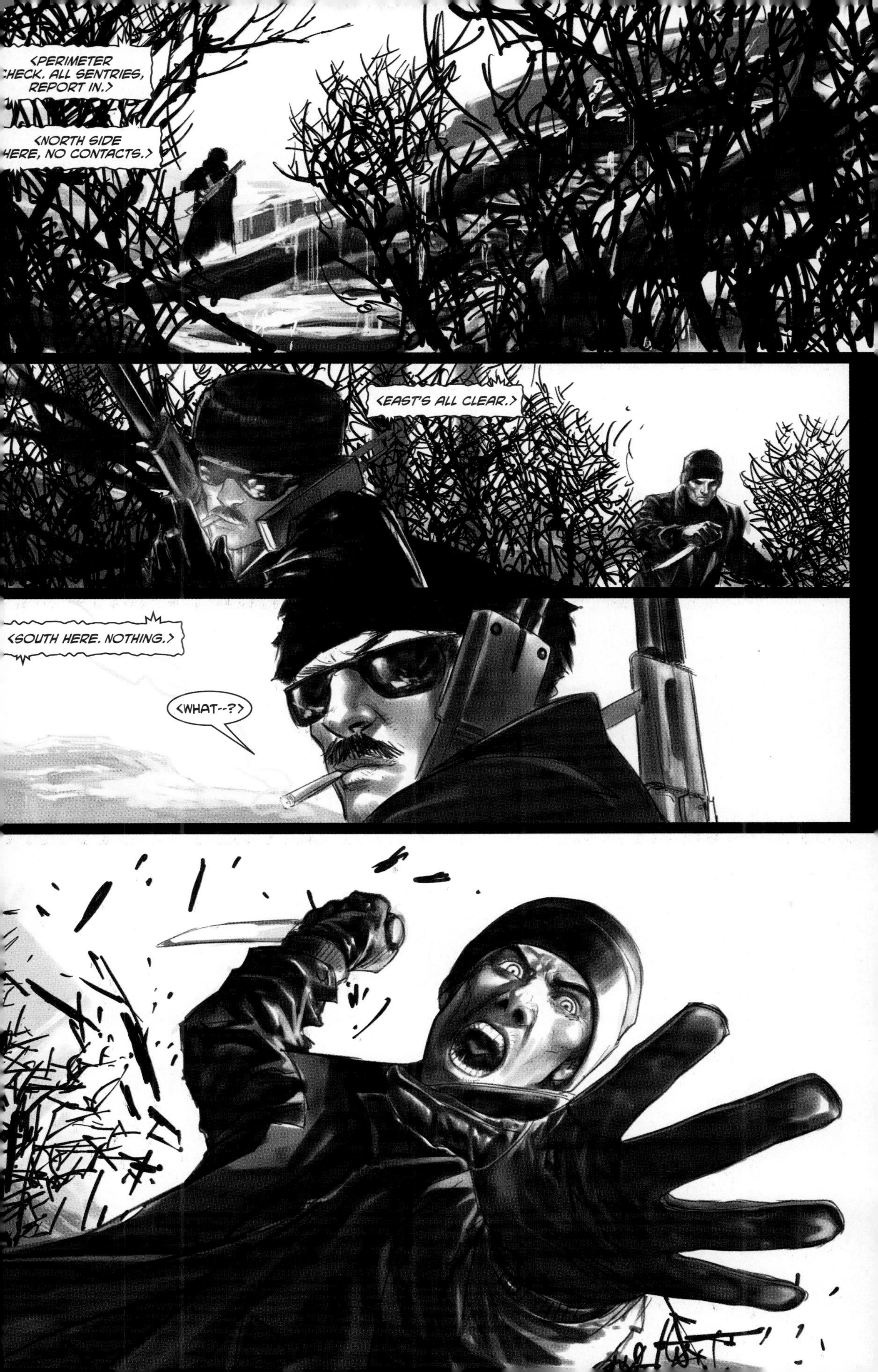

<PERIMETER CHECK. ALL SENTRIES, REPORT IN.>
<NORTH SIDE HERE, NO CONTACTS.>
<EAST'S ALL CLEAR.>
<SOUTH HERE. NOTHING.>
<WHAT--?>

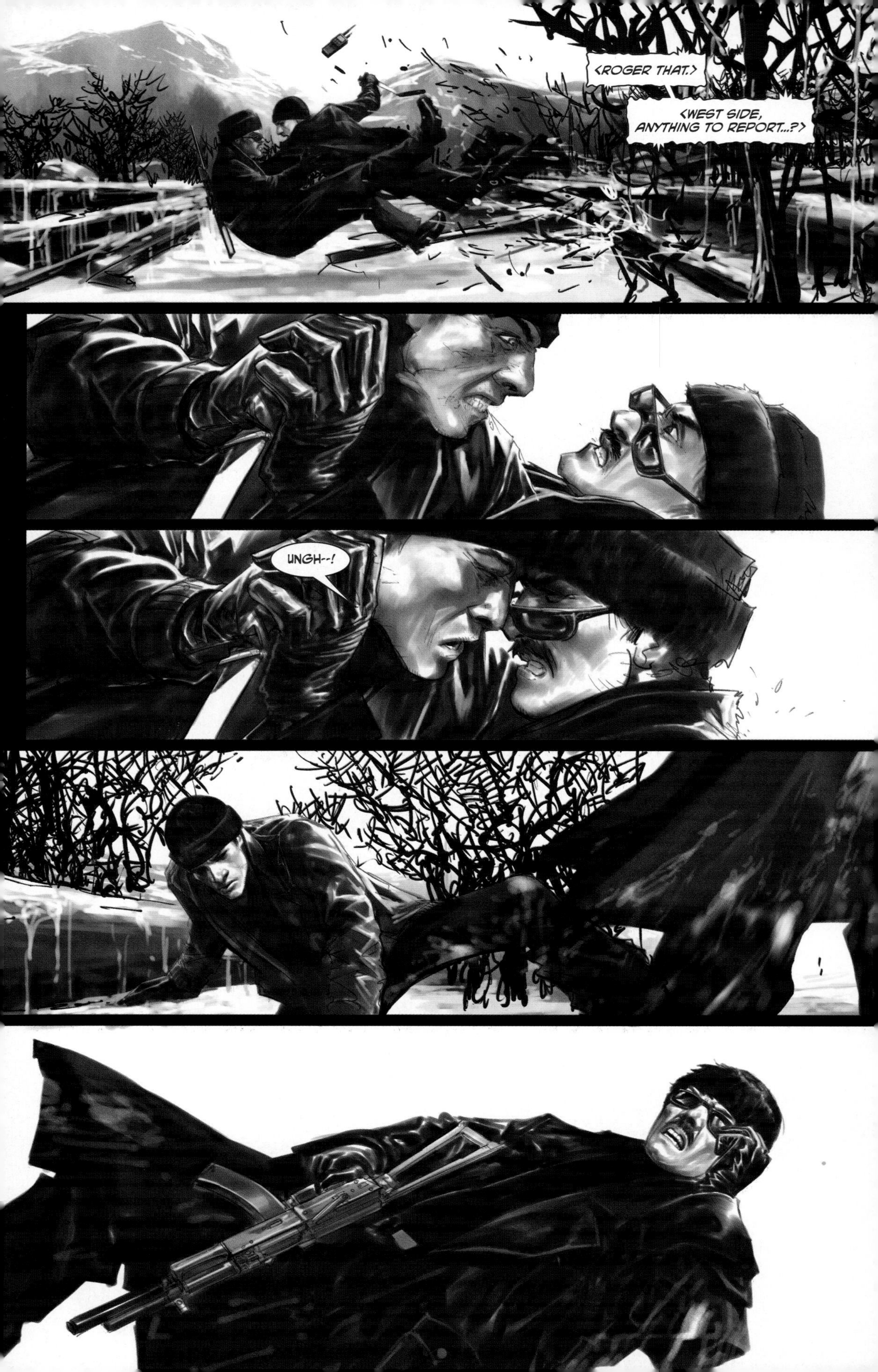
<ROGER THAT.>
<WEST SIDE, ANYTHING TO REPORT...?>
UNGH--!

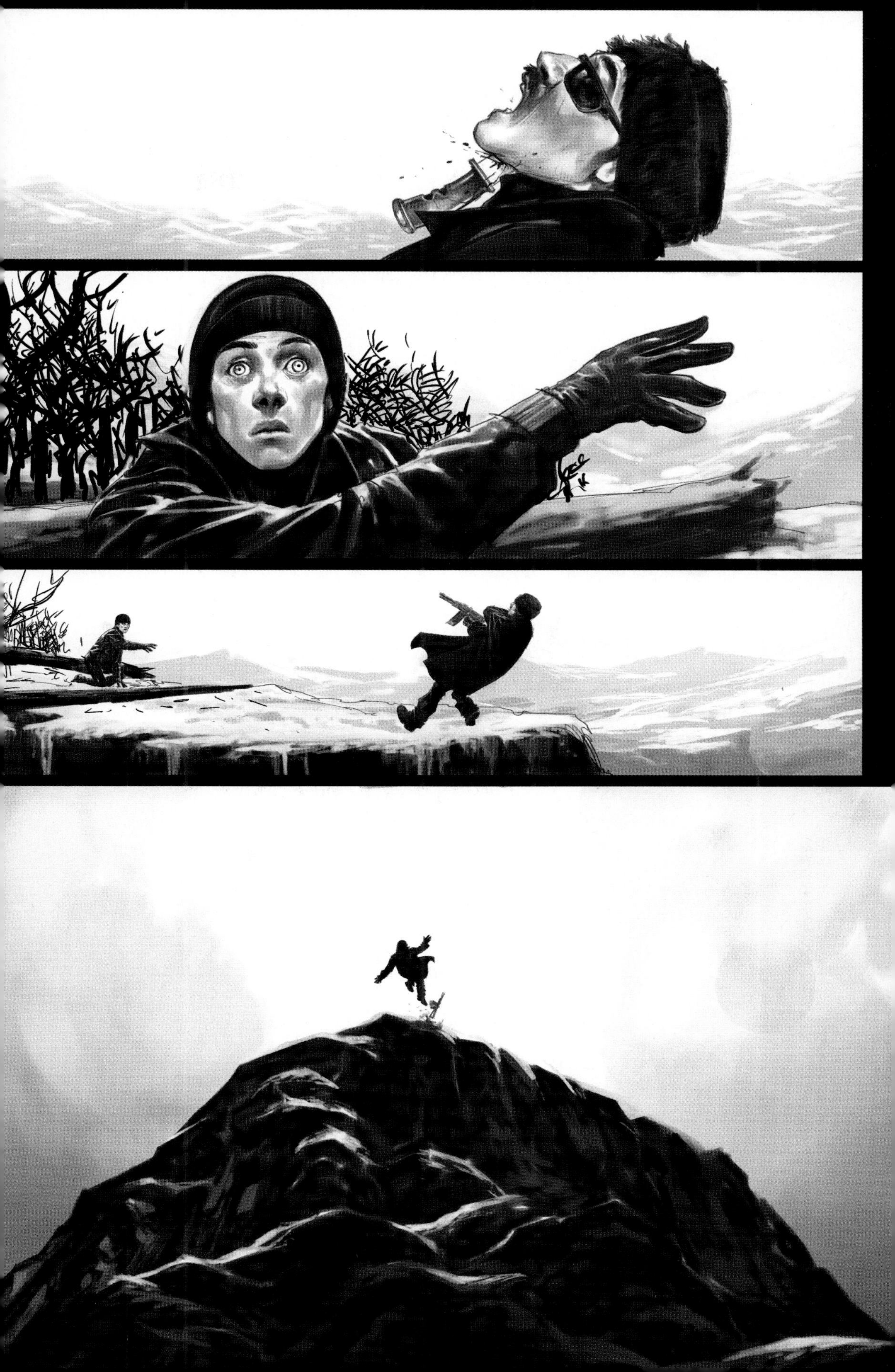

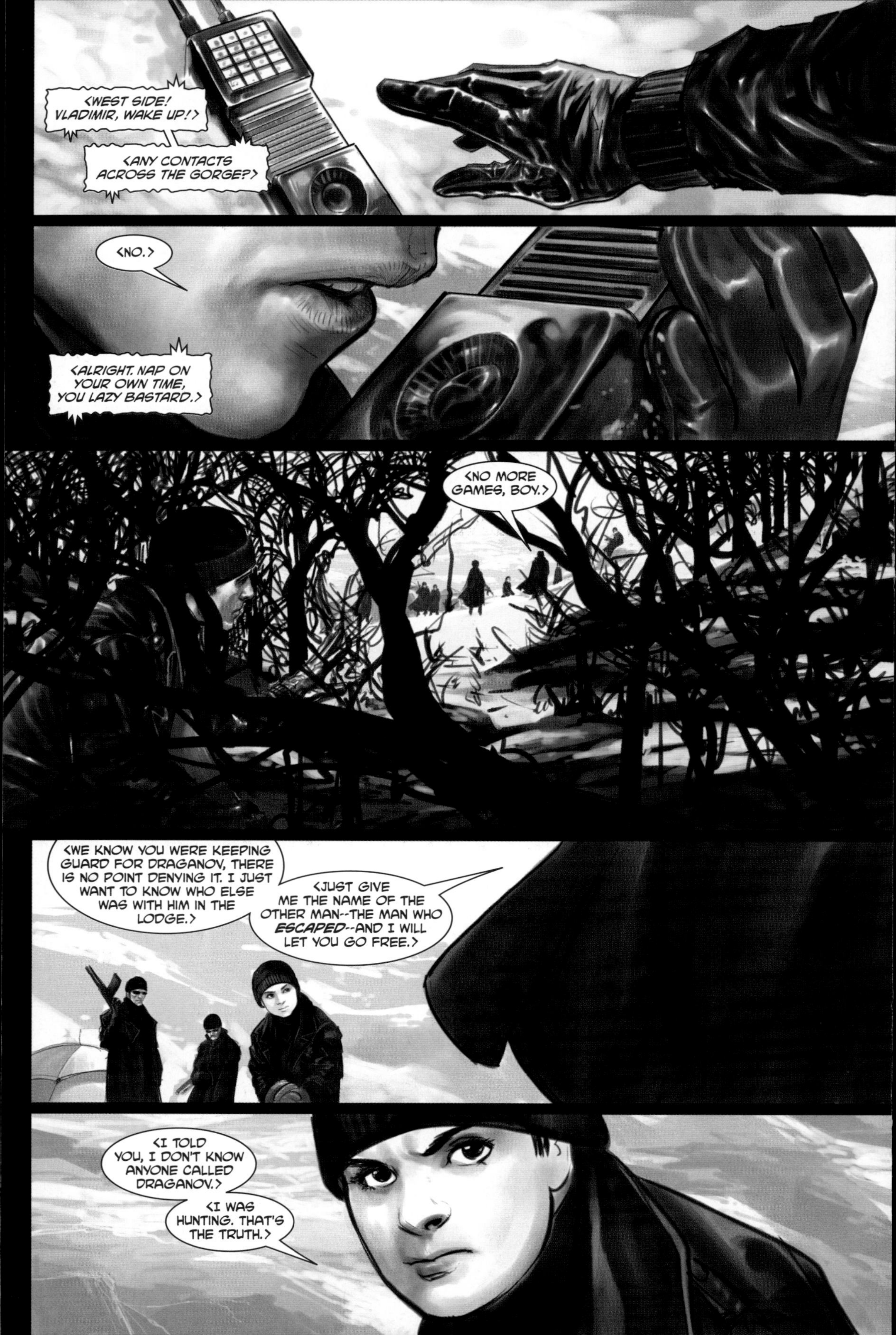
<WEST SIDE! VLADIMIR, WAKE UP!>
<ANY CONTACTS ACROSS THE GORGE?>
<NO.>
<ALRIGHT. NAP ON YOUR OWN TIME, YOU LAZY BASTARD.>
<NO MORE GAMES, BOY.>
<WE KNOW YOU WERE KEEPING GUARD FOR DRAGANOV, THERE IS NO POINT DENYING IT. I JUST WANT TO KNOW WHO ELSE WAS WITH HIM IN THE LODGE.>
<JUST GIVE ME THE NAME OF THE OTHER MAN--THE MAN WHO ESCAPED--AND I WILL LET YOU GO FREE.>
<I TOLD YOU, I DON'T KNOW ANYONE CALLED DRAGANOV.>
<I WAS HUNTING. THAT'S THE TRUTH.>

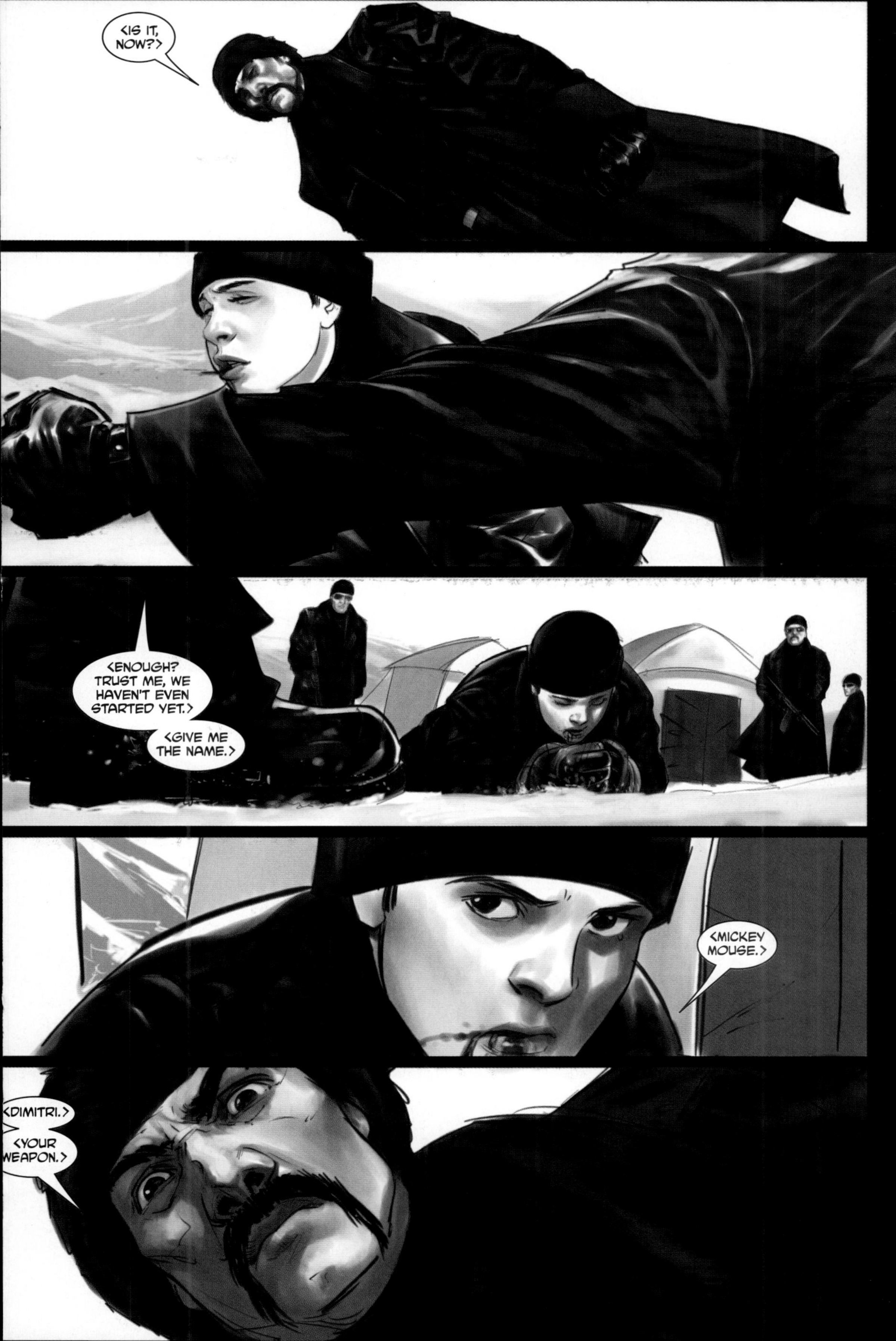
<IS IT, NOW?>
<ENOUGH? TRUST ME, WE HAVEN'T EVEN STARTED YET.>
<GIVE ME THE NAME.>
<MICKEY MOUSE.>
<DIMITRI.>
<YOUR WEAPON.>

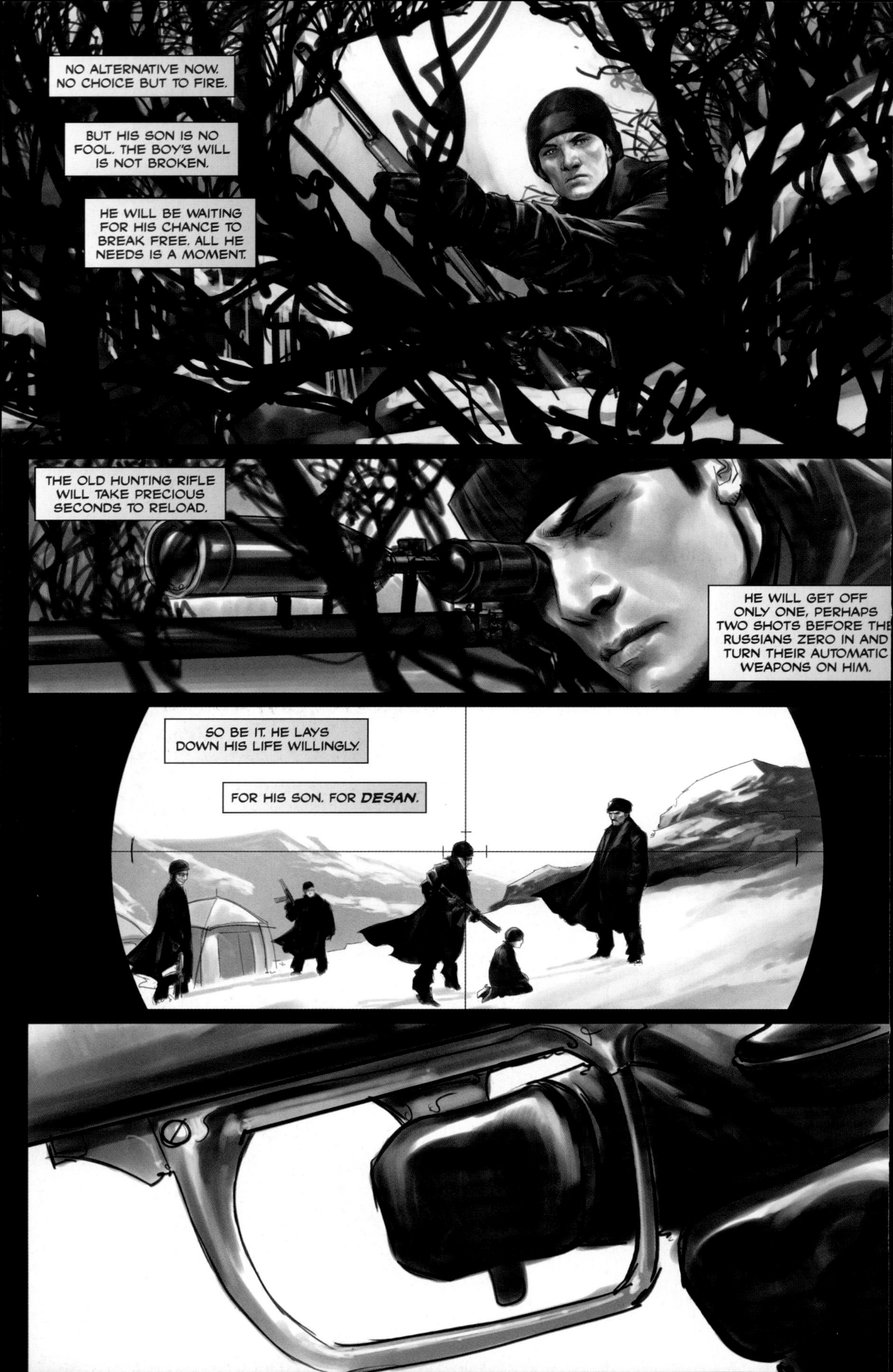
NO ALTERNATIVE NOW. NO CHOICE BUT TO FIRE.
BUT HIS SON IS NO FOOL. THE BOY'S WILL IS NOT BROKEN.
HE WILL BE WAITING FOR HIS CHANCE TO BREAK FREE. ALL HE NEEDS IS A MOMENT.
THE OLD HUNTING RIFLE WILL TAKE PRECIOUS SECONDS TO RELOAD.
HE WILL GET OFF ONLY ONE, PERHAPS TWO SHOTS BEFORE THE RUSSIANS ZERO IN AND TURN THEIR AUTOMATIC WEAPONS ON HIM.
SO BE IT. HE LAYS DOWN HIS LIFE WILLINGLY.
FOR HIS SON. FOR ***DESAN***.

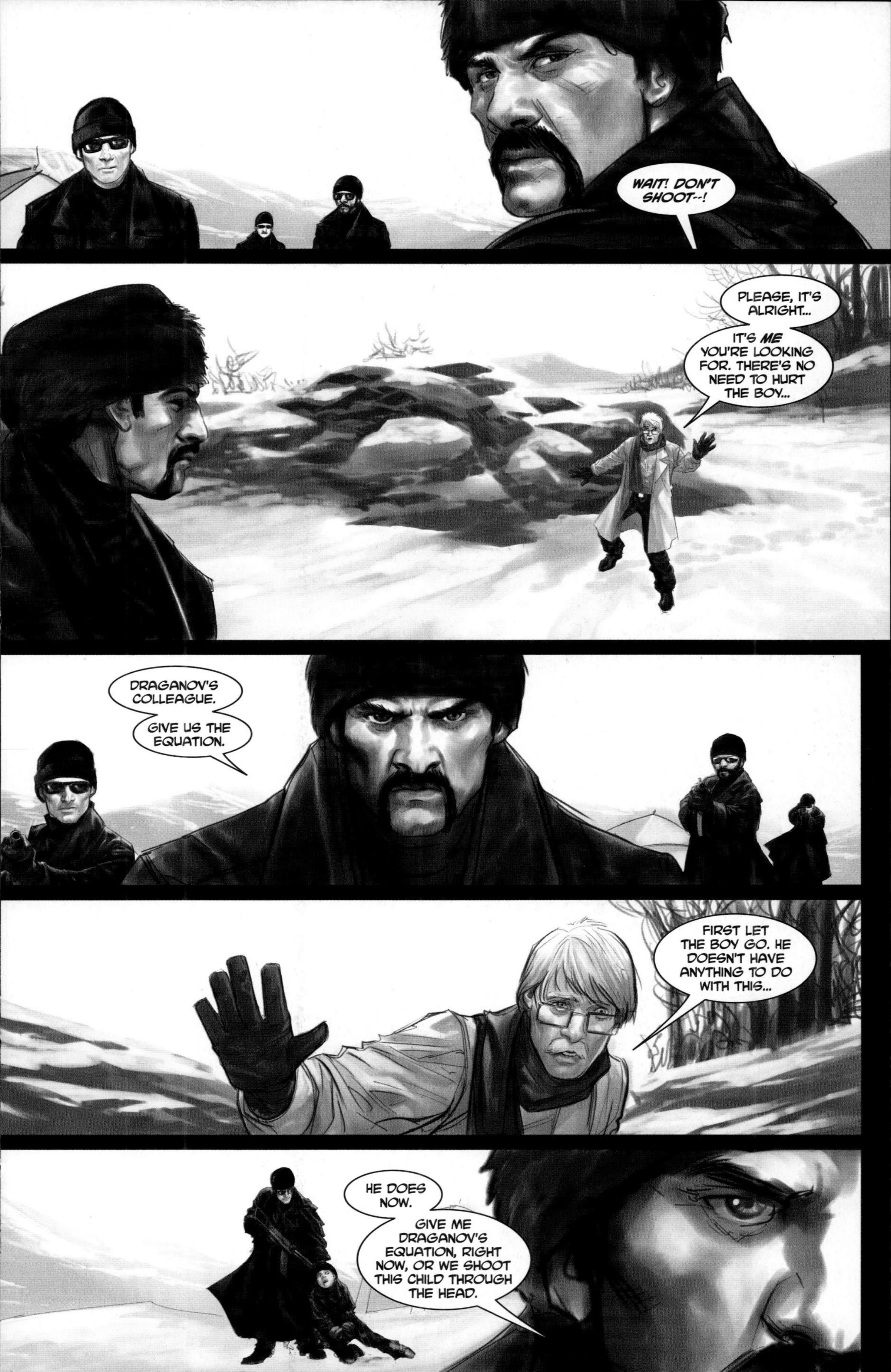
WAIT! DON'T SHOOT--!
PLEASE, IT'S ALRIGHT...
IT'S *ME* YOU'RE LOOKING FOR. THERE'S NO NEED TO HURT THE BOY...
DRAGANOV'S COLLEAGUE.
GIVE US THE EQUATION.
FIRST LET THE BOY GO. HE DOESN'T HAVE ANYTHING TO DO WITH THIS...
HE DOES NOW.
GIVE ME DRAGANOV'S EQUATION, RIGHT NOW, OR WE SHOOT THIS CHILD THROUGH THE HEAD.

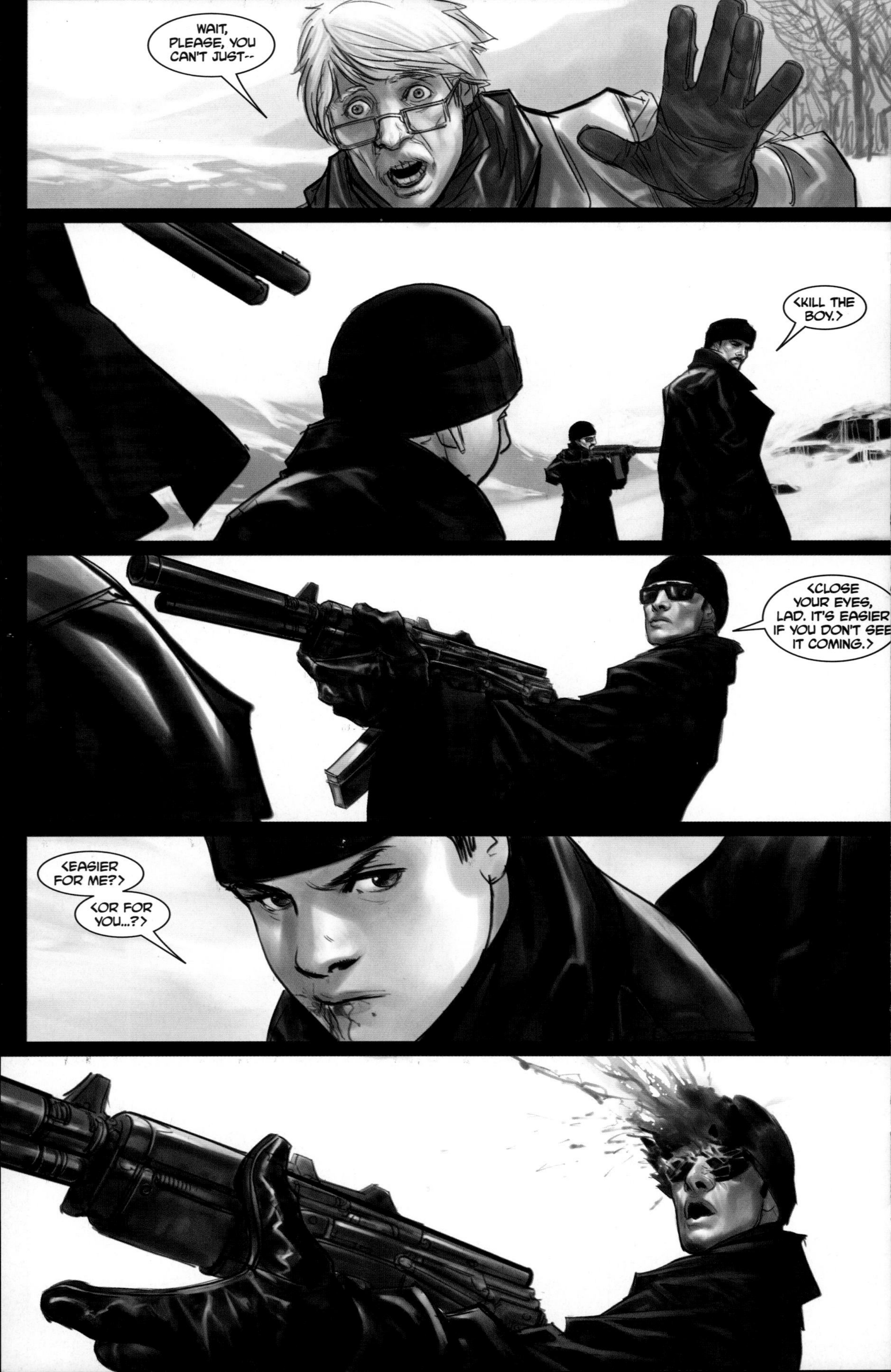
WAIT, PLEASE, YOU CAN'T JUST--
<KILL THE BOY.>
<CLOSE YOUR EYES, LAD. IT'S EASIER IF YOU DON'T SEE IT COMING.>
<EASIER FOR ME?>
<OR FOR YOU...?>

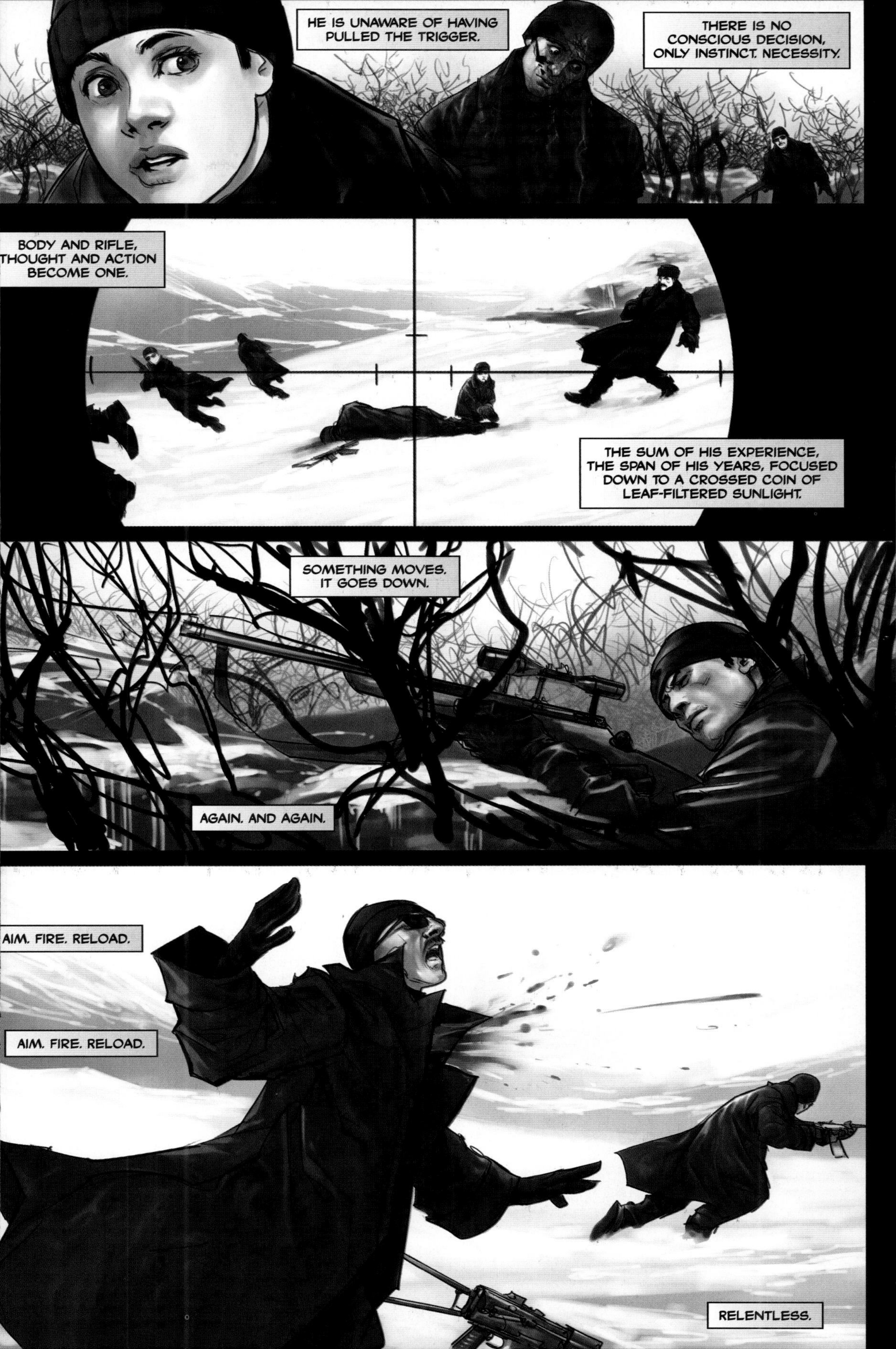
HE IS UNAWARE OF HAVING PULLED THE TRIGGER.
THERE IS NO CONSCIOUS DECISION, ONLY INSTINCT. NECESSITY.
BODY AND RIFLE, THOUGHT AND ACTION BECOME ONE.
THE SUM OF HIS EXPERIENCE, THE SPAN OF HIS YEARS, FOCUSED DOWN TO A CROSSED COIN OF LEAF-FILTERED SUNLIGHT.
SOMETHING MOVES. IT GOES DOWN.
AGAIN. AND AGAIN.
AIM. FIRE. RELOAD.
AIM. FIRE. RELOAD.
RELENTLESS.

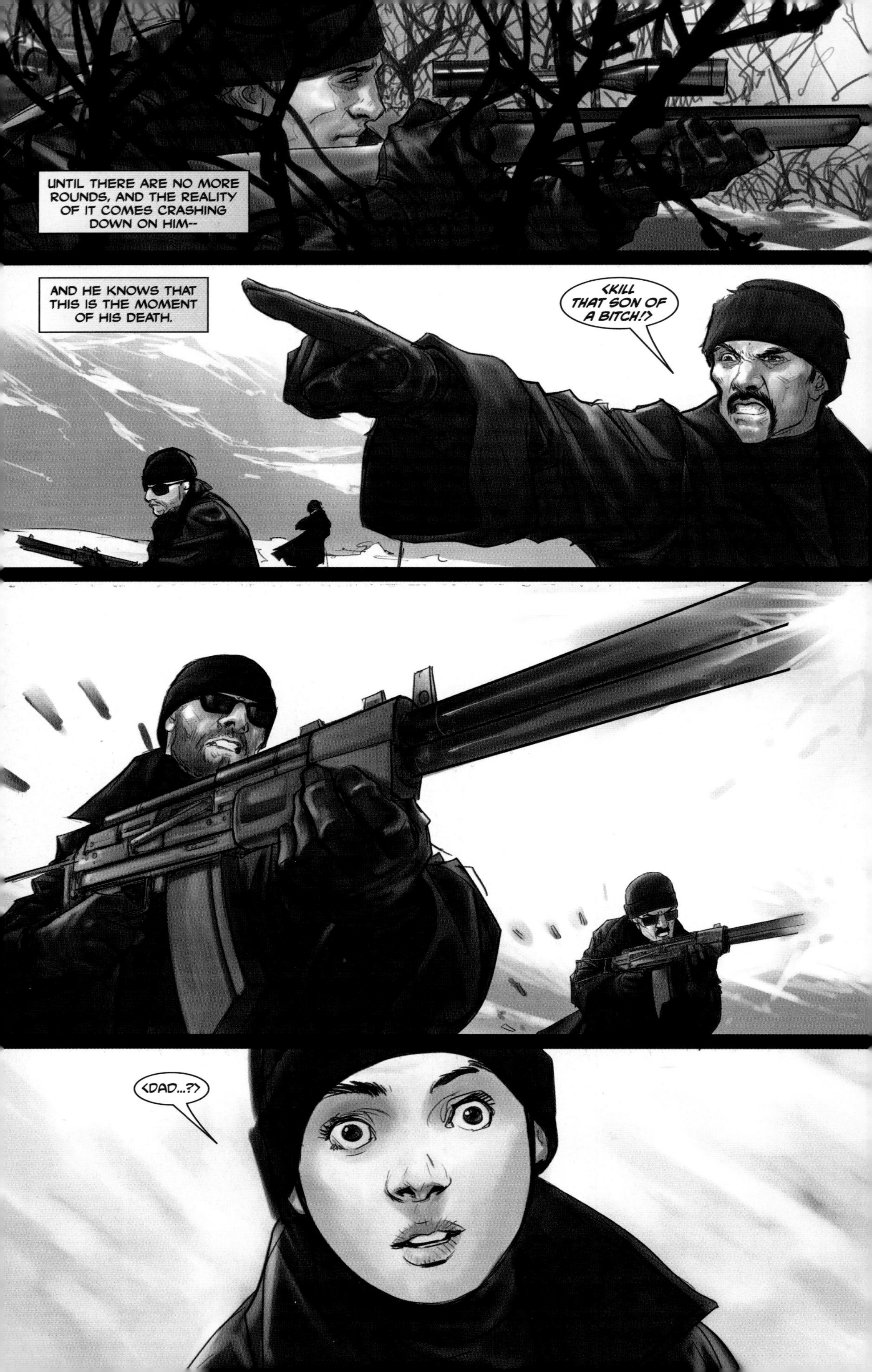
UNTIL THERE ARE NO MORE ROUNDS, AND THE REALITY OF IT COMES CRASHING DOWN ON HIM--
AND HE KNOWS THAT THIS IS THE MOMENT OF HIS DEATH.
<KILL THAT SON OF A BITCH!>
<DAD...?>

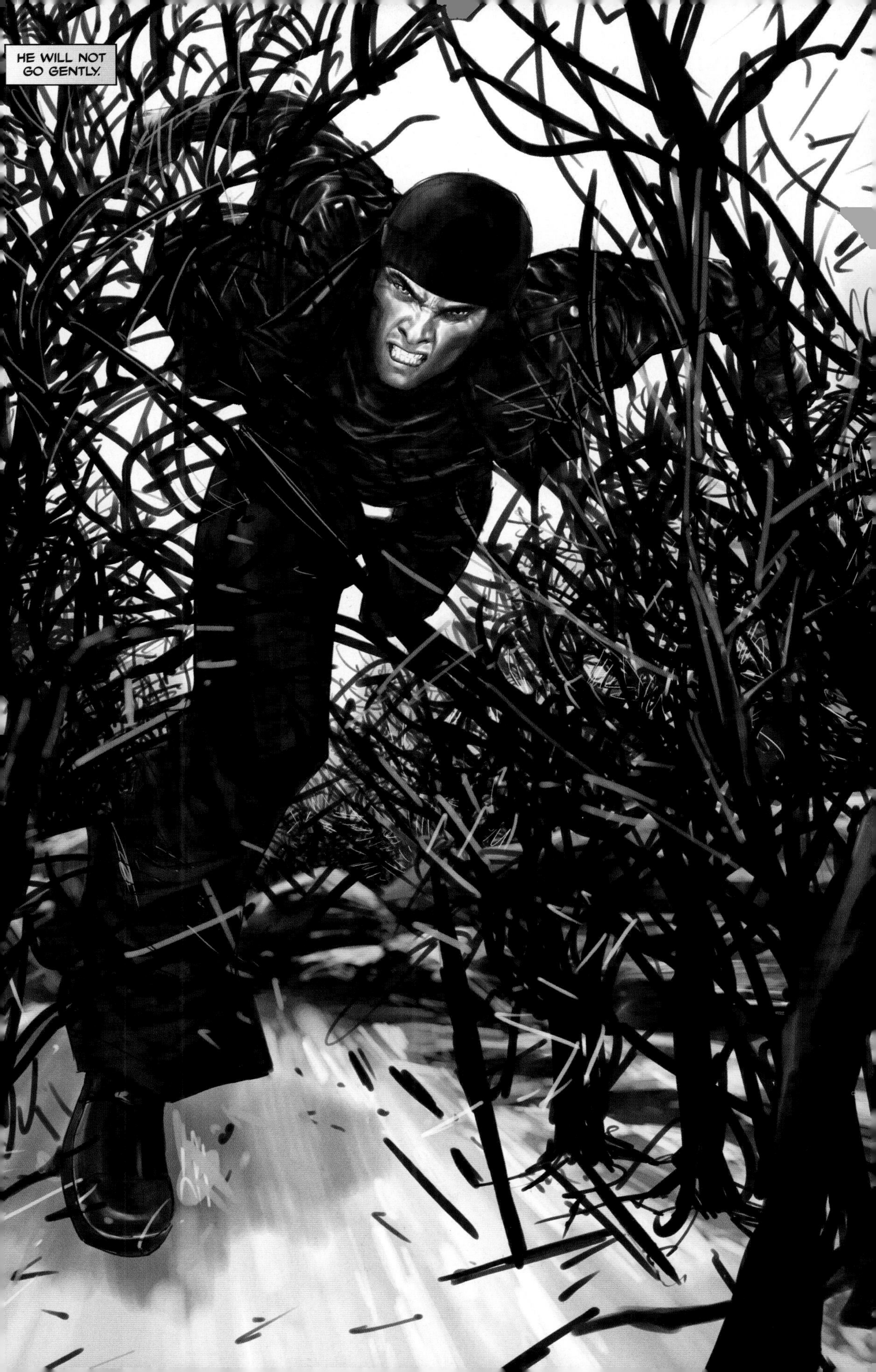
HE WILL NOT GO GENTLY.

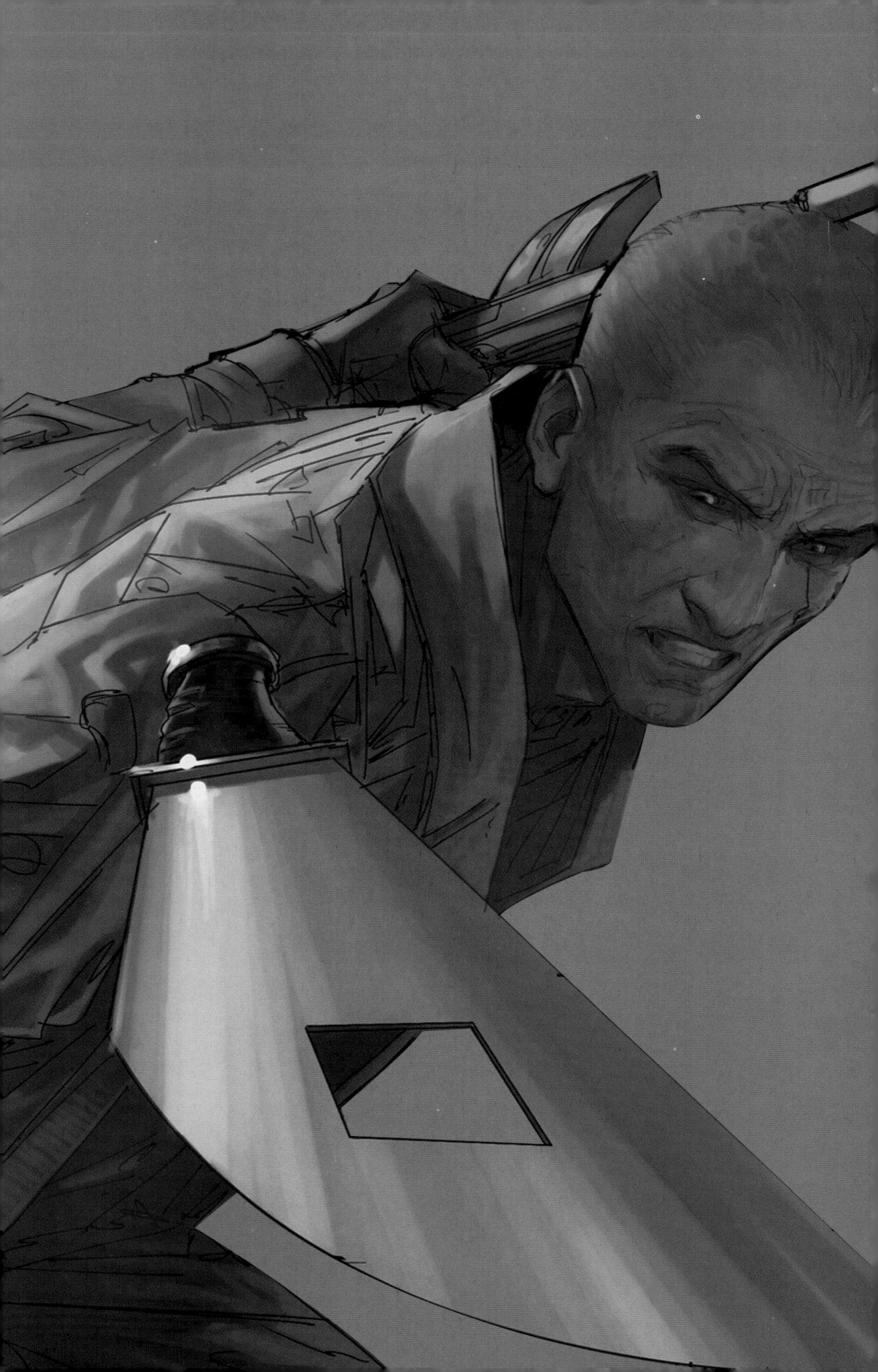

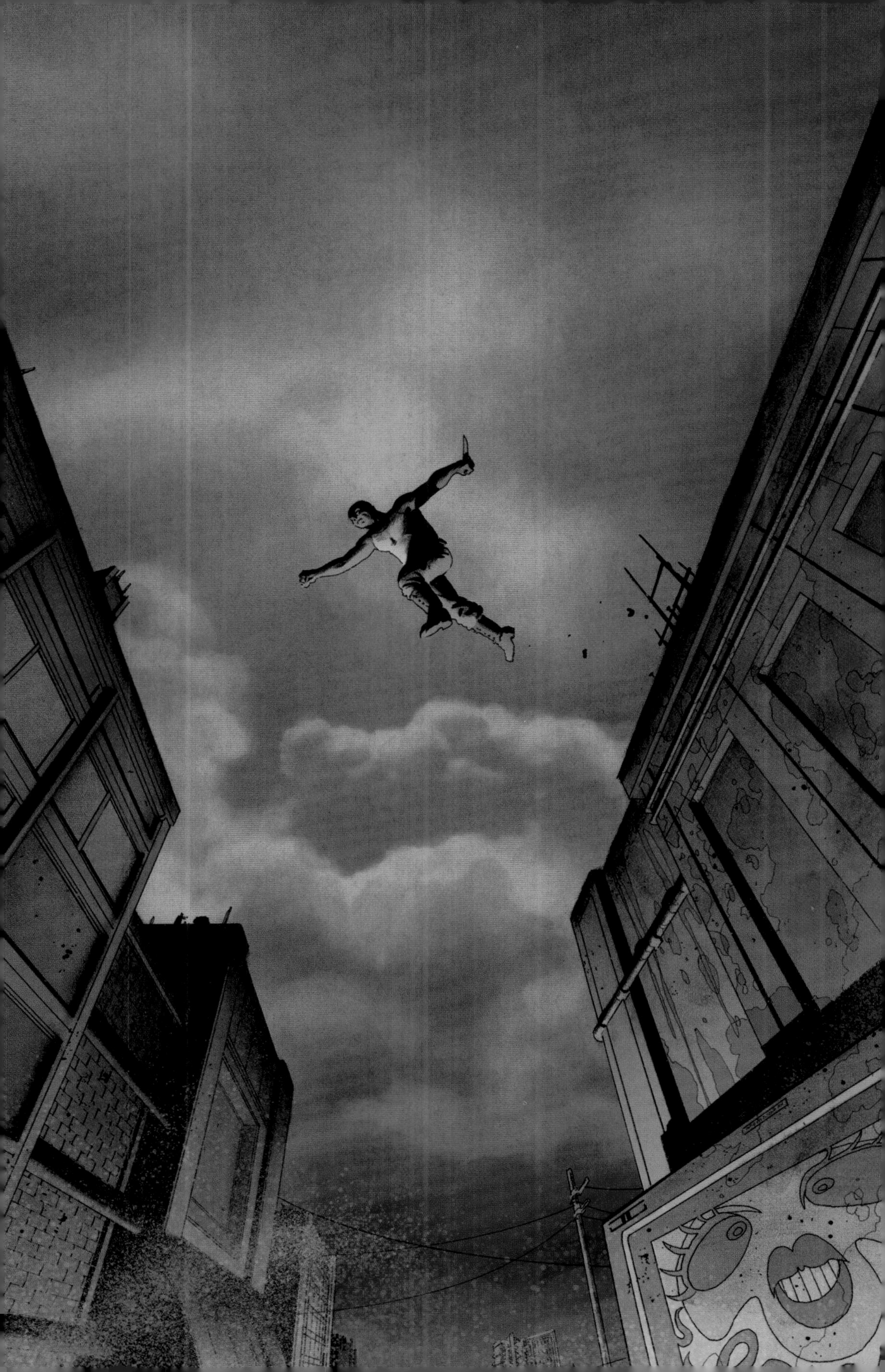

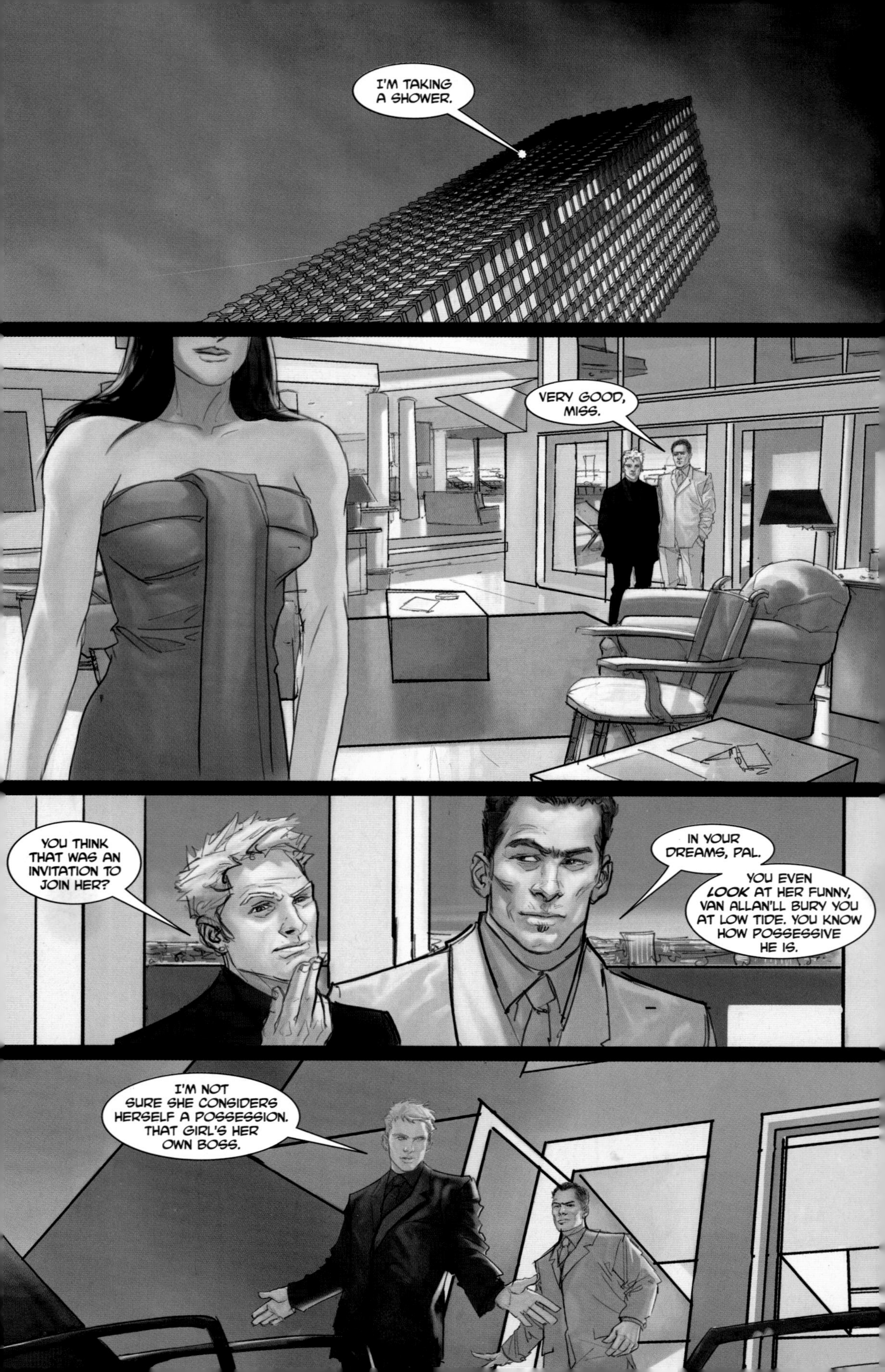

I'M TAKING A SHOWER.
VERY GOOD, MISS.
YOU THINK THAT WAS AN INVITATION TO JOIN HER?
IN YOUR DREAMS, PAL.
YOU EVEN LOOK AT HER FUNNY, VAN ALLAN'LL BURY YOU AT LOW TIDE. YOU KNOW HOW POSSESSIVE HE IS.
I'M NOT SURE SHE CONSIDERS HERSELF A POSSESSION. THAT GIRL'S HER OWN BOSS.

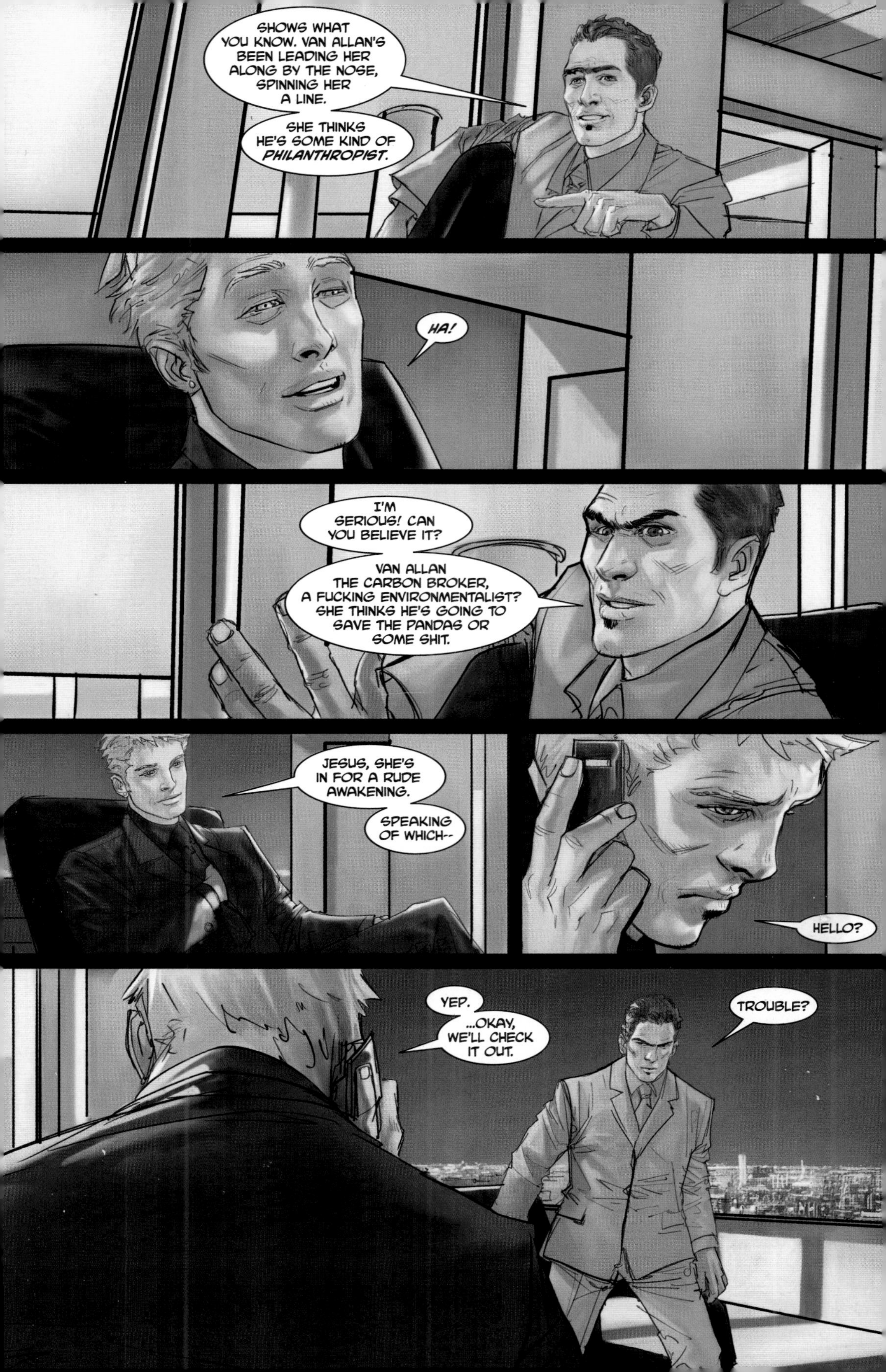
SHOWS WHAT YOU KNOW. VAN ALLAN'S BEEN LEADING HER ALONG BY THE NOSE, SPINNING HER A LINE.
SHE THINKS HE'S SOME KIND OF PHILANTHROPIST.
HA!
I'M SERIOUS! CAN YOU BELIEVE IT?
VAN ALLAN THE CARBON BROKER, A FUCKING ENVIRONMENTALIST? SHE THINKS HE'S GOING TO SAVE THE PANDAS OR SOME SHIT.
JESUS, SHE'S IN FOR A RUDE AWAKENING.
SPEAKING OF WHICH--
HELLO?
YEP. ...OKAY, WE'LL CHECK IT OUT.
TROUBLE?

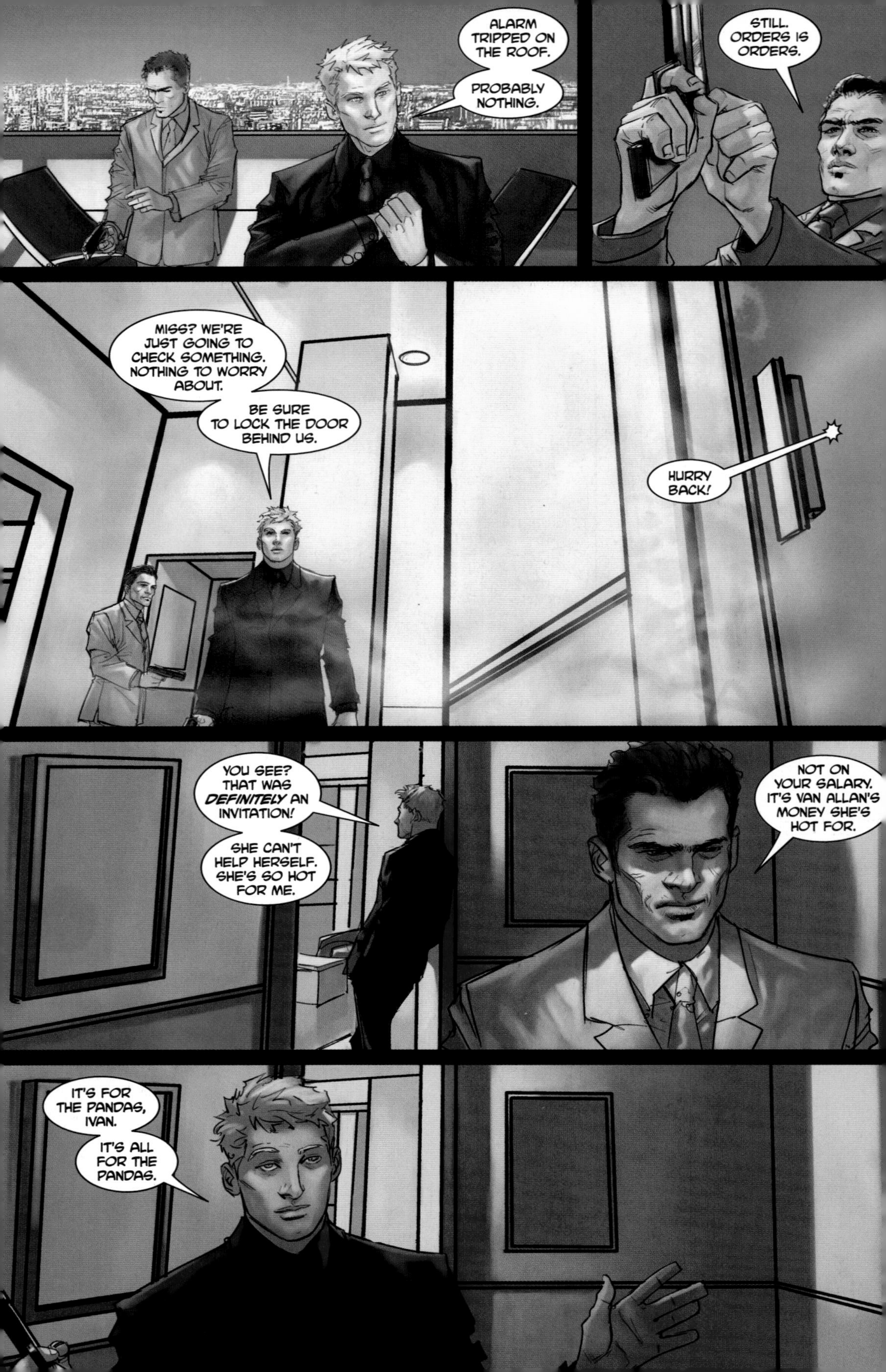
ALARM TRIPPED ON THE ROOF.
PROBABLY NOTHING.
STILL. ORDERS IS ORDERS.
MISS? WE'RE JUST GOING TO CHECK SOMETHING. NOTHING TO WORRY ABOUT.
BE SURE TO LOCK THE DOOR BEHIND US.
HURRY BACK!
YOU SEE? THAT WAS *DEFINITELY* AN INVITATION!
SHE CAN'T HELP HERSELF. SHE'S SO HOT FOR ME.
NOT ON YOUR SALARY. IT'S VAN ALLAN'S MONEY SHE'S HOT FOR.
IT'S FOR THE PANDAS, IVAN.
IT'S ALL FOR THE PANDAS.

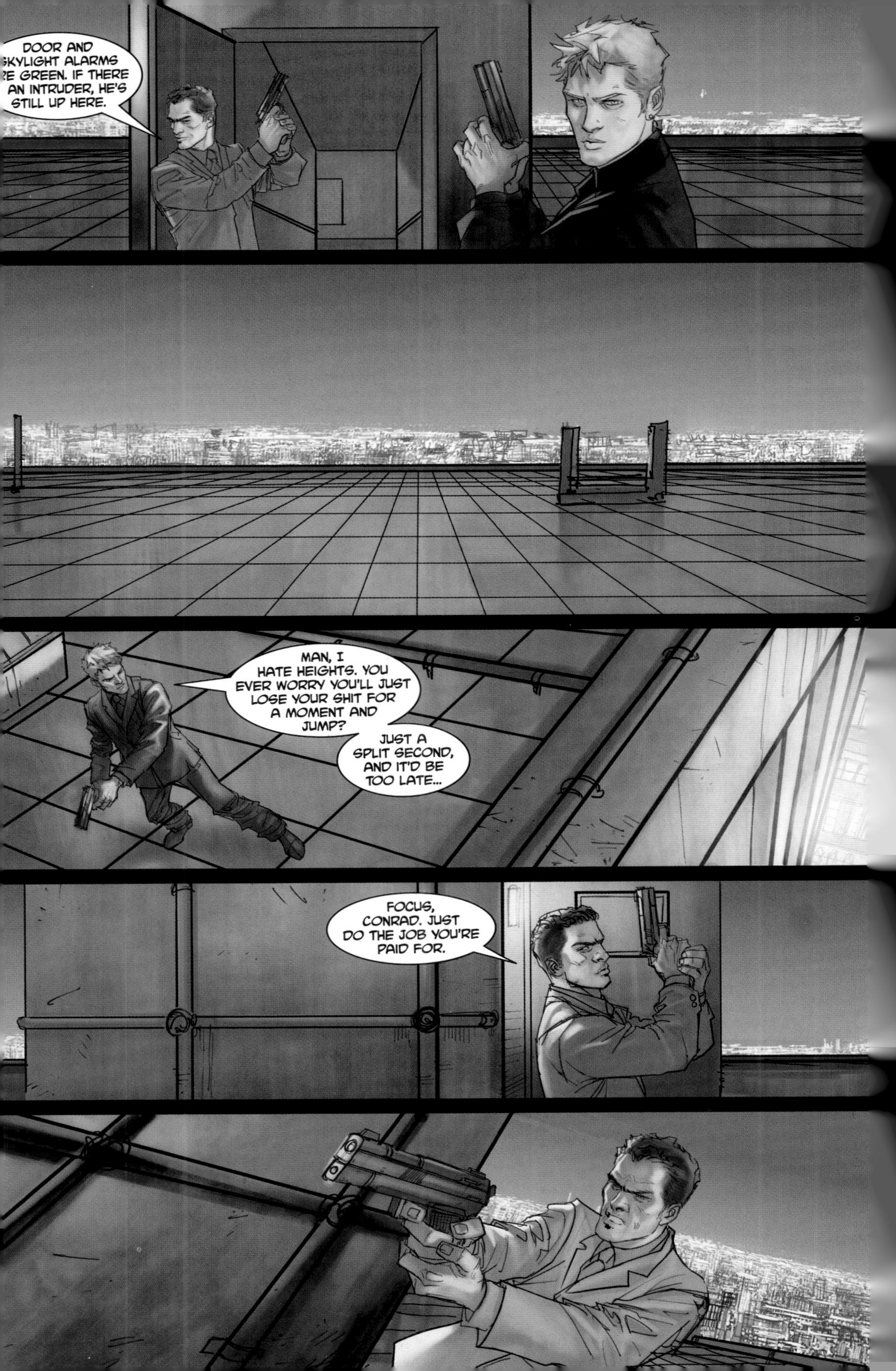

DOOR AND SKYLIGHT ALARMS RE GREEN. IF THERE AN INTRUDER, HE'S STILL UP HERE.
MAN, I HATE HEIGHTS. YOU EVER WORRY YOU'LL JUST LOSE YOUR SHIT FOR A MOMENT AND JUMP?
JUST A SPLIT SECOND, AND IT'D BE TOO LATE...
FOCUS, CONRAD. JUST DO THE JOB YOU'RE PAID FOR.

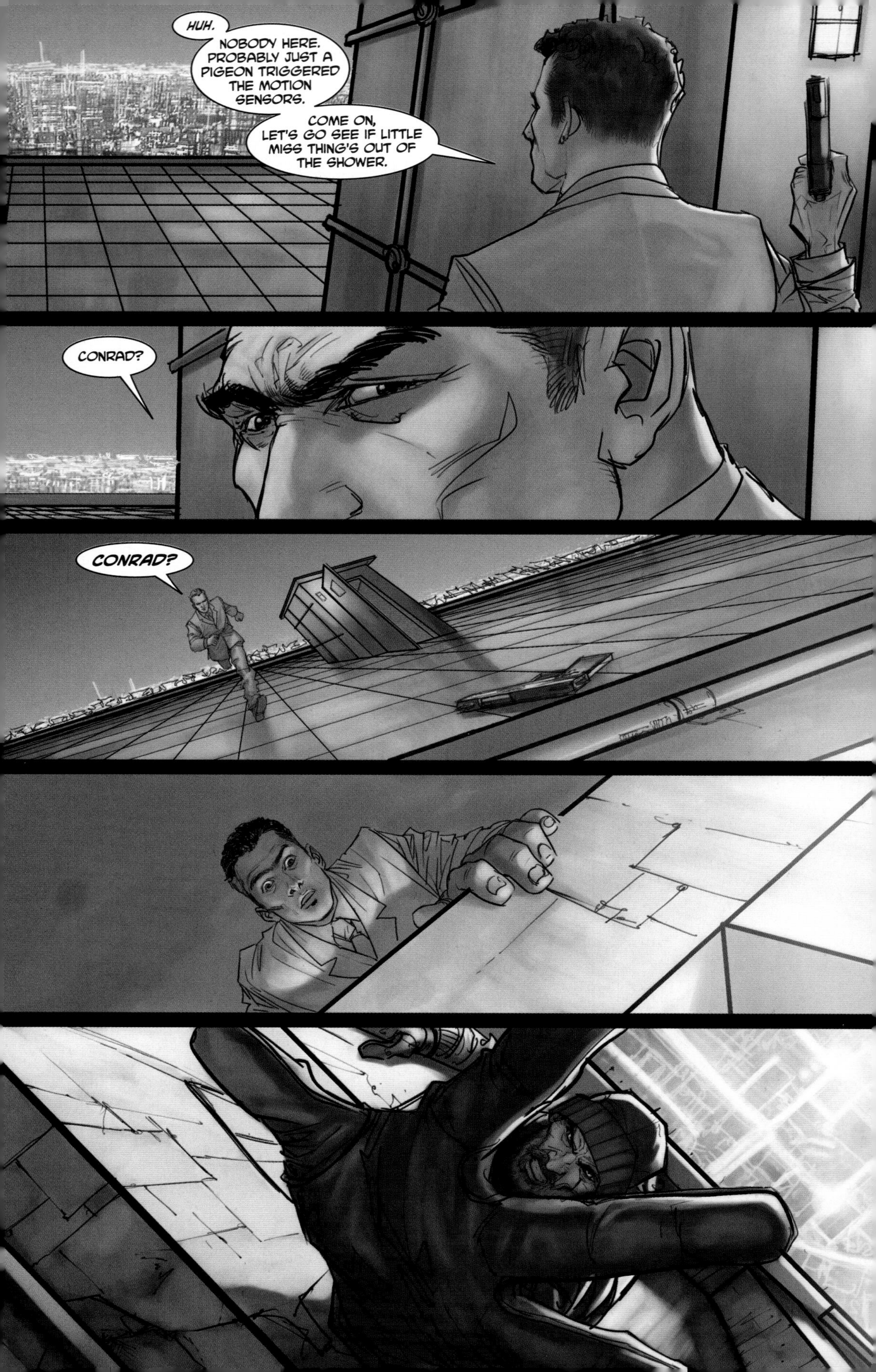
HUH.
NOBODY HERE. PROBABLY JUST A PIGEON TRIGGERED THE MOTION SENSORS.
COME ON, LET'S GO SEE IF LITTLE MISS THING'S OUT OF THE SHOWER.
CONRAD?
CONRAD?

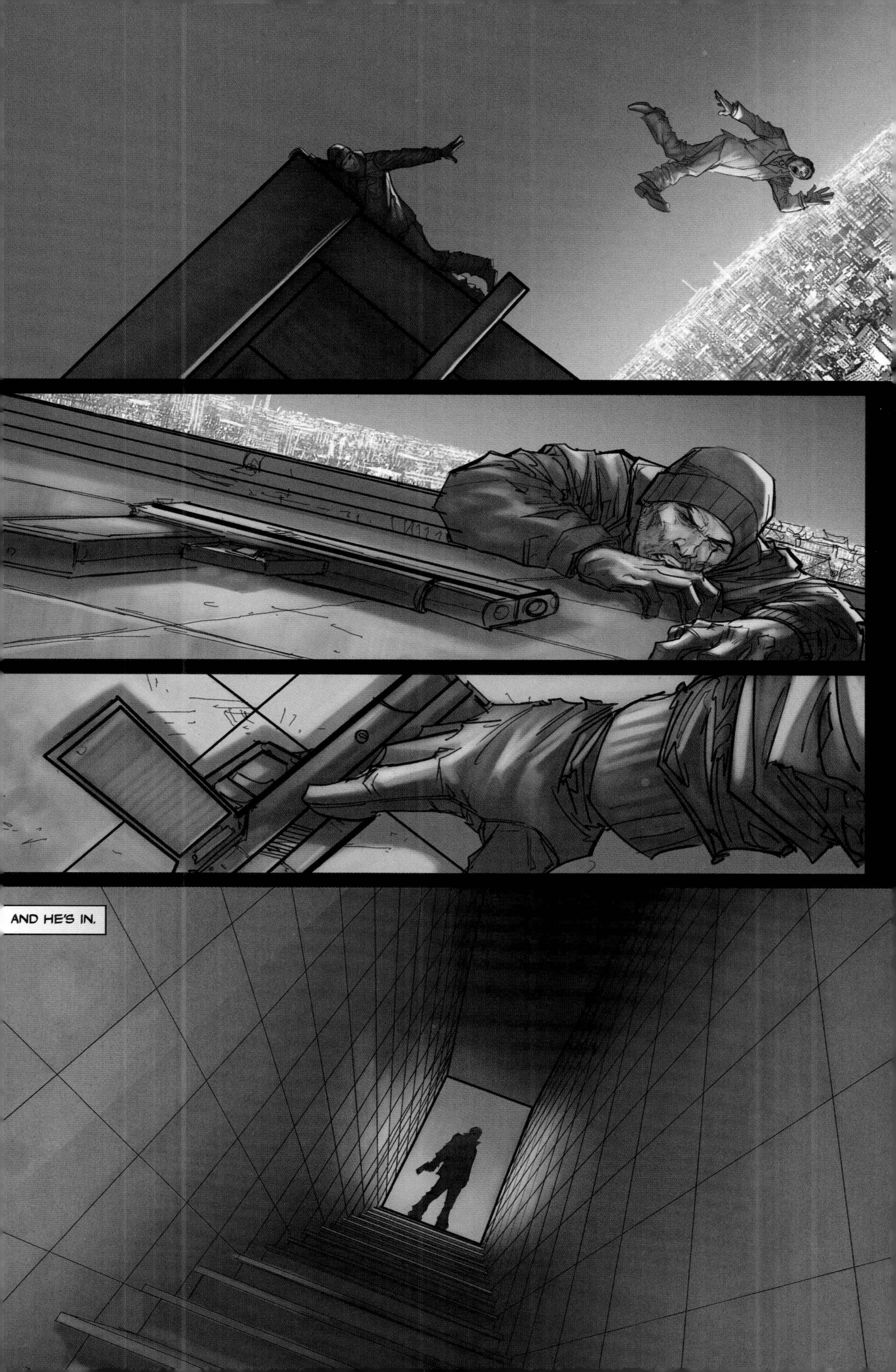
AND HE'S IN.

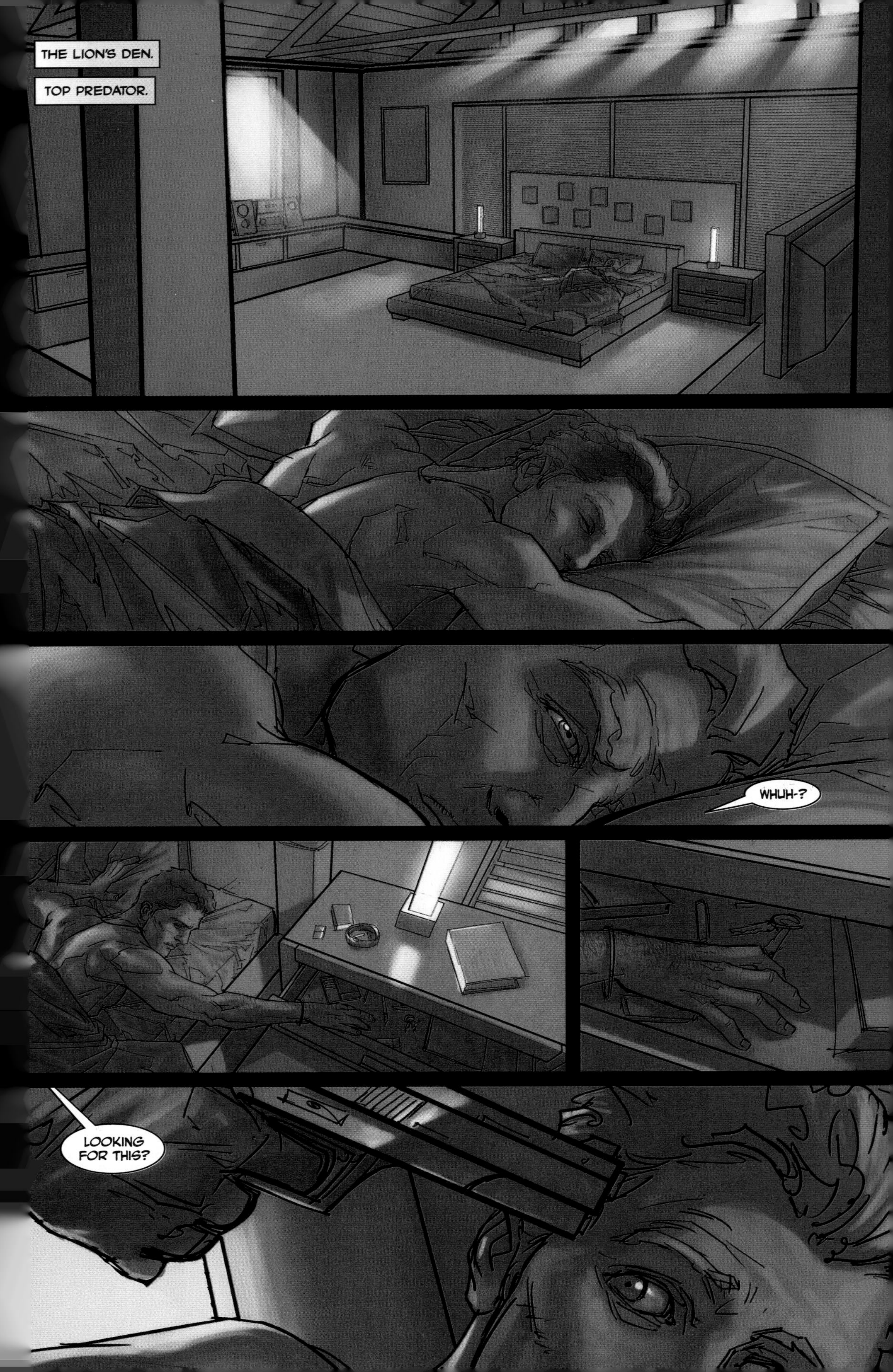
THE LION'S DEN.
TOP PREDATOR.
WHUH-?
LOOKING FOR THIS?

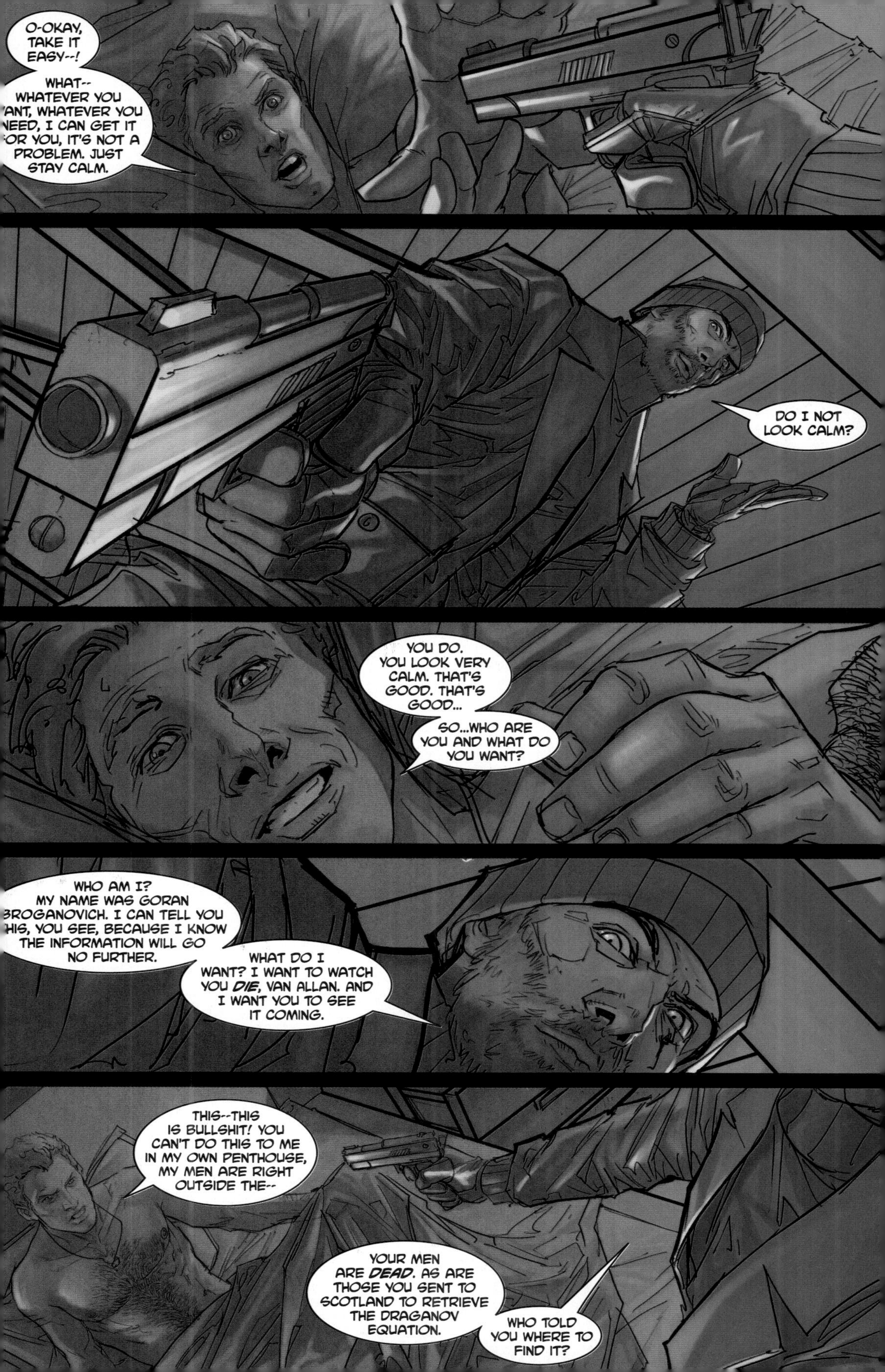
O-OKAY, TAKE IT EASY--!
WHAT-- WHATEVER YOU WANT, WHATEVER YOU NEED, I CAN GET IT FOR YOU, IT'S NOT A PROBLEM. JUST STAY CALM.
DO I NOT LOOK CALM?
YOU DO. YOU LOOK VERY CALM. THAT'S GOOD. THAT'S GOOD...
SO...WHO ARE YOU AND WHAT DO YOU WANT?
WHO AM I? MY NAME WAS GORAN BROGANOVICH. I CAN TELL YOU THIS, YOU SEE, BECAUSE I KNOW THE INFORMATION WILL GO NO FURTHER.
WHAT DO I WANT? I WANT TO WATCH YOU *DIE*, VAN ALLAN. AND I WANT YOU TO SEE IT COMING.
THIS--THIS IS BULLSHIT! YOU CAN'T DO THIS TO ME IN MY OWN PENTHOUSE, MY MEN ARE RIGHT OUTSIDE THE--
YOUR MEN ARE *DEAD*. AS ARE THOSE YOU SENT TO SCOTLAND TO RETRIEVE THE DRAGANOV EQUATION.
WHO TOLD YOU WHERE TO FIND IT?

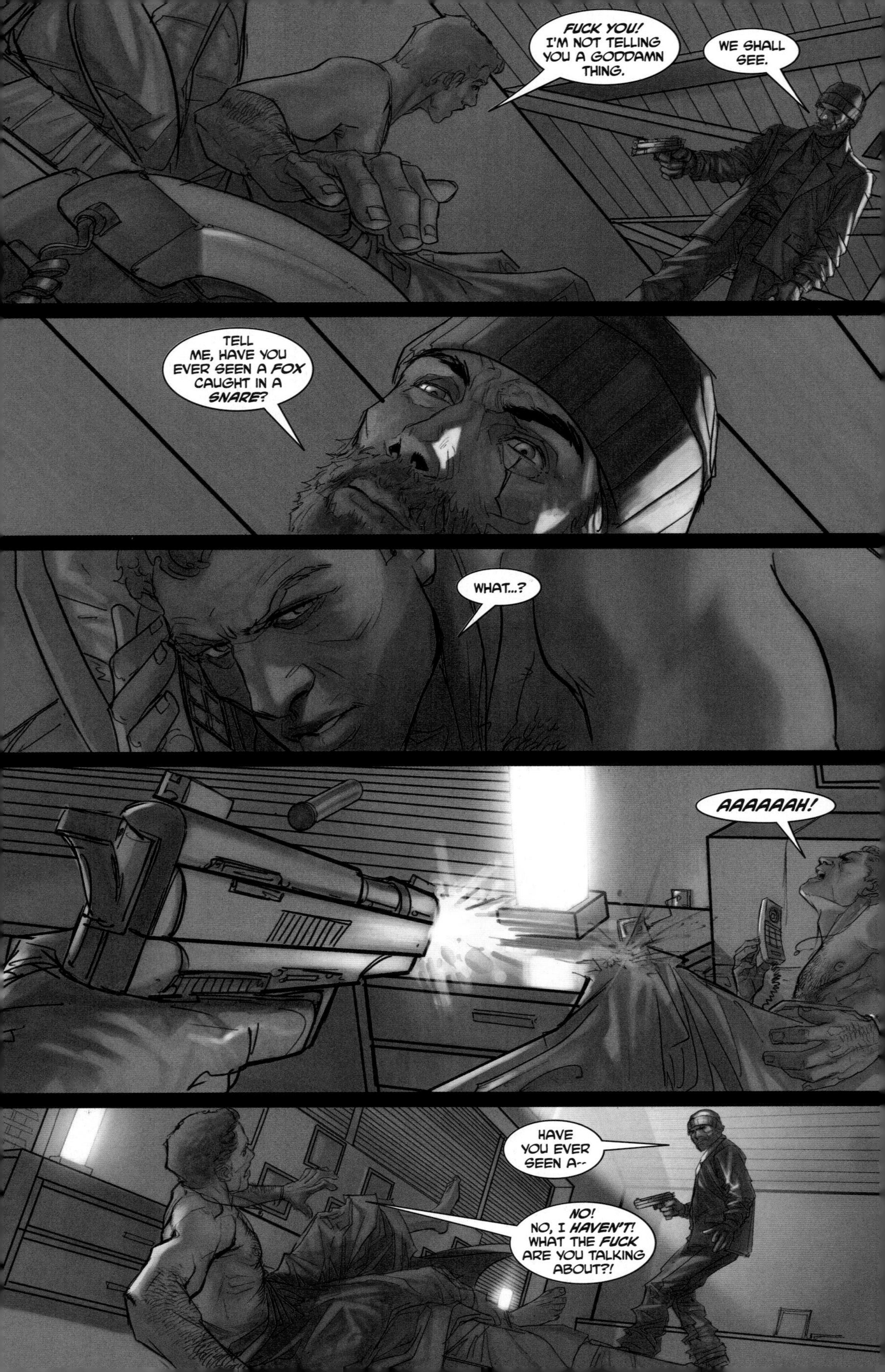
FUCK YOU! I'M NOT TELLING YOU A GODDAMN THING.
WE SHALL SEE.
TELL ME, HAVE YOU EVER SEEN A FOX CAUGHT IN A SNARE?
WHAT...?
AAAAAAH!
HAVE YOU EVER SEEN A--
NO! NO, I HAVEN'T! WHAT THE FUCK ARE YOU TALKING ABOUT?!

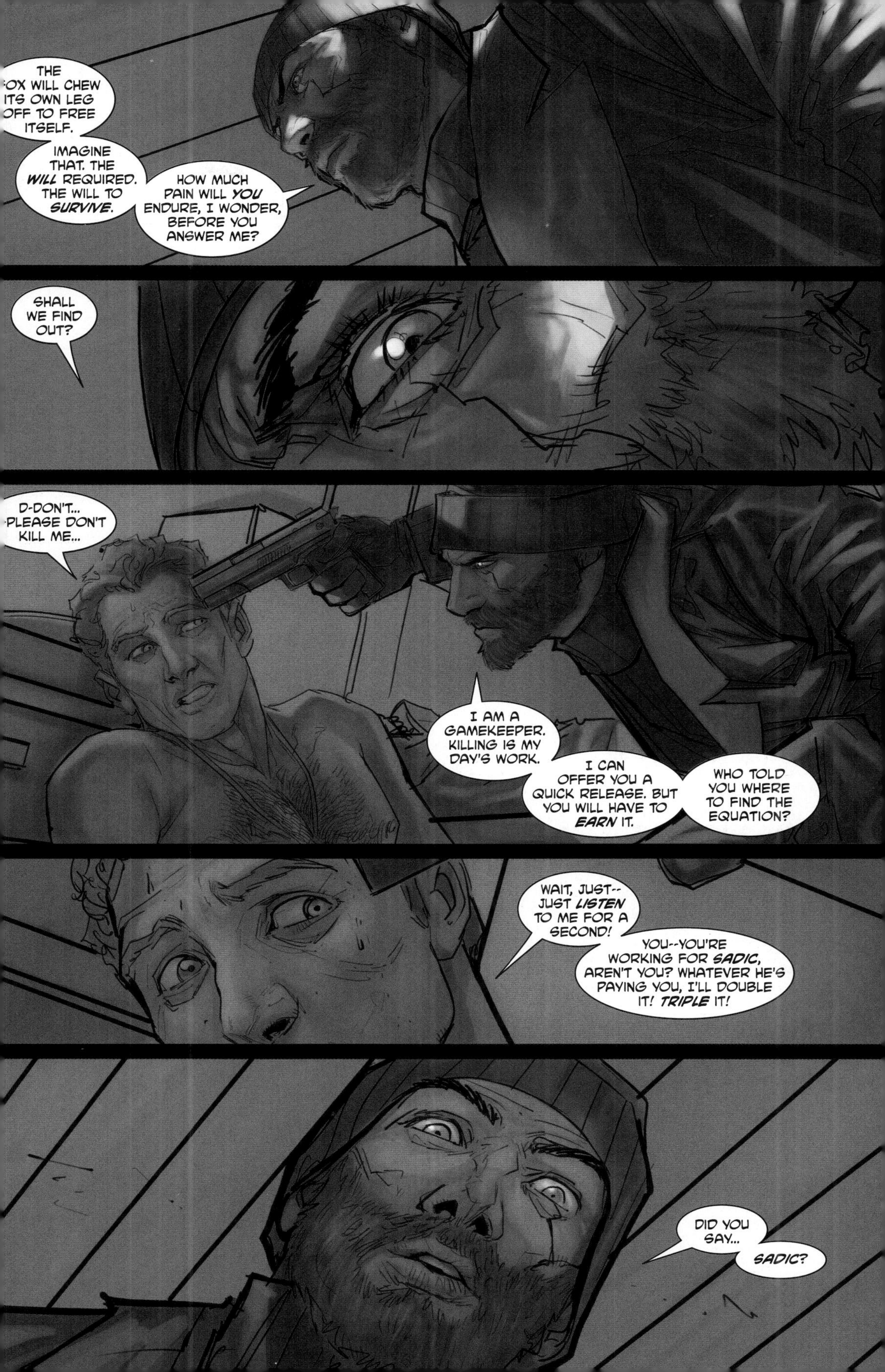
THE FOX WILL CHEW ITS OWN LEG OFF TO FREE ITSELF.
IMAGINE THAT. THE *WILL* REQUIRED. THE WILL TO *SURVIVE*.
HOW MUCH PAIN WILL *YOU* ENDURE, I WONDER, BEFORE YOU ANSWER ME?
SHALL WE FIND OUT?
D-DON'T... PLEASE DON'T KILL ME...
I AM A GAMEKEEPER. KILLING IS MY DAY'S WORK.
I CAN OFFER YOU A QUICK RELEASE. BUT YOU WILL HAVE TO *EARN* IT.
WHO TOLD YOU WHERE TO FIND THE EQUATION?
WAIT, JUST-- JUST *LISTEN* TO ME FOR A SECOND!
YOU--YOU'RE WORKING FOR *SADIC*, AREN'T YOU? WHATEVER HE'S PAYING YOU, I'LL DOUBLE IT! *TRIPLE* IT!
DID YOU SAY...
SADIC?

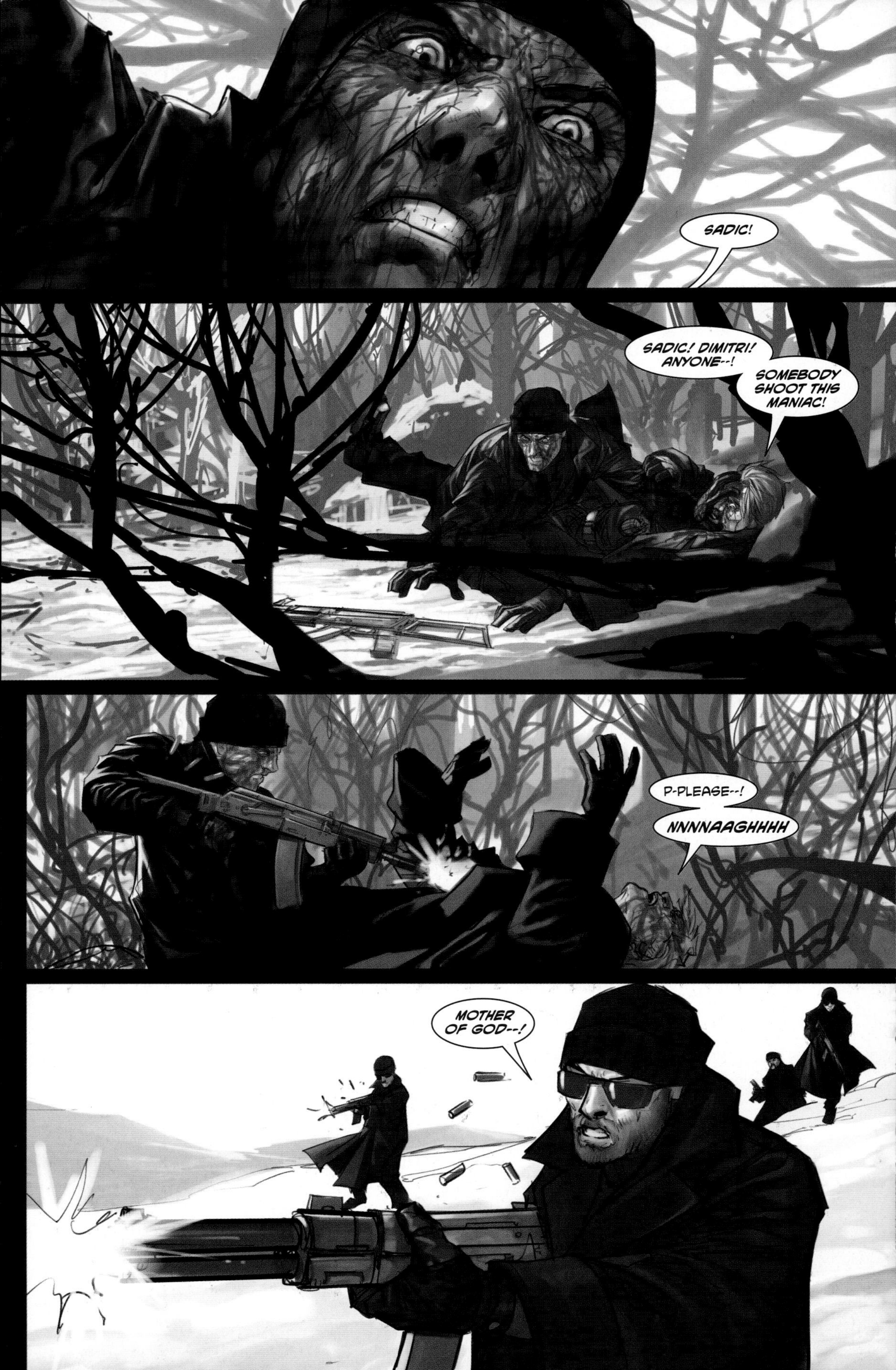
SADIC!
SADIC! DIMITRI! ANYONE--!
SOMEBODY SHOOT THIS MANIAC!
P-PLEASE--!
NNNNAAGHHHH
MOTHER OF GOD--!

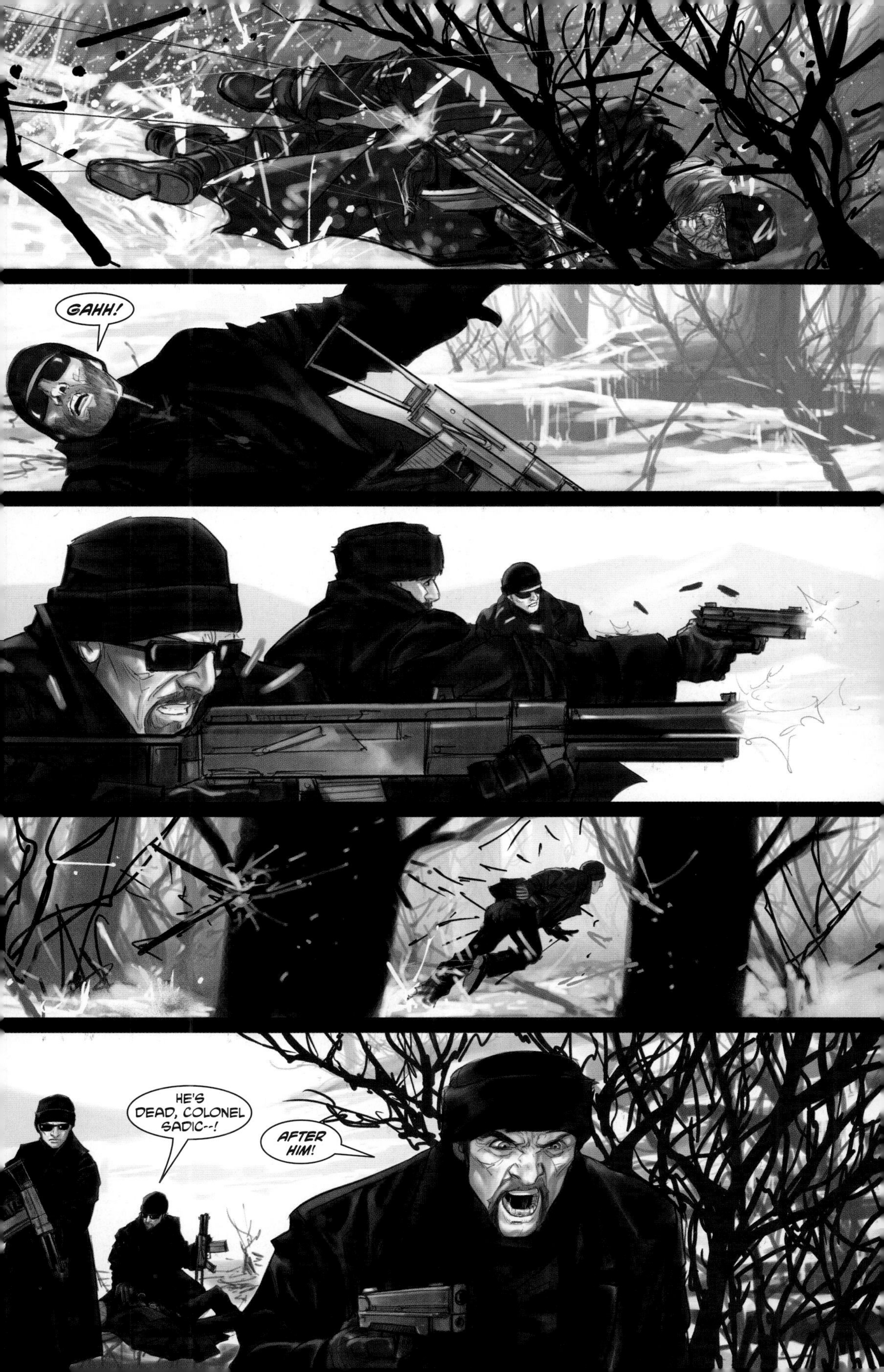
GAHH!
HE'S DEAD, COLONEL SADIC--!
AFTER HIM!

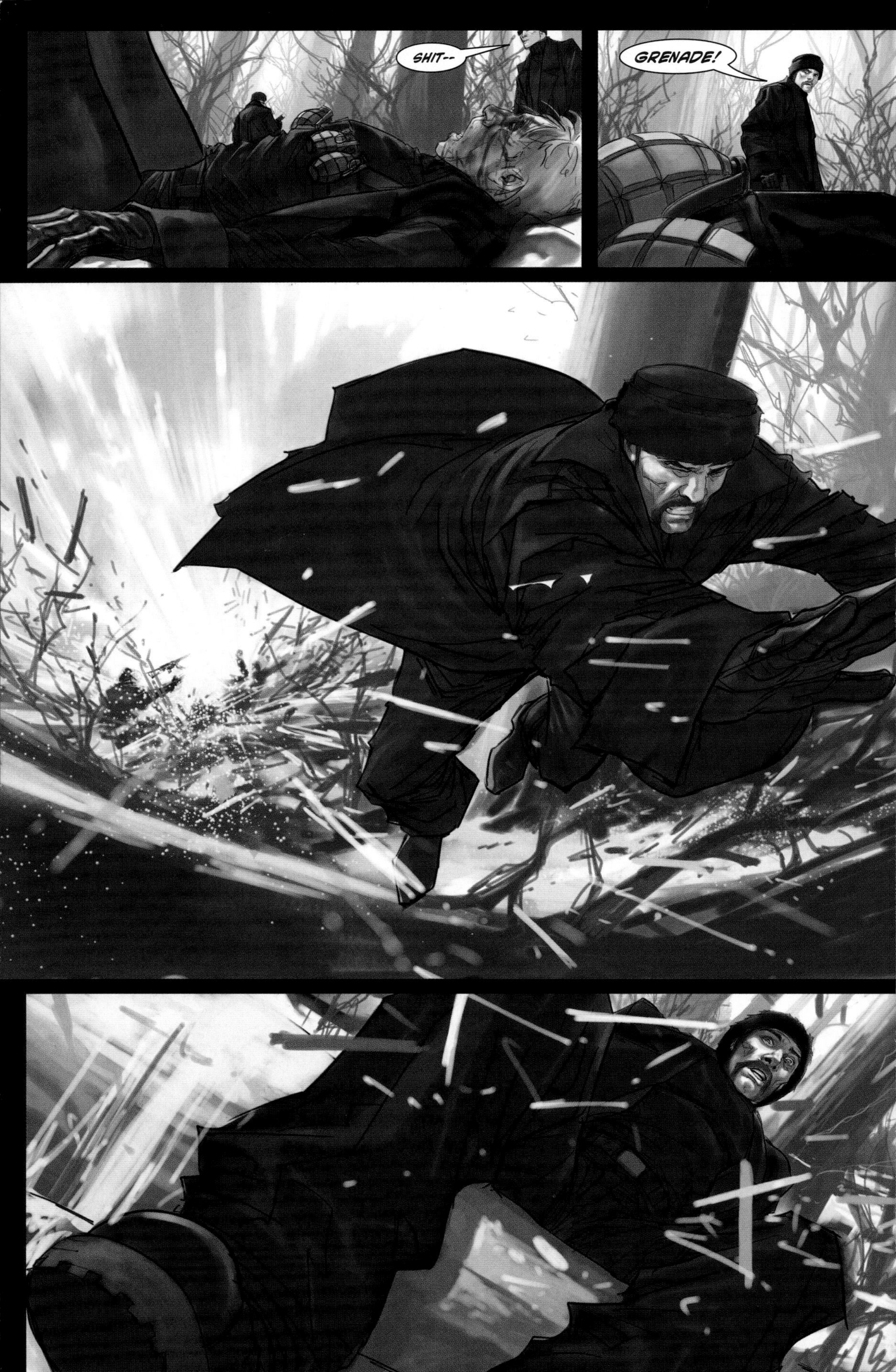
SHIT--
GRENADE!

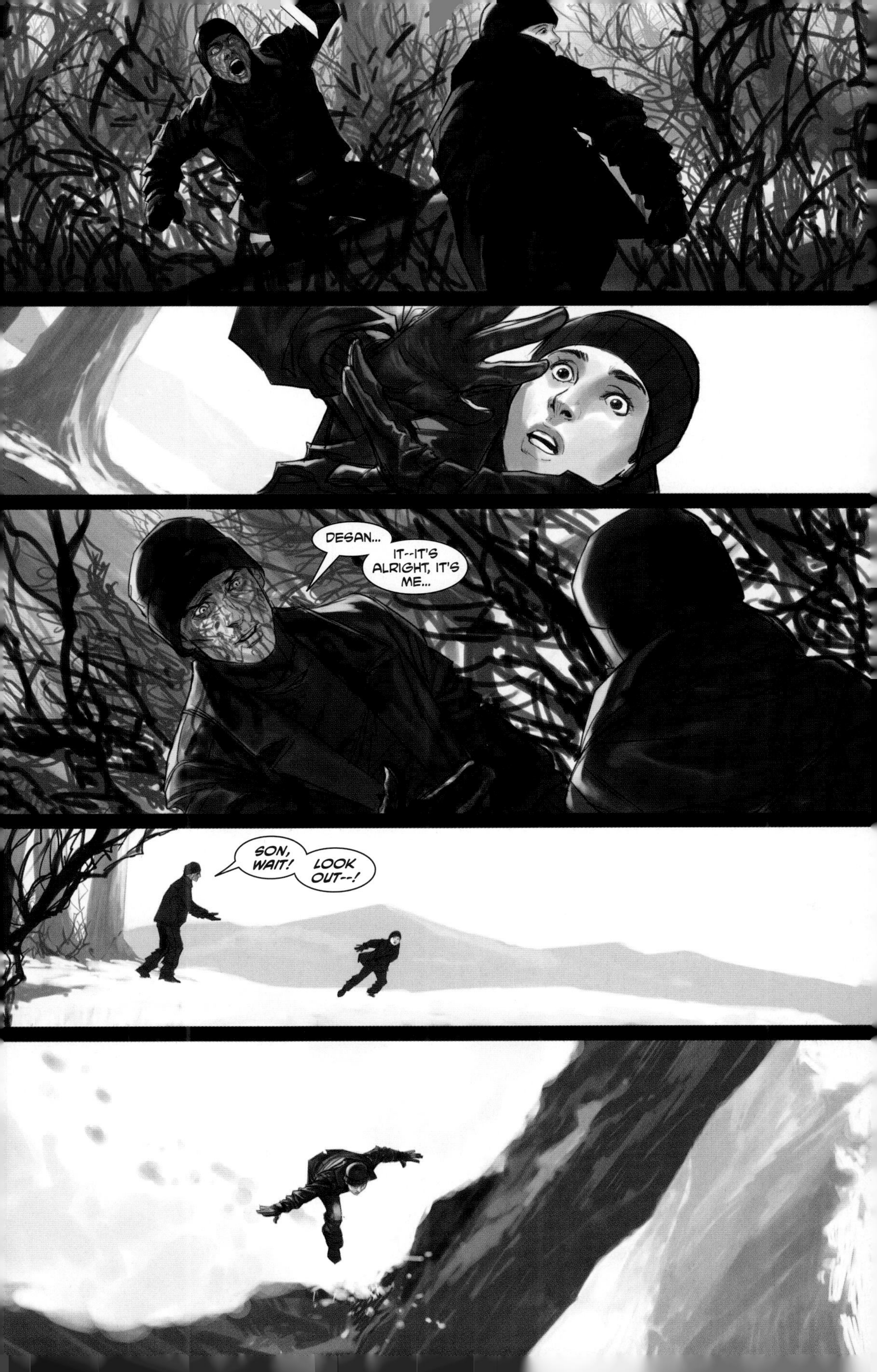
DESAN...
IT--IT'S ALRIGHT, IT'S ME...
SON, WAIT!
LOOK OUT--!

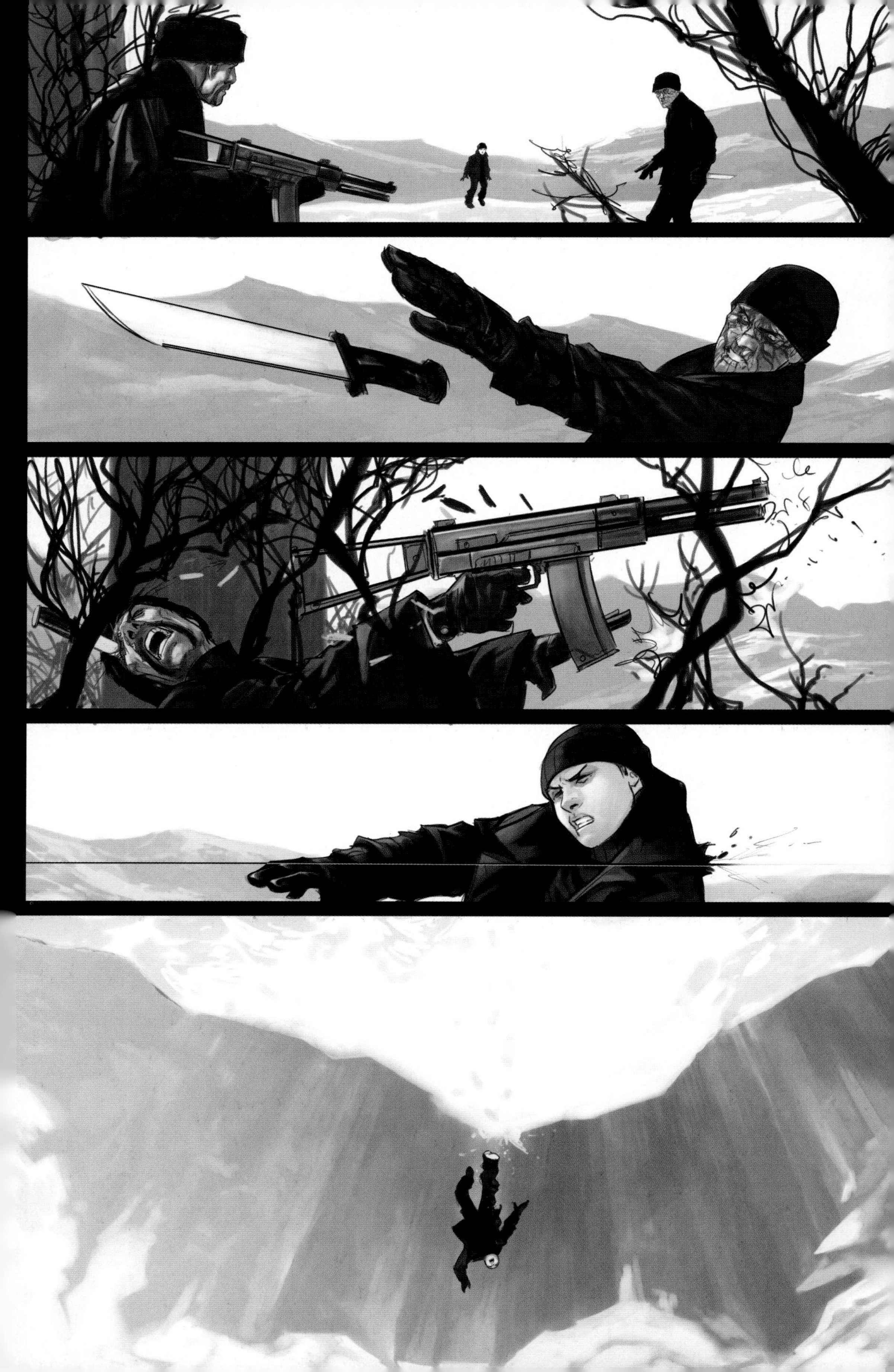

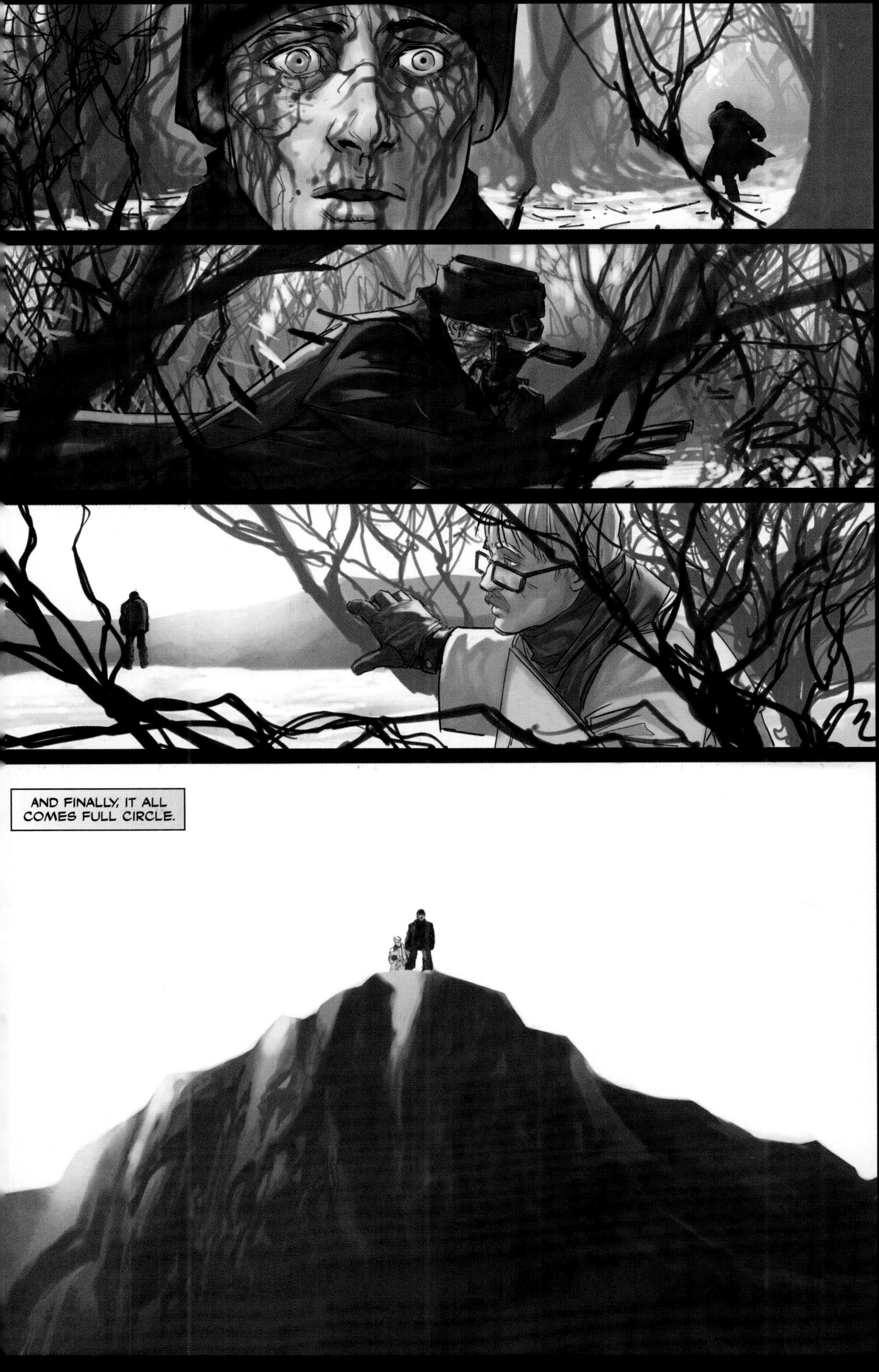
AND FINALLY, IT ALL COMES FULL CIRCLE.

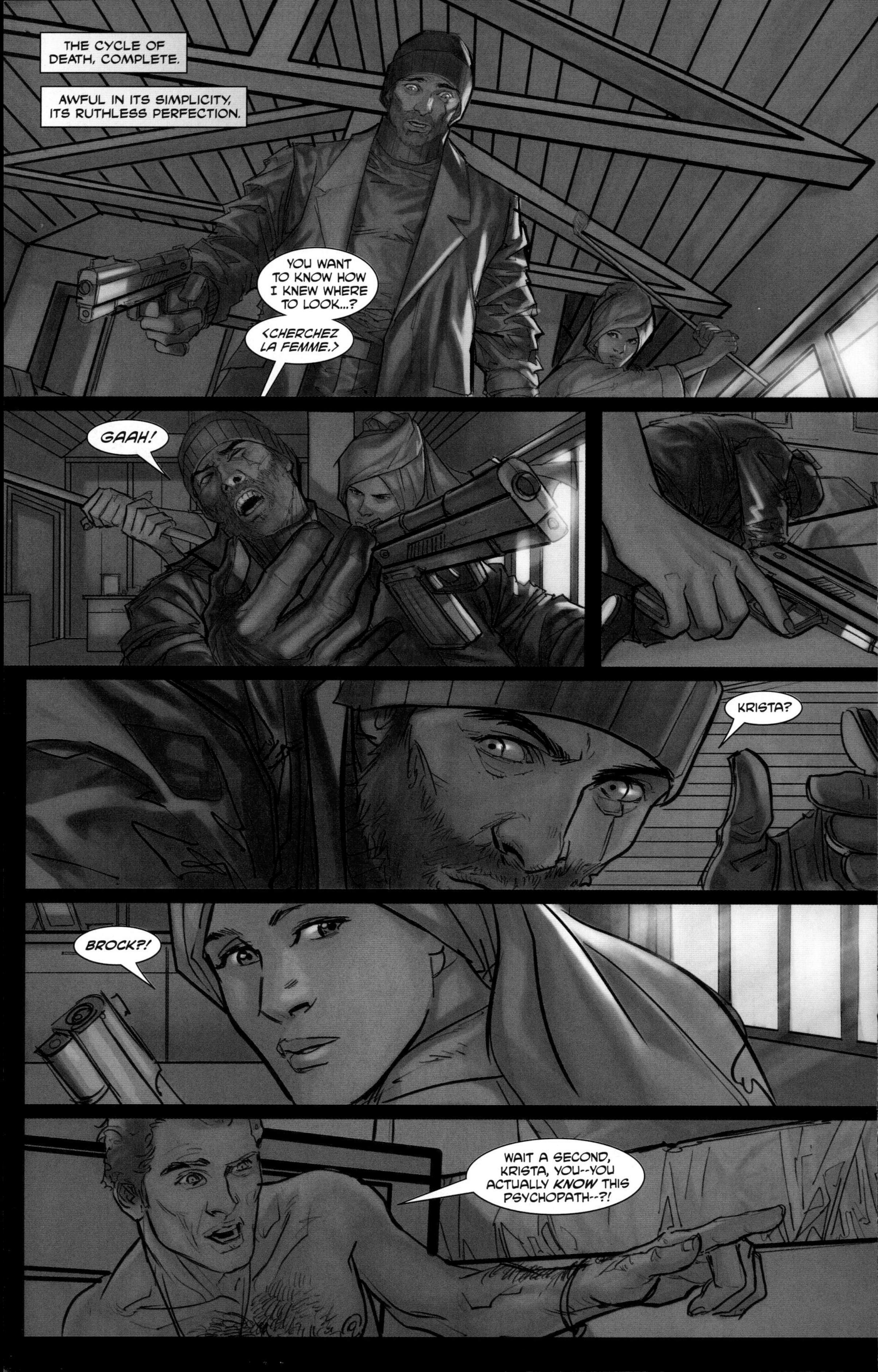
THE CYCLE OF DEATH, COMPLETE.
AWFUL IN ITS SIMPLICITY, ITS RUTHLESS PERFECTION.
YOU WANT TO KNOW HOW I KNEW WHERE TO LOOK...?
<CHERCHEZ LA FEMME.>
GAAH!
KRISTA?
BROCK?!
WAIT A SECOND, KRISTA, YOU--YOU ACTUALLY KNOW THIS PSYCHOPATH--?!

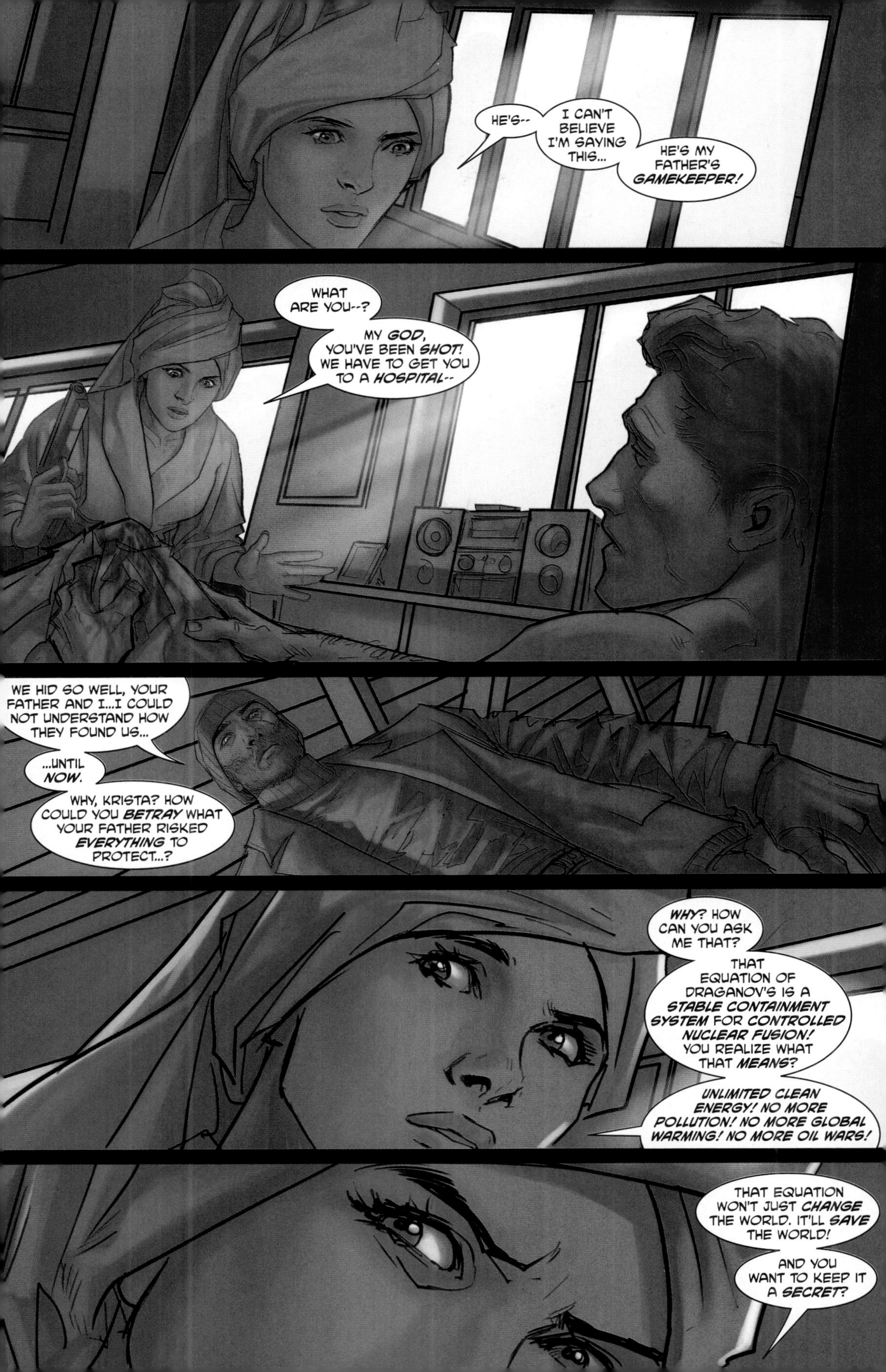
HE'S--
I CAN'T BELIEVE I'M SAYING THIS...
HE'S MY FATHER'S GAMEKEEPER!
WHAT ARE YOU--?
MY GOD, YOU'VE BEEN SHOT! WE HAVE TO GET YOU TO A HOSPITAL--
WE HID SO WELL, YOUR FATHER AND I...I COULD NOT UNDERSTAND HOW THEY FOUND US...
...UNTIL NOW.
WHY, KRISTA? HOW COULD YOU BETRAY WHAT YOUR FATHER RISKED EVERYTHING TO PROTECT...?
WHY? HOW CAN YOU ASK ME THAT?
THAT EQUATION OF DRAGANOV'S IS A STABLE CONTAINMENT SYSTEM FOR CONTROLLED NUCLEAR FUSION! YOU REALIZE WHAT THAT MEANS?
UNLIMITED CLEAN ENERGY! NO MORE POLLUTION! NO MORE GLOBAL WARMING! NO MORE OIL WARS!
THAT EQUATION WON'T JUST CHANGE THE WORLD. IT'LL SAVE THE WORLD!
AND YOU WANT TO KEEP IT A SECRET?

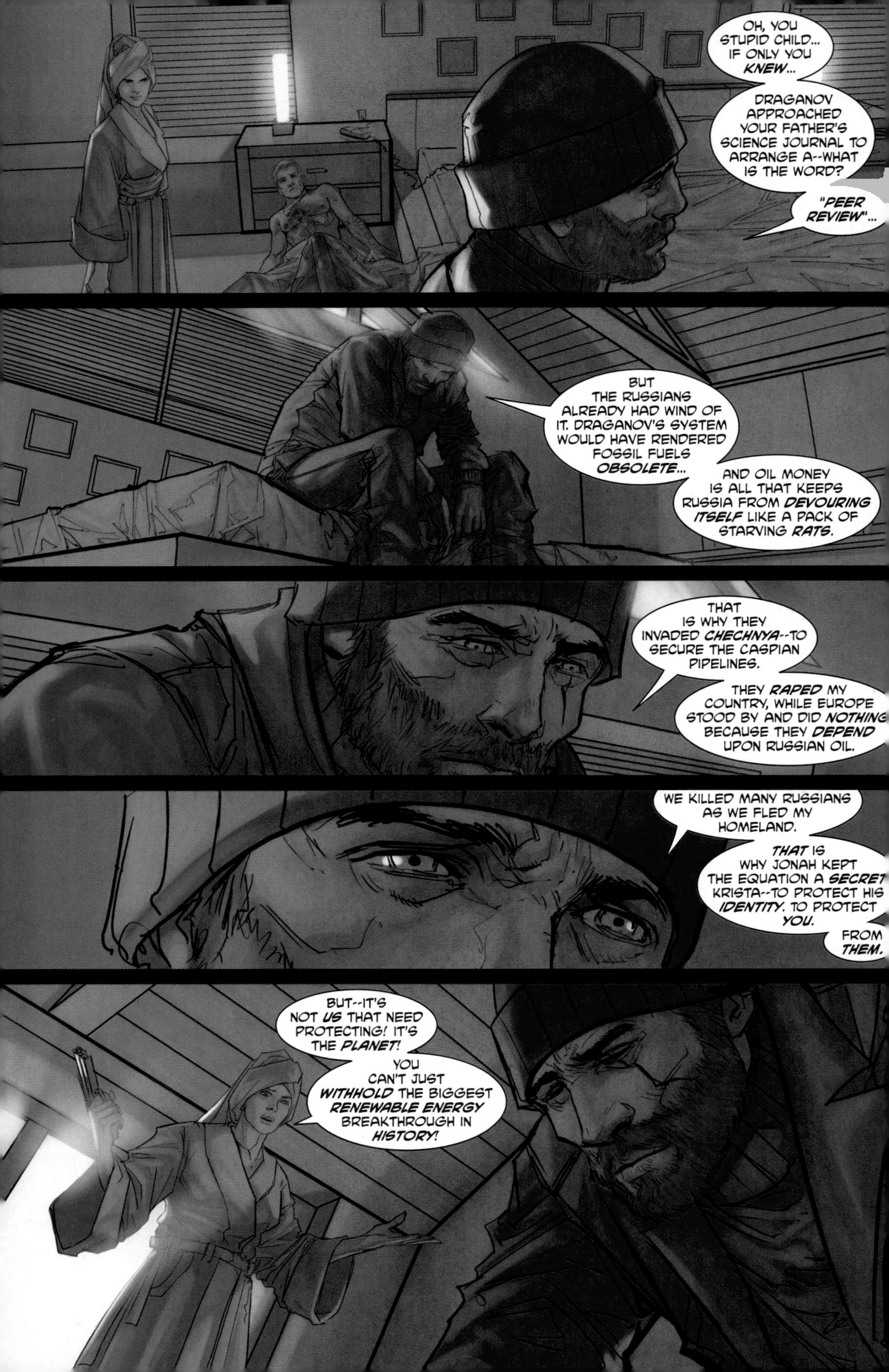
OH, YOU STUPID CHILD... IF ONLY YOU KNEW...
DRAGANOV APPROACHED YOUR FATHER'S SCIENCE JOURNAL TO ARRANGE A--WHAT IS THE WORD?
"PEER REVIEW"...
BUT THE RUSSIANS ALREADY HAD WIND OF IT. DRAGANOV'S SYSTEM WOULD HAVE RENDERED FOSSIL FUELS OBSOLETE...
AND OIL MONEY IS ALL THAT KEEPS RUSSIA FROM DEVOURING ITSELF LIKE A PACK OF STARVING RATS.
THAT IS WHY THEY INVADED CHECHNYA--TO SECURE THE CASPIAN PIPELINES.
THEY RAPED MY COUNTRY, WHILE EUROPE STOOD BY AND DID NOTHING BECAUSE THEY DEPEND UPON RUSSIAN OIL.
WE KILLED MANY RUSSIANS AS WE FLED MY HOMELAND.
THAT IS WHY JONAH KEPT THE EQUATION A SECRET KRISTA--TO PROTECT HIS IDENTITY. TO PROTECT YOU.
FROM THEM.
BUT--IT'S NOT US THAT NEED PROTECTING! IT'S THE PLANET!
YOU CAN'T JUST WITHHOLD THE BIGGEST RENEWABLE ENERGY BREAKTHROUGH IN HISTORY!

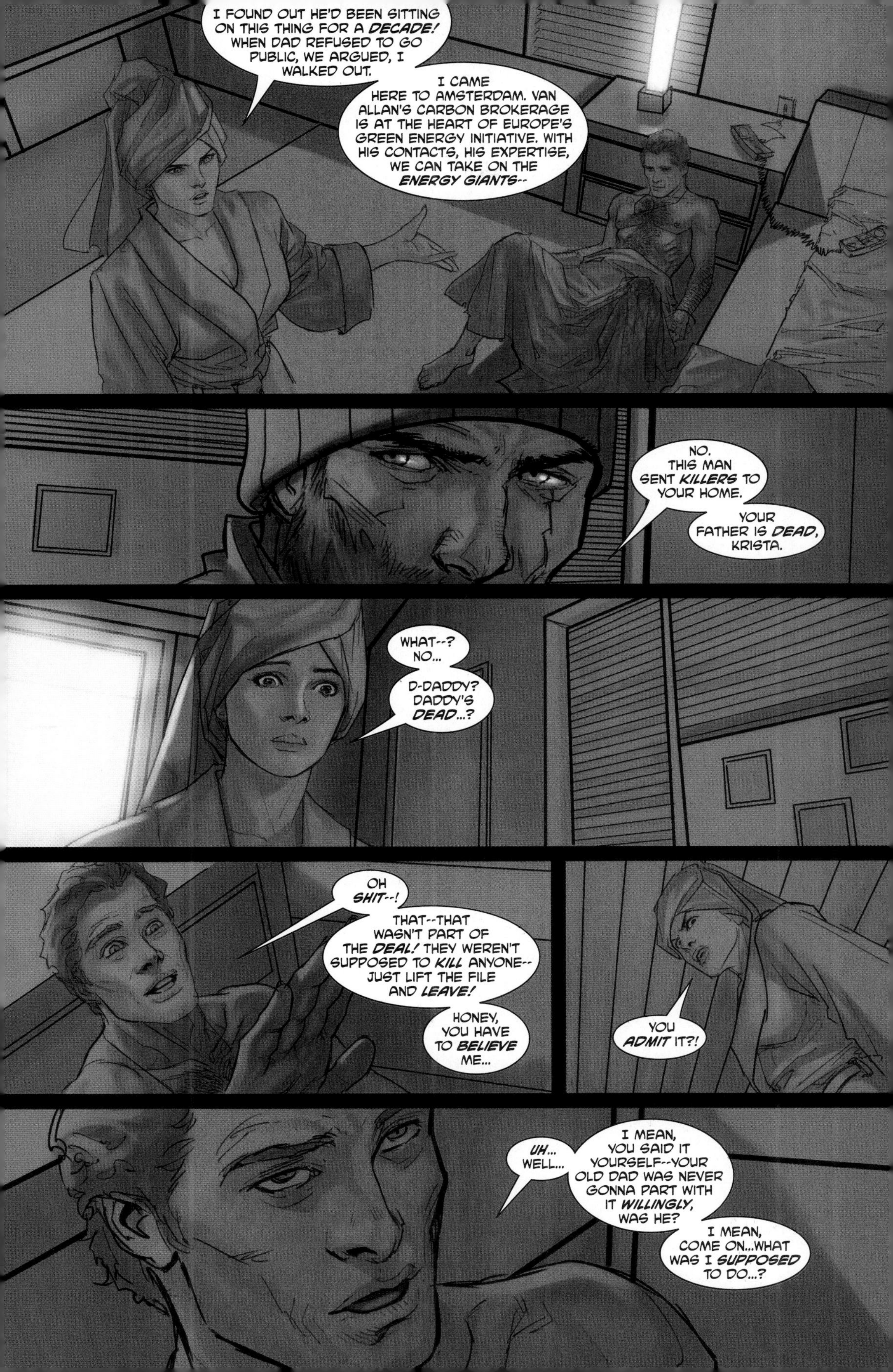
I FOUND OUT HE'D BEEN SITTING ON THIS THING FOR A *DECADE!* WHEN DAD REFUSED TO GO PUBLIC, WE ARGUED, I WALKED OUT.
I CAME HERE TO AMSTERDAM. VAN ALLAN'S CARBON BROKERAGE IS AT THE HEART OF EUROPE'S GREEN ENERGY INITIATIVE. WITH HIS CONTACTS, HIS EXPERTISE, WE CAN TAKE ON THE *ENERGY GIANTS*--
NO. THIS MAN SENT *KILLERS* TO YOUR HOME.
YOUR FATHER IS *DEAD*, KRISTA.
WHAT--? NO...
D-DADDY? DADDY'S *DEAD*...?
OH *SHIT*--!
THAT--THAT WASN'T PART OF THE *DEAL!* THEY WEREN'T SUPPOSED TO *KILL* ANYONE--JUST LIFT THE FILE AND *LEAVE!*
HONEY, YOU HAVE TO *BELIEVE* ME...
YOU *ADMIT* IT?!
UH... WELL...
I MEAN, YOU SAID IT YOURSELF--YOUR OLD DAD WAS NEVER GONNA PART WITH IT *WILLINGLY*, WAS HE?
I MEAN, COME ON...WHAT WAS I *SUPPOSED* TO DO...?

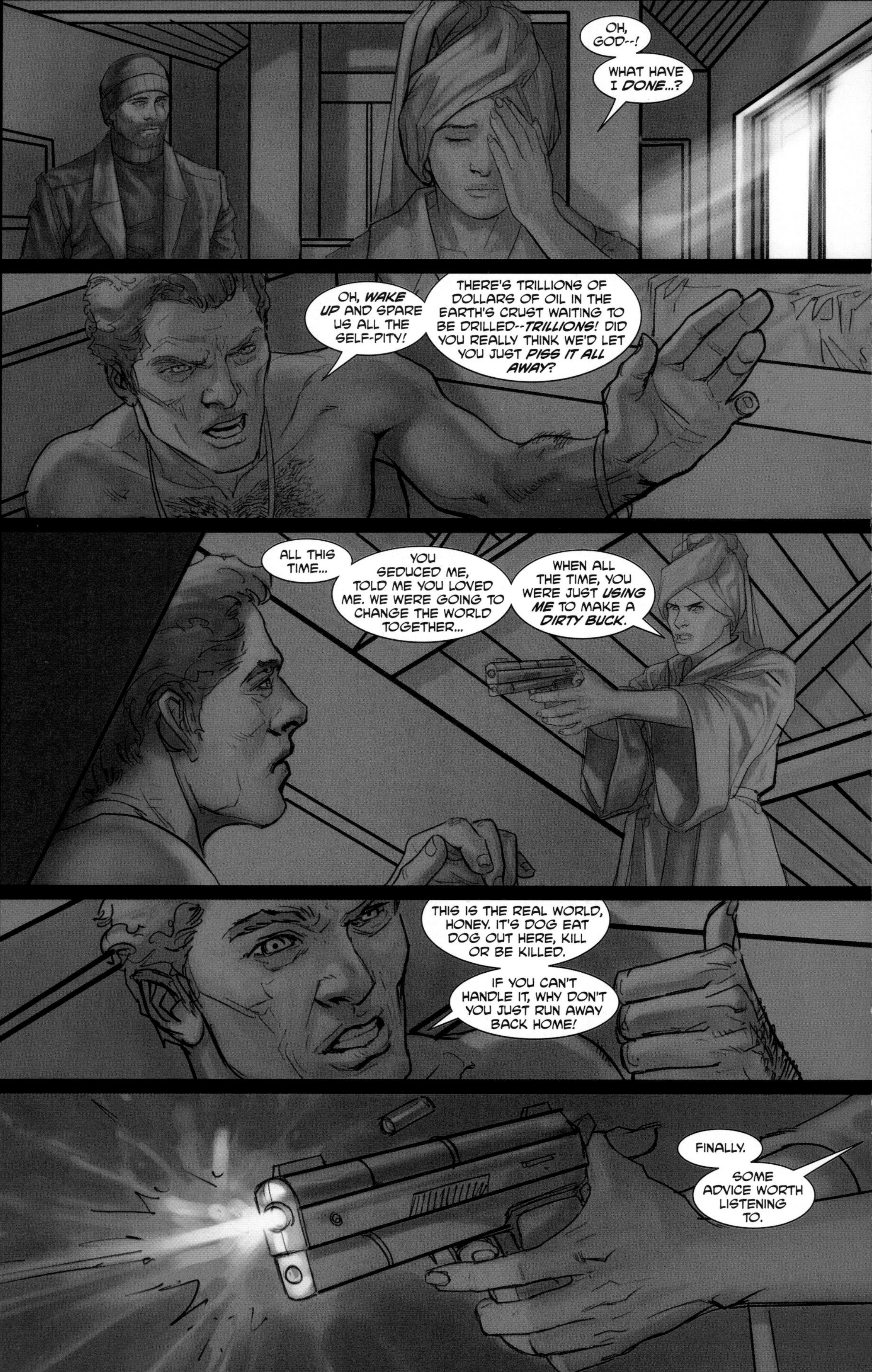
OH, GOD--!
WHAT HAVE I *DONE*...?
OH, *WAKE UP* AND SPARE US ALL THE SELF-PITY!
THERE'S TRILLIONS OF DOLLARS OF OIL IN THE EARTH'S CRUST WAITING TO BE DRILLED--*TRILLIONS!* DID YOU REALLY THINK WE'D LET YOU JUST *PISS IT ALL AWAY?*
ALL THIS TIME...
YOU SEDUCED ME, TOLD ME YOU LOVED ME. WE WERE GOING TO CHANGE THE WORLD TOGETHER...
WHEN ALL THE TIME, YOU WERE JUST *USING ME* TO MAKE A *DIRTY BUCK*.
THIS IS THE REAL WORLD, HONEY. IT'S DOG EAT DOG OUT HERE, KILL OR BE KILLED.
IF YOU CAN'T HANDLE IT, WHY DON'T YOU JUST RUN AWAY BACK HOME!
FINALLY.
SOME ADVICE WORTH LISTENING TO.

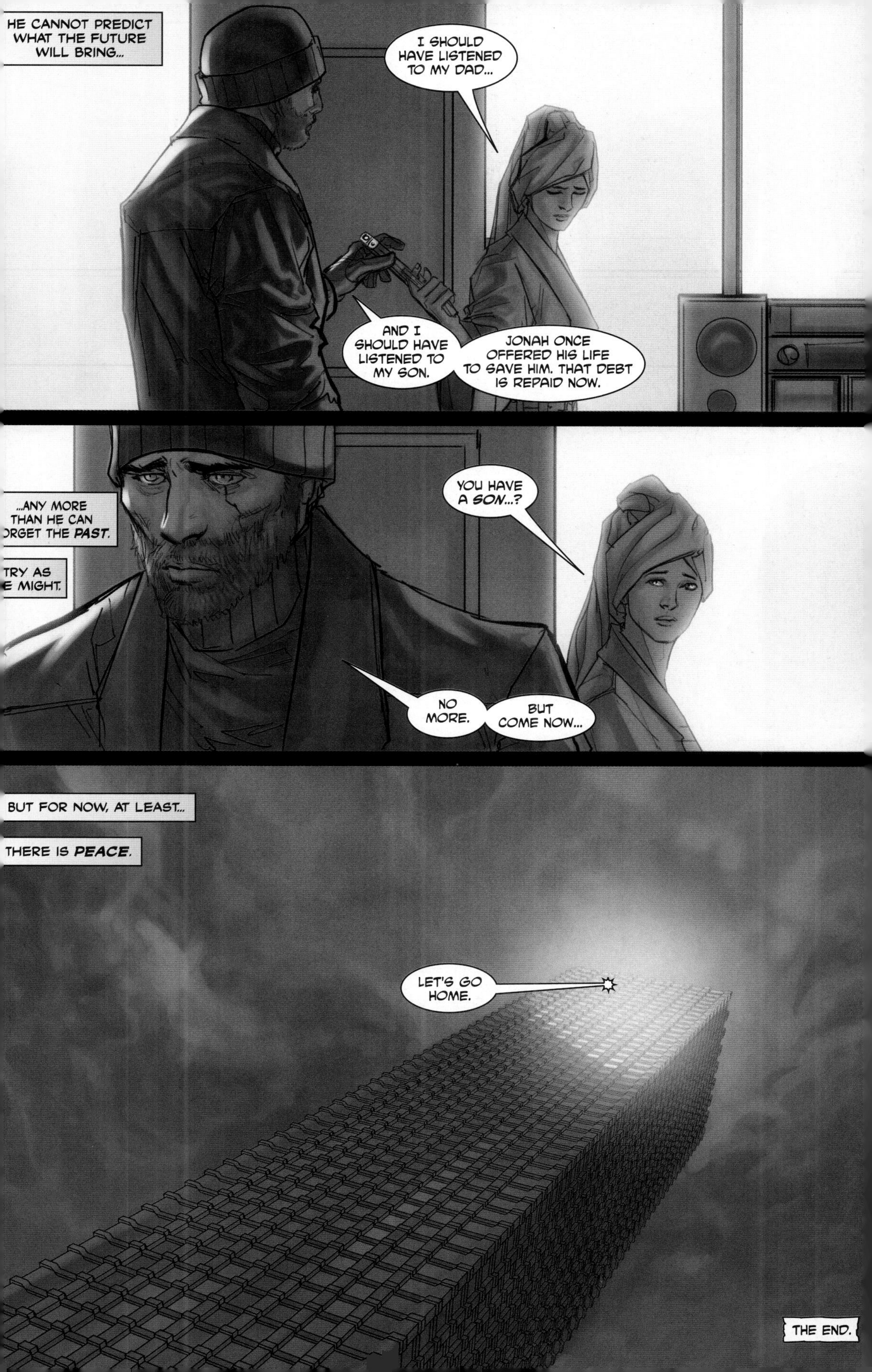
HE CANNOT PREDICT WHAT THE FUTURE WILL BRING...
I SHOULD HAVE LISTENED TO MY DAD...
AND I SHOULD HAVE LISTENED TO MY SON.
JONAH ONCE OFFERED HIS LIFE TO SAVE HIM. THAT DEBT IS REPAID NOW.
...ANY MORE THAN HE CAN
ORGET THE PAST.
TRY AS
E MIGHT.
YOU HAVE A SON...?
NO MORE.
BUT COME NOW...
BUT FOR NOW, AT LEAST...
THERE IS PEACE.
LET'S GO HOME.
THE END.

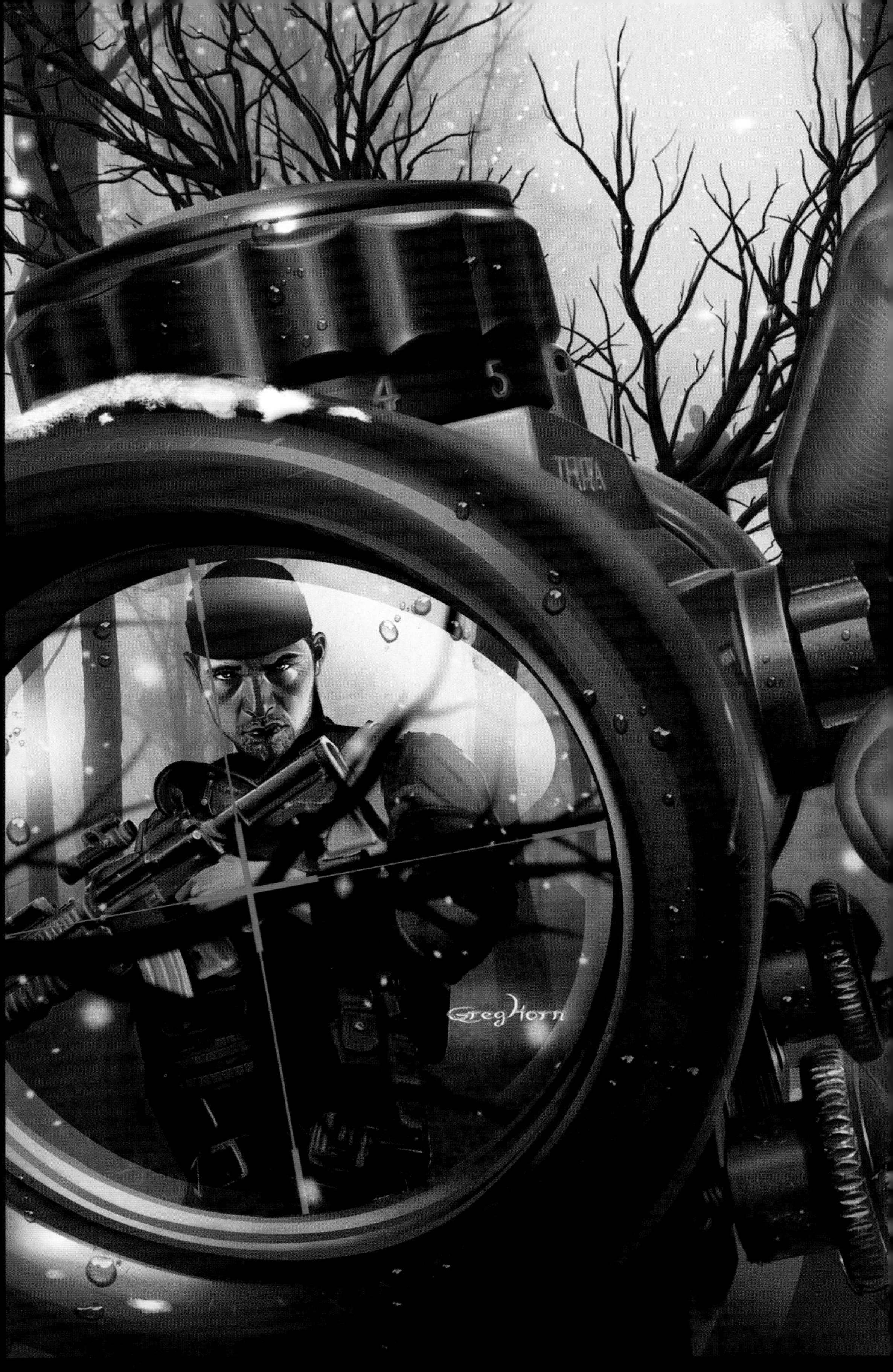
GregHorn

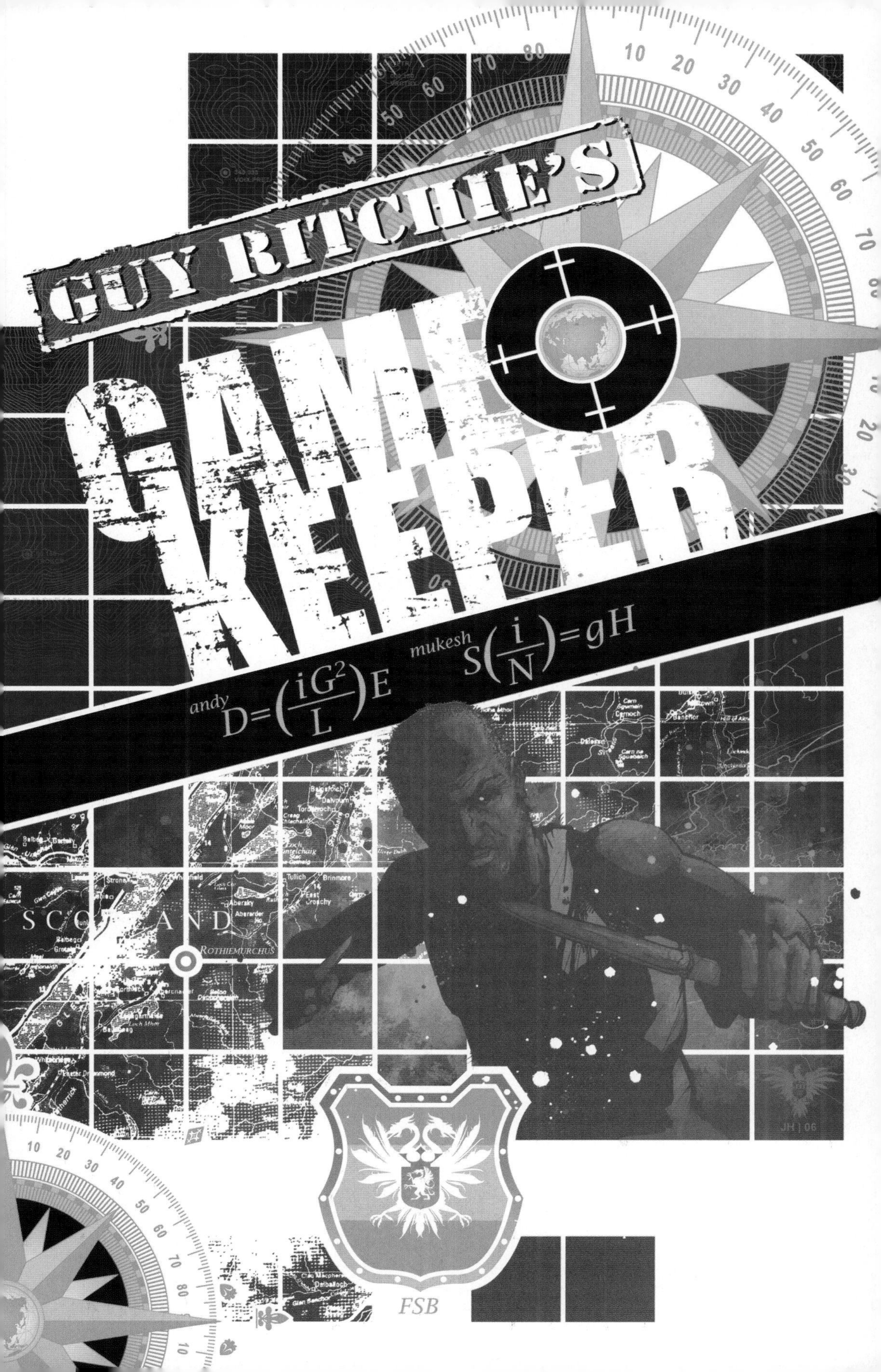

GUY RITCHIE'S
GAMEKEEPER
andy $D=\left(\frac{iG^2}{L}\right)E$
mukesh $S\left(\frac{i}{N}\right)=gH$
SCOTLAND
ROTHIEMURCHUS
FSB
JH | 06

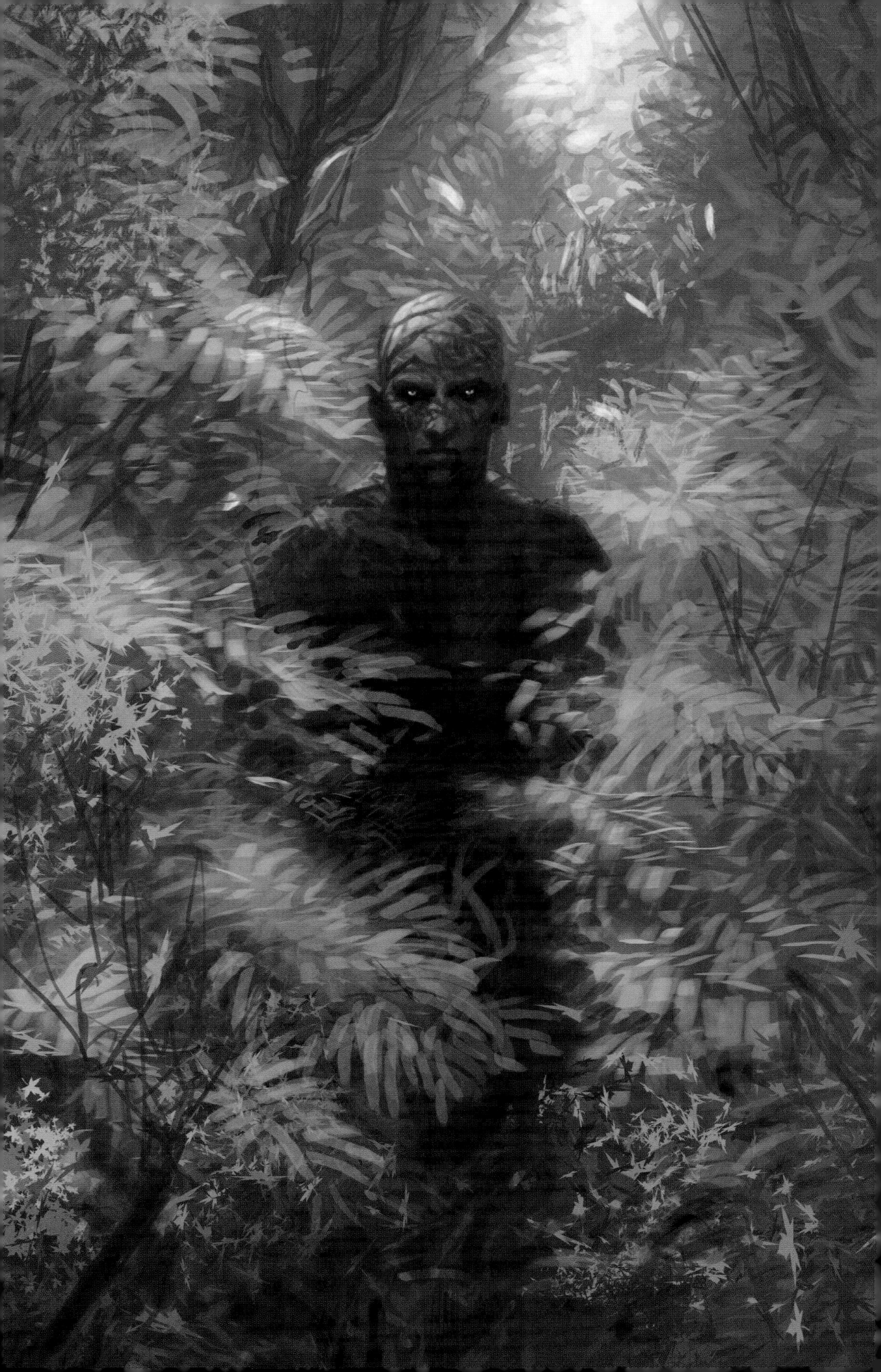

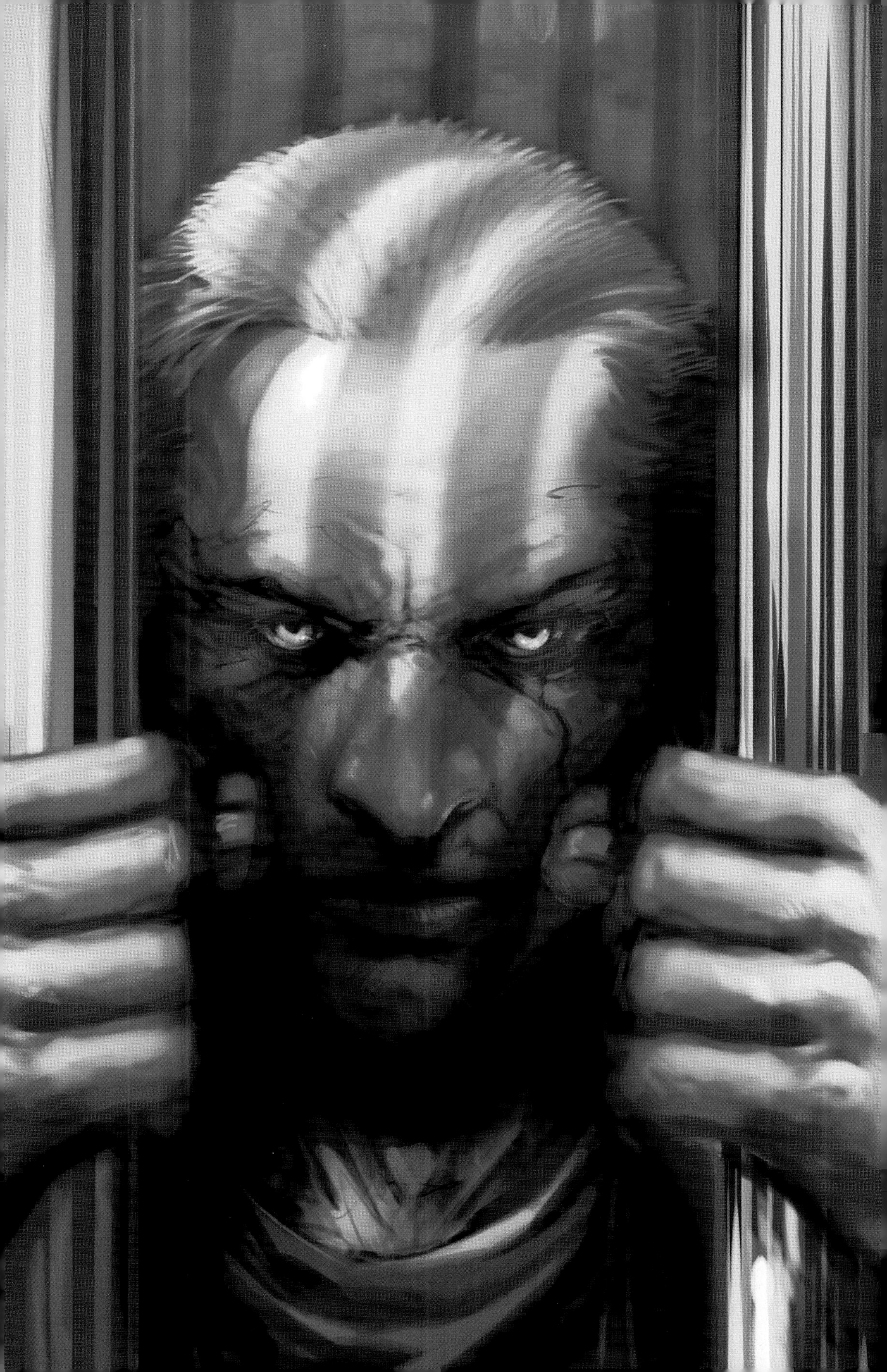

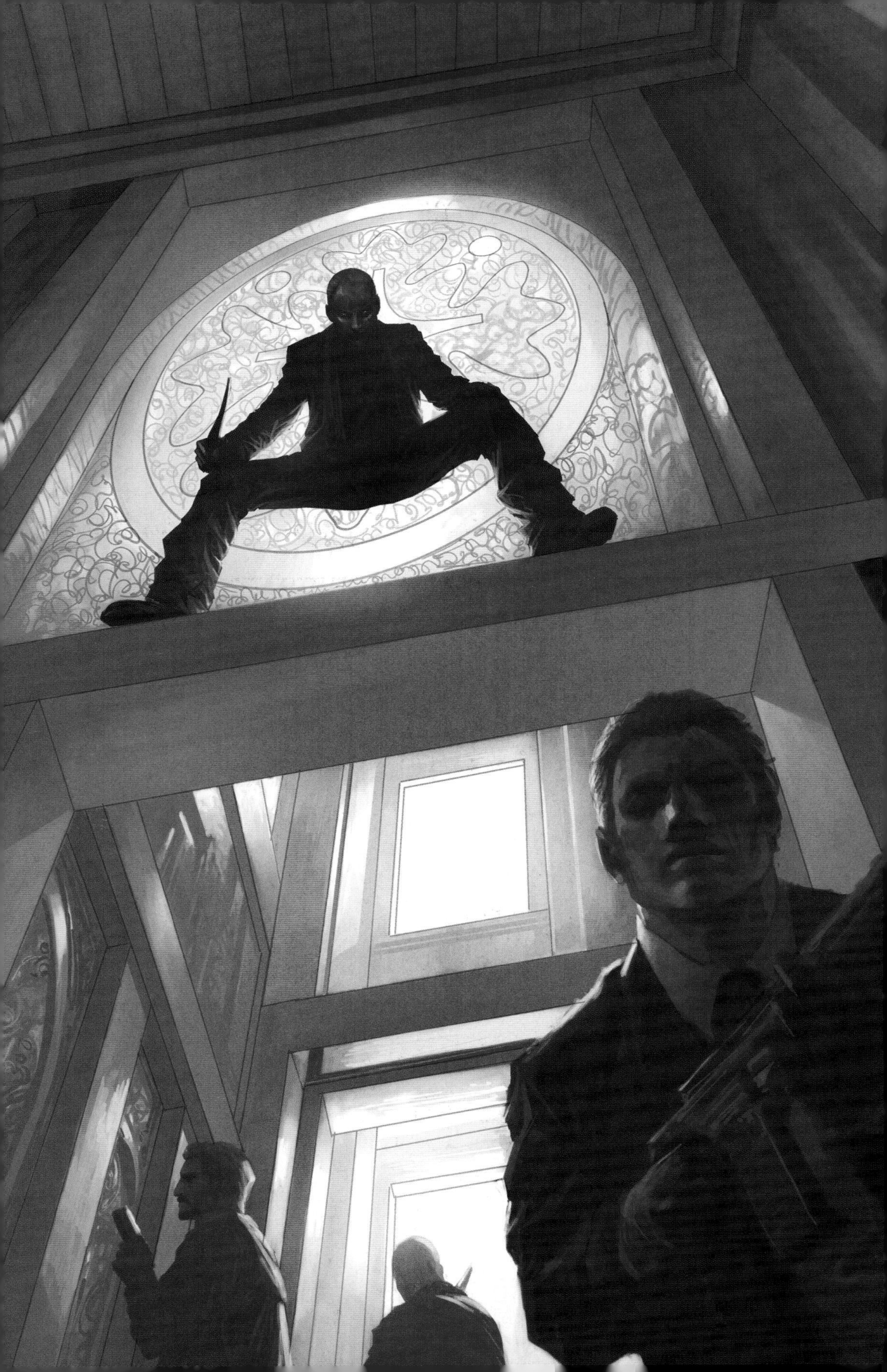

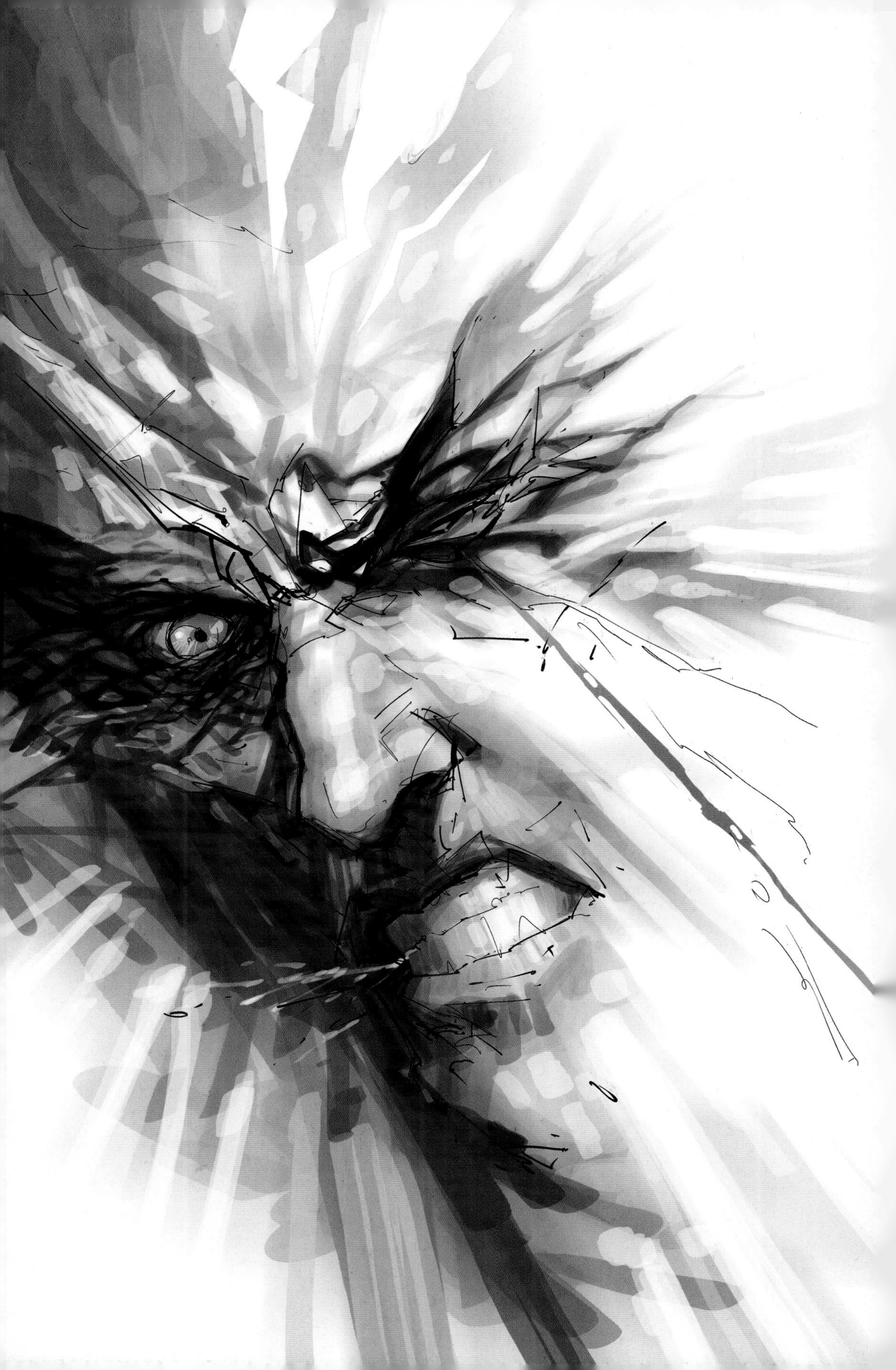

GAMEKEEPER #1

ANDY DIGGLE SCRIPT EXCERPT

PAGE NINE
(Five Panels)

Panel 1
Jonah calls out to SETH, a rough-looking farmhand who approaches them.

JONAH :   SETH! PUT HIM TO WORK IN THE STABLES. HE CAN BED
                 DOWN IN THE HAY LOFT UNTIL HE CAN BE QUARTERED.

SETH :   RIGHT YOU ARE, SIR.

      (link):   THIS WAY, LAD.

Panel 2
Brock and Jonah confer in the foreground, watching as Darren follows Seth off
towards the stables in the background. Brock looks troubled.

BROCK :   I SHOULD HAVE RUN HIM OFF.

JONAH :   NO, NO, WE NEED ALL THE HANDS WE CAN GET
                 AROUND HERE. ESPECIALLY SINCE, YOU KNOW...

      (link) :   SINCE KRISTA WENT AWAY.

Panel 3
Two-shot of Brock and Jonah. Jonah look up at him, but Brock seems lost in a
distant sadness...

JONAH :   BESIDES, EVERYONE DESERVES A SECOND CHANCE,
                 DON'T THEY?
      (link) :   BROCK...?

Panel 4
Move in close on Brock, not answering,
lost in memory, his eyes hollow and grieving...

Panel 5
Brock's POV, looking at Darren, who turns to look
back at us over his shoulder with a grateful smile.

CAPTION :   "THERE ARE NO SECOND
                      CHANCES..."

PAGE TEN
(Five Panels)

Panel 1
FLASHBACK. THE COMPOSITION OF THIS PANEL SHOULD MIRROR THAT OF
THE PREVIOUS PANEL AS CLOSELY AS POSSIBLE (i.e. Page 9, panel 4). It's a
"mirroring" effect we'll use to slide into flashbacks smoothly.
The art and coloring style for all flashback sequences needs to be clearly distinct
from the "present day" sequences—perhaps just penciled without inks, and/or
with ragged panel borders, and/or with faded, washed-out coloring. Whatever
works for you—as long as it works! Every subsequent flashback in the opening
5-issue arc will be a continuation of the scene we're establishing here.
We've jumped back 10 years into the past, to the cold Caucasus Mountain pine
forests of southern Chechnya. As previous, this panel is composed from Brock's
POV. His 10-year old son DESAN is up ahead, mirroring the position of Darren in
the previous panel. Desan stands with his back to us, looking back over his shoulder at us with the same expression. He's wielding a single-shot, bolt-action hunting rifle with a telescopic scope. Desan is a serious-minded boy with a tough,
flinty strength behind his eyes.

DESAN: SURE THERE ARE!
        (link) : SO WHAT IF I MISS--I CAN ALWAYS TAKE
                 ANOTHER SHOT AT IT.

Panel 2
Desan's POV, looking back at BROCK—10 years and a lifetime younger. He still has
some of his hair; but more significantly, he has not yet been ground down by the
burden of horrors that await him. He is a rough, earthy father, honest and happy,
with a face that cracks easily into a smile. Teaching his son to hunt with a rifle—in
this part of the world, as natural and wholesome as a game of catch in the back
yard. He is every boy's memory of their father; smiling patiently, lovingly.

BROCK :   IF YOU MISS--OR JUST WOUND IT--THE BUCK WILL VANISH
          FASTER THAN THE BLINK OF AN EYE.

          (link) :   YOU'LL WASTE HALF A DAY TRYING TO
                     TRACK IT DOWN AGAIN, AND IT IT'LL
                     BE ALL THE MORE WARY WHEN YOU DO.

Panel 3
Two-shot. Desan hands Brock the rifle.
BROCK :   NO, THERE'S A GOOD REASON WHY
          A HUNTING RIFLE ONLY HOLDS ONE
          BULLET. YOU WAIT FOR YOUR SHOT.
(link) :   PATIENCE IS THE HUNTER'S WEAPON.
DESAN :   THAT'S WHAT YOU ALWAYS SAY--
          AND EVERYTHING TAKES TEN
          TIMES LONGER!

Panel 4
Closer on Brock. He racks the rifle bolt, ejecting an
unspent .303 cartridge. His smile is fading, grim
bitterness settling over him like a rain cloud...
BROCK :   THIS IS OUR LIFE NOW, DESAN.
          WE DON'T KILL, WE DON'T EAT.
(link) :   THE NATURE OF THE MOUNTAINS
           IS NOT TO FORGIVE.

Panel 5
 Close on Desan, sulking now, his smile evaporated.
A shadow has been cast on both of their hearts...
DESAN :   THEN WE SHOULD GO BACK
          TO THE CITY.

PAGE ELEVEN
(Four Panels)

Panel 1
Brock turns away from his son, grief hollowing his eyes. Haunted by bitter
memory. He doesn't want his son to see the emotion on his face—but we do. We
will leave the reader to imagine what might have happened to the boy's
mother...

BROCK :   SOMETIMES, DESAN, YOU SOUND SO MUCH LIKE
                   YOUR MOTHER IT KILLS ME.

Panel 2
View from behind the two of them as they move forward through the deep
forest. Desan in foreground panel left, Brock in mid-ground panel right, a few
yards ahead of Desan. Brock suddenly crouches, intense and dynamic, waving
one hand down and behind to signal Desan to hit the dirt. We can see that the
ground suddenly drops away up ahead, but we can't see what lies beyond—

DESAN :   GOD REST HER--

BROCK :   GET DOWN!

Panel 3
Very low angle, POV from below the lip of the drop-off in front of them. Both of
them lie in the pine-needle dirt, peering down over the edge of a low cliff. Desan
is confused; Brock is utterly alert and intense, his eyes boring down into us like
diamond drills—

DESAN :   WHAT IS IT? I CAN SMELL BURNING--

BROCK :   SHH!

Panel 4
BIG. SAME ANGLE. PULL BACK to reveal a
shallow cliff-face, dropping away to a hollow in the
forest. Some kind of rooftop in the foreground.
Black smoke rising from it, although we can't yet
tell if it's from a chimney or something else...

PAGE TWELVE
(Three Panels)

Panel 1

BIG! Almost a full-page splash. Pull back from previous to reveal a wide establishing shot of the scene. A wooden hunting lodge/log cabin sits in a hollow in the
forest, surrounded to the rear by low cliffs rising to about 30 feet at the highest
point. Brock and Desan lie at the lip of the cliff, tiny in the panel. The lodge itself
is on fire, flames roaring from the blown-out windows, thick black-and-orange
smoke boiling from the roof. SIX MEN stand in the clearing around the lodge,
watching it burn. They are Russian FSB (Secret Service) agents, dressed in
civilian clothes but carrying snub-nosed Kalashnikov AKS-74U assault rifles.
One of the six Russians stands forward of the others, standing over a seventh
man who kneels before him. Although we're probably too far away to see what's
happening in detail, the kneeling man is being tortured...

Panel 2

Full-width panel across the foot of the page. Move in closer on the torture scene.
SADIC is a brutal and ruthless FSB officer. DRAGANOV is the man being
tortured—a thin, elderly academic. Sadic has twisted one of Draganov's hands
behind his back, and is cutting off one of his fingers with a combat knife.
Draganov SCREAMS, helpless. The other FSB agents just stand and watch,
stony-faced...

CAPTION :   TEN YEARS AND A LIFETIME LATER,
                 HE CAN STILL SMELL THE SMOKE.

Panel 3
  Small inset panel. Extreme close on Draganov—his eyes squeezed shut,
SCREAMING in agony...

                    CAPTION :   HEAR THE SCREAMING.

PAGE THIRTEEN
(Four Panels)

Panel 1
BACK TO THE PRESENT. It's NIGHT. BROCK suddenly bolts
upright in bed, staring right at us, alert and intense in the semi-darkness—

CAPTION :   SENSE MEMORY.

CAPTION :   THE HORSES--

Panel 2
Brock shoves open the door of the rough wooden shack on
the estate grounds—his humble home. He's pulling on a jacket—

CAPTION :   THE HORSES ARE SCREAMING.

Panel 3
BIG! The Morgans' stables are ON FIRE! A dozen farmhands try to
fight the flames with water buckets and blankets, but it's out of control.
In the foreground, SETH the stable-hand YELLS—

SETH :(jagged)   FIRE! THE STABLES ARE ON FIRE!

        (link) : EVERYBODY UP!

Panel 4
View looking out through the stable doors as farmhands are forced back by the
intense heat. Flames in the foreground.

PAGE FOURTEEN
(Four Panels)

Panel 1
DARREN scurries away from the burning stable towards one of the outbuildings. It's dark out here, and he's little more than a silhouette. He speaks into a mobile phone. He looks worried, sick with guilt at what he's done...

RADIO JAG (no tail) : IS IT DONE...?

DARREN :   AND DUSTED--STABLE'S GONE UP LIKE GUY FAWKES
      NIGHT. THE HORSES, THOUGH, THEY'RE STILL IN THERE...

Panel 2
Darren ducks back behind the outbuilding, hidden from view of the stables.

RADIO JAG (no tail) : FOCUS. EMERGENCY SERVICES--WHAT'S THEIR E.T.A.?

DARREN :   THEY MUST BE AN HOUR OFF EASY,
      IT'S THE ARSE END OF NOWHERE OUT HERE.

RADIO JAG (no tail) : AND THE MAIN HOUSE...?

Panel 3
Darren peeks out from behind the outbuilding, his face semi-lit by the firelight from the burning stables in the distance.

DARREN :   BURGLAR ALARMS HAVE ALL GONE DOOLALLY,
      AND EVERYONE'S OUTSIDE FIGHTING THE FIRE.

    (link) : IN OTHER WORDS, IT'S WIDE OPEN.

RADIO JAG (no tail) : GOOD WORK.
              (link)   : ALRIGHT, MEET US AT THE
                   RENDEZVOUS POINT...

Panel 4
BIG! Low angle upshot for dramatic impact. Deep in the dark woods elsewhere on the estate grounds, TWO MERCENARIES are readying their weapons —compact Heckler & Koch G36C assault rifles with fat cylindrical silencers/suppressors, laser-spot designators, entry flashlights and night-vision scopes. Serious hardware. The two men are professional British mercenaries, dressed in dark civilian clothing and black kevlar vests, their faces smudged with dark camo paint. Both wear radio mike/earpiece headsets and black woolen beanie hats which, we will later discover, can be rolled down into SWAT-style face-covering balaclavas. These two men are Alpha team—let's call them Alpha 1 and Alpha 2. We'll be meeting Bravo and Charlie teams later...

ALPHA 1 :   IT'S TIME.

PAGE FIFTEEN
(Four Panels)

Panel 1

DARREN runs from behind the outbuilding, away from the stables and house, heading for the deep blackness of the woods beyond...

Panel 2

BROCK lurks in the shadow of a tree, crouched, alert as a predatory animal, his eyes narrowing suspiciously—he's spotted Darren...

Panel 3

Darren approaches the lone Alpha 1 merc in a shadowy woodland clearing...

DARREN :   ALRIGHT, I'VE DONE IT JUST LIKE YOU SAID.
                NOW WHEN DO I GET ME MONEY...?

ALPHA 1 :   RELAX, SUNSHINE.
                YOU'LL GET WHAT'S COMING TO YOU.

Panel 4

Close on Darren as the second merc, Alpha 2, suddenly pulls a GARROTTE around his throat! Darren's eyes bulge with terror as the wire bites into the skin of his throat. We can see Alpha 2 intimately close behind the boy, straining to choke the life out of him...

ALPHA 2 :   PAYMENT IN FULL.

RT EXPLORATIONS BY MUKESH SINGH

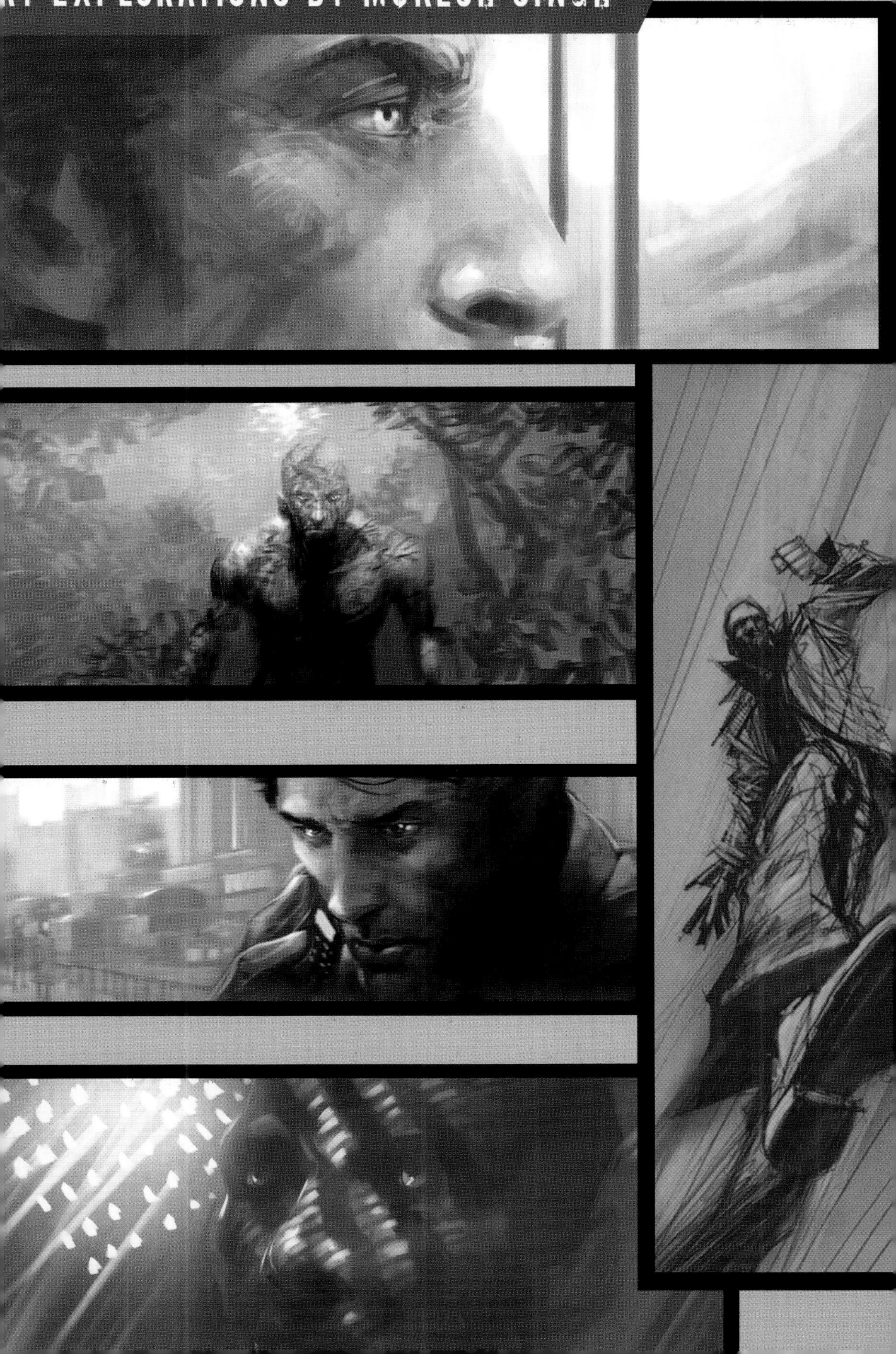

ART EVOLUTION

EDITORIAL COMMENTARY

Panel 1:

As per note on previous page either blow off his head some more or turn him face down.
Ha - that's a funny note.

Panel 3:

In pencils, let's make sure that this dude's face is very visible, and that his expression of "Bravo I suddenly realizes he's about to die" is brought out.

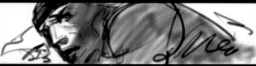

Panel 1:

Where is Bravo 4/Brock? We want to see him in this panel looming over the crawling away dude (and then pnl 2 will make sense which, as of now, is a bit confusing.)

Panel 3:

Who is he talking to? Turn him to talk to the reader – put the reader in the position of the dying merc with this terrifying executioner crouching over us. It'd be a really cool, effective shot.

Panel 4:

This too is coming off as a cool shot but not one that terrifies in the context of the story. How can we make the reader more interactive with these last two panels, know that we are about to get tortured?! It's a big moment – it should be very actively engaging and putting the reader in the place of the victim is a good way to accomplish that.

BROCK'S EVOLUTION

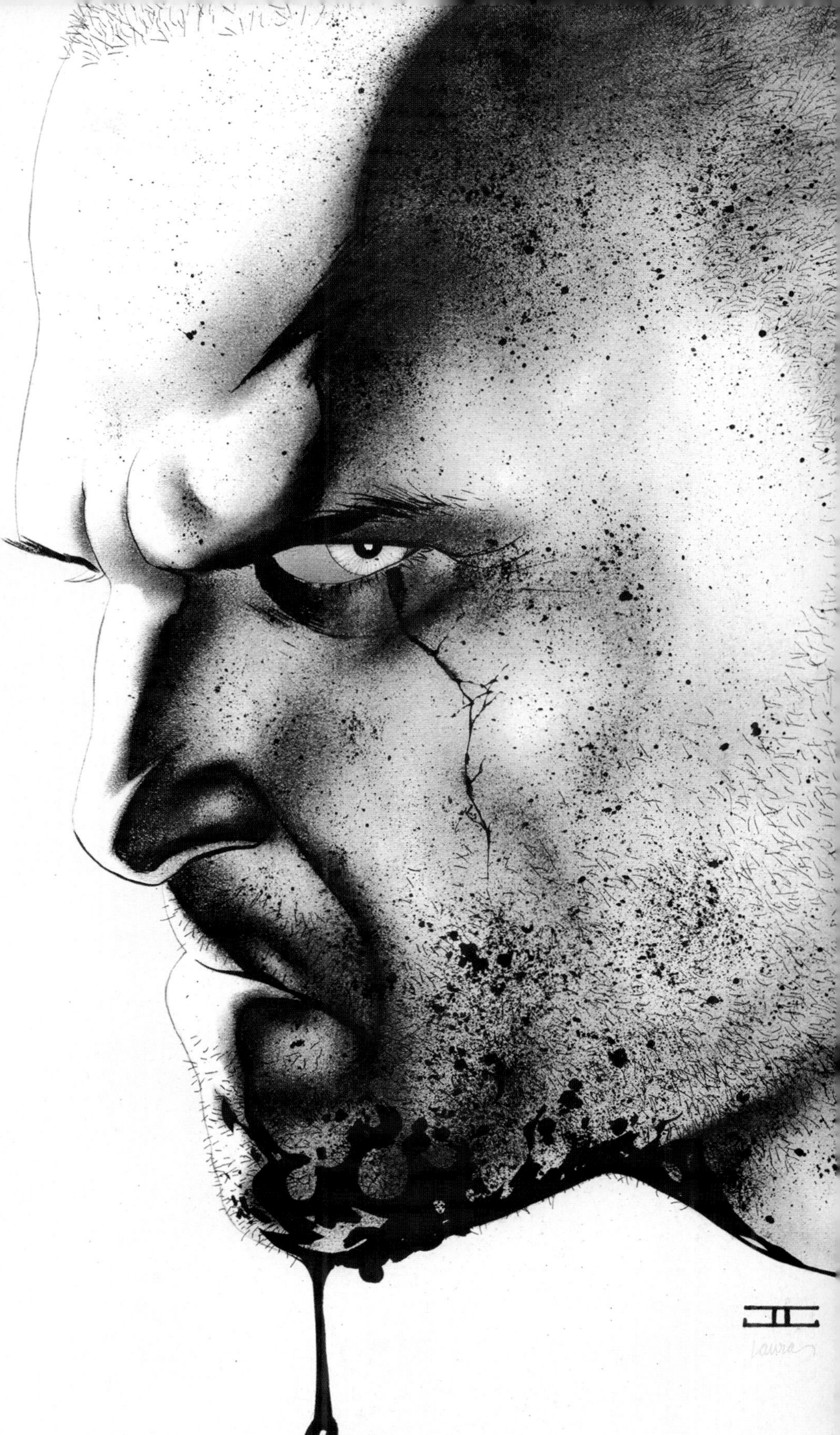